From the Royal to the Republican Body

From the Royal to the Republican Body

Incorporating the Political in Seventeenth- and Eighteenth-Century France

Edited by Sara E. Melzer
and Kathryn Norberg

UNIVERSITY OF CALIFORNIA PRESS

Berkeley / Los Angeles / London

University of California Press
Berkeley and Los Angeles, California

University of California Press, Ltd.
London, England

Parts of this book were published in earlier versions.

Chapter 2: Excerpted from Abby Zanger, *Scenes from the Marriage of Louis XIV: Nuptial Fictions and the Making of Absolutist Power* (Palo Alto: Stanford University Press, 1997).

Chapter 3: Previously published as Mark Franko, "Double Bodies: Androgyny and Power in the Performances of Louis XIV," *TDR / The Drama Review* 38, no. 4 (winter 1994): 71–82. Reprinted with permission by MIT Press Journals.

Chapter 8: A longer version of this essay appeared in chapter 5 of Sarah Maza, *Private Lives and Public Affairs: The Causes Célèbres of Prerevolutionary France* (Berkeley: University of California Press, 1993).

Library of Congress Cataloging-in-Publication Data

From the royal to the republican body: incorporating the political in seventeenth- and eighteenth-century France / edited by Sara E. Melzer and Kathryn Norberg.

p. cm.

Includes bibliographic references and index.

ISBN 0–520–20806–4 (alk. paper).—ISBN 0–520–20807–2 (pbk.: alk. paper)

1. France—Civilization—Political aspects. 2. France—History—Bourbons, 1589–1789. 3. Body, Human—Symbolic aspects—France. 4. France—Court and courtiers—Social life and customs. 5. Symbolism in politics—France. 6. Despotism—France.

I. Melzer, Sara E. II. Norberg, Kathryn, 1948– .

DC33.4.F89 1998

944'.033—DC21 97–22678

CIP

MN

Printed in the United States of America

9 8 7 6 5 4 3 2 1

The paper used in this publication is both acid-free and totally chlorine-free (TCF). It meets the minimum requirements of American Standard for Information Sciences—Permanence of Paper for Printed Library Materials, ANSI Z39.48–1984.

Contents

Illustrations

Introduction

SARA E. MELZER AND KATHRYN NORBERG

Few states were as body centered as seventeenth- and eighteenth-century France. The rhetoric, rites, and rhythm of political life derived from bodies. Political discourse abounded in body metaphors. Under the Bourbon monarchs, guildsmen spoke of their "corporation," and magistrates, of their "corps." Legal theorists talked about the "body politic," while royal apologists described the king as the "head" and his subjects as "members." The Jacobin republicans were no less body minded. Even though they rejected the king and replaced him with the nation, they still needed to embody authority (as either Hercules or Marianne), and they still talked about the "great body of the nation."

The most important rituals of the state also centered on bodies. At the coronation ceremony, the bishop of Reims anointed the king's body with the holy chrism. The king in turn touched, and supposedly cured, the bodies of scrofula sufferers.[1] The royal entry allowed city dwellers to glimpse the king as he passed under triumphal arches that celebrated the corporal themes of Bourbon fertility and potency.[2] Engagements, weddings,

1. Marc Bloch, *The Royal Touch: Sacred Monarchy and Scrofula in England and France*, trans. J. E. Anderson (London: Routledge, 1973); Richard Jackson, *Vive le Roi! A History of the French Coronation from Charles V to Charles X* (Chapel Hill: University of North Carolina Press, 1984); *Le Sacre des rois: Actes du colloque international d'histoire sur les sacres et couronnements royaux* (Paris: Les Belles Lettres, 1985).

2. See Lawrence Bryant, *The King and the City in the Parisian Royal Entry Ceremony: Politics, Ritual, and Art in the Renaissance* (Geneva: Librairie Droz, 1986). The ritual of the *lit de justice* also focused on the body—the king's body; see Sarah Hanley, *The Lit de Justice*

and births of royal family members occasioned public festivals and regular celebration of Bourbon fecundity. Of course, the revolutionary republicans despised these monarchical rites and abolished them. But they created new rituals in which bodies played just as important a role. Bare-breasted statues embodied the state at the great Jacobin celebrations, and the nude portraits David did of Marat and Lepelletier de St. Fargeau became icons of the Jacobin regime.[3]

Under the monarchy, however, the body had a special resonance. Bourbon absolutism invested power not in anonymous institutions, as today, but in a body, that of the king. All authority flowed from the royal person, and proximity to the king equaled power. Consequently, at Versailles courtiers competed to be near his royal presence. They vied to participate in the ceremony of the *levée*, especially in the sixth *entrée*, during which they might have the enormous privilege of standing close enough to the king to hold his candle.[4]

Outside Versailles, French subjects had little hope of physical contact with the king, but his body was still a subject of speculation and concern. Was the king ill? Did he drink too much? Did he suffer from impotence, or was he too promiscuous?[5] The monarch's appetites had political significance, for a sudden death or an interruption in the royal line could bring on civil disturbances or foreign war. Frenchmen believed that the king's health reflected on, perhaps even determined, the welfare of the realm. If the king were fertile, agriculture and commerce would prosper; if he were impotent, the kingdom too would be unproductive.[6]

Clearly, a special affinity existed between the king's body and his king-

---

of the Kings of France: Constitutional Ideology in Legend, Ritual, and Discourse (Princeton: Princeton University Press, 1983); Abby Zanger, *Scenes from the Marriage of Louis XIV: Nuptial Fictions and the Making of Absolutist Power* (Stanford: Stanford University Press, 1997); and Jean-Marie Apostolidès, *Le Roi-machine: Spectacle et politique au temps de Louis XIV* (Paris: Editions de Minuit, 1981).

3. Mona Ozouf, *La Fête révolutionnaire* (Paris: Gallimard, 1976). On the paintings of Marat and Lepelletier de St. Fargeau, see Lynn Hunt, *The Family Romance of the French Revolution* (Berkeley: University of California Press, 1992), 74–75. Marat's nude image also figured in revolutionary pageantry; see Marie-Hélène Huet, *Rehearsing the Revolution: The Staging of Marat's Death*, trans. Robert Hurley (Berkeley: University of California Press, 1982).

4. This ceremony is examined in Norbert Elias, *The Court Society*, trans. Edmund Jephcott (New York: Pantheon Books, 1983), 78–85.

5. On speculation concerning the king's health, see Thomas Kaiser's essay "Louis *le Bien-Aimé* and the Rhetoric of the Royal Body" in this volume.

6. In her forthcoming book on depopulationist delusions in eighteenth-century France, Carol Blum explores the connections believed to exist between the king's health and the material well-being of the country. On speculation regarding Louis XVI's potency, see Antoine de Baecque, *Le Corps de l'histoire: Métaphores et politique, 1770–1800* (Paris: Calmann-Lévy, 1993).

dom, an affinity promoted by the legal fiction of the king's "two bodies." According to medieval law, the king had a material or "natural" body and an invisible or "sacred" body. The material body died, but the sacred body lived on, for it consisted of all the king's subjects, united harmoniously in the fiction of an immaterial, figurative "body politic."[7] The sacred body was the incarnation of the realm, just as the Host was the incarnation of Jesus Christ. The relationship between the king's two bodies was made visible at the king's funeral. When he died, not one but two bodies—the second an effigy—were displayed before his mourners.[8] They cried, "The king is dead; long live the king," seeing in the "natural" body being buried the immortality of the "sacred" body of the state.

Imaging the state in terms of the king's body made it difficult to conceive of the state as a separate entity. King Louis XIV articulated this fusion when he said, "In France, the nation is not a separate body but resides entirely in the person of the King"; and as Louis XV announced to the rebellious Parisian magistrates, "The rights and interests of the nation, which you dare to render as a body separate from the Monarch, are, of necessity, united with mine and remain uniquely in my hands."[9] Small wonder, then, that the defining gesture of the Jacobin republic would be the beheading of the king, an act that signified the end not just of the monarchy but of a certain kind of society as well.[10]

If the king's body had great political significance, so too did the bodies of his subjects. As sites of signification and symbolization, subject bodies constituted a valuable "political resource," one that neither the old nor the new regime could afford to ignore.[11] By disciplining the body, the monarchy mastered the mind—and nowhere did it do this more effectively than at Versailles. The noble who longed to hold the candle at the

7. See Ernst H. Kantorowicz, *The King's Two Bodies: A Study in Mediaeval Political Theology* (Princeton: Princeton University Press, 1957). For a very useful analysis of Kantorowicz's influence on French history, see Ralph E. Giesey, *Cérémonial et puissance souveraine: France, XVe–XVIIe siècles* (Paris: Armand Colin, 1987), 9–19.

8. See Ralph E. Giesey, *The Royal Funeral Ceremony in France* (Geneva: Librairie Droz, 1960). An extensive bibliography exists, and the studies of Giesey, Lawrence Bryant, Sarah Hanley, and Richard Jackson provide meticulous and insightful analyses of the key ceremonies.

9. Cited in Pierre Goubert, *L'Ancien Régime*, vol. 1 (Paris: Armand Colin, 1969), 11.

10. Many historians have argued that the great novelty of the Revolution was the trial of the monarch. Like Lynn Hunt, we tend to believe that the significant event was not the trial but the king's execution; see Hunt, *Family Romance*, 12, 53–67. On the king's trial and execution, see David P. Jordan, *The King's Trial: The French Revolution vs. Louis XVI* (Berkeley: University of California Press, 1979).

11. The expression is Dorinda Outram's in *The Body and the French Revolution: Sex, Class, and Political Culture* (New Haven: Yale University Press, 1989), 1.

sixth *entrée* of the *levée* had been effectively harnessed to Bourbon absolutism. The aristocrat who learned to bow, speak, and dance in accordance with court (that is, royal) protocol had learned to obey. Courtiers' bodies became symbolic surfaces upon which Bourbon rule was inscribed. Their flesh bore the marks—the elaborate wigs, the high heels, the restrained demeanor—of royal will. Their movements—patterned and precise—recreated the disciplined designs of Versailles's music, dance, and architecture.

Eventually, the Jacobin republicans rejected this courtly body and tried to construct a new, republican body. They banished the marks of absolutism—the nobles' swords, the priests' collars, the aristocrats' knee breeches, and the courtly *vous* form of address—replacing them with egalitarian, tricolored sashes, workingmen's knee-breeches, and the fraternal *tu*. By these means, the Jacobins hoped to inscribe bodies instead with the marks of republican virtue.

Considering the centrality of the body in seventeenth- and eighteenth-century France, it is not surprising that the first scholars to study body politics—Norbert Elias, Ernst Kantorowicz, and Michel Foucault—all focused on this period.[12] The essays in this volume build on this work. Some, following Kantorowicz, examine the transformation of the king's body into a royal spectacle, one that commanded the vast resources of art, ceremony, and ritual. Others, using Foucault, analyze how state power inscribed itself on the bodies of French subjects through performance, ritual, and text. The influence of Elias is seen in analyses of etiquette as a disciplinary tool of court society and its impact on the body. All of the essays collected here add to our understanding of body politics by refining our conception of state power and by enlarging our definition of the body.

If Foucault located state power on the scaffold, many of our authors

12. Key studies by these scholars that have particular relevance to our project include Elias, *Court Society;* idem, *Power and Civility: The Civilizing Process*, trans. Edmund Jephcott (New York: Pantheon Books, 1983); Kantorowicz, *The King's Two Bodies;* and Michel Foucault, *Surveiller et punir: Naissance de la prison* (Paris: Gallimard, 1975). For a critical assessment of Elias's work, see Outram, *The Body and the French Revolution*, 6–26; and Roger Chartier, "Social Figuration and Habitus: Reading Elias," in *Cultural History: Between Practices and Representations*, trans. Lydia G. Cochrane (New York: Polity Press, 1988), 71–95. Of course, not all analyses of the political significance of the body focus on Bourbon France. Body history has centered on many different periods, times, and places, as an important collection of essays, *Fragments for the History of the Body*, ed. M. Feher, 3 vols. (New York: Zone Books, 1989), amply demonstrates.

find it on the stage.[13] Versailles, they demonstrate, was a vast theater, where discipline was expressed in the form of social ritual, music, dance, and drama.[14] Dance occupies an unusually large place in this collection because it played an unusually important role at Versailles. At the court, everyone danced: the king himself took dance lessons for twenty-five years and starred in the ballets that punctuated court life.[15] His performances constituted the premier spectacle at Versailles, and his courtiers struggled to dance with the same self-control and grace. This was a struggle not simply in terms of technique and practice; for in courtly dancing, from elaborate ballets to social dance, the only music permitted by the king was a stiff, regimented French music. Both literally and figuratively, therefore, the king called the tune and the courtiers danced to it.

The performing arts were, to use Foucault's phrase, one of the premier "technologies of power" of seventeenth- and eighteenth-century France. Foucault, indeed, implies that the state is invincible and omnipotent, always successful in disciplining bodies; in his reading, there is little room for resistance or change.[16] In fact, however, these "technologies of power" were not always effective; sometimes they encouraged not obedience, but active resistance. Which leads us to the overriding question addressed in this volume: When do bodies change? How can "new" bodies—that is, new gestures, dress, dance, behaviors—ever emerge? By exploring the flaws and contradictions inherent in Bourbon body politics, the essays in this collection show how the incomplete and inconsistent inscription of Bourbon power on bodies permitted the emergence of a new kind of body in the late eighteenth century.

Just as these essays paint a more nuanced picture of state power, so

13. See Foucault, *Surveiller et punir*, 3–4; and idem, "The Subject and Power," *Critical Inquiry* 8 (1982): 777–96.

14. Clifford Geertz's work on the politics of display is relevant to an understanding of the grand but fundamentally weak monarchy of Louis XIV; see his *Negara: The Theatre State in Nineteenth-Century Bali* (Princeton: Princeton University Press, 1980). Also relevant is Guy Debord's notion of a "société de spectacle." Versailles was indeed a society where social relations were mediated through spectacle, through the great pageants such as the Carrousel of 1662 or the Enchanted Island. See Debord, *La Société du spectacle* (Paris: Champ Libre, 1967).

15. See Mark Franko, *Dance as Text: Ideologies of the Baroque Body* (Cambridge: Cambridge University Press, 1993); also Régine Astier, "Louis XIV, 'Premier Danseur,'" in *Sun King: The Ascendancy of French Culture During the Reign of Louis XIV*, ed. David Lee Rubin (Washington, D.C.: Folger Shakespeare Library, 1992); and Apostolidès, *Roi-machine*.

16. For a good summary and critique of Foucault's views on power, see Mark Cousins and Althar Hussain, *Michel Foucault* (London: Macmillan, 1984), 225–52. For a more complete critique of Foucault's work, see the three-volume collection of essays on Foucault edited by Barry Smart, *Michel Foucault: Assessments* (London: Routledge, 1995).

they also explore a more complicated notion of bodies. When Foucault and Elias wrote, race and gender were not important categories of scholarly inquiry. No one thought to include (as do our contributors) Louisiana slaves or Caribbean women among French subjects. Nor did anyone think to describe Louis XIV's body politics as inherently gendered, even though Bourbon propaganda relied almost entirely on symbols of virility and potency.[17]

In "The Body Politics of French Absolutism," Jeffrey Merrick argues that Bourbon absolutism painted the monarch as a strong, virile, self-sufficient father. In an analysis of three theorists of Bourbon absolutism, Jean Bodin, Jacques-Bénigne Bossuet, and Jacob-Nicolas Moreau, Merrick shows that all three linked "personal order in the male self with public order in . . . the state." They compared the king to a male head of household who ruled over a potentially unruly extended family. This patriarchal image, Merrick argues, enhanced the king's legitimacy, but it could also undermine authority, for it opened the monarchy to charges of effeminacy, irrationality, and lust.

When the young Louis XIV took power, royal propagandists laid particular stress on the virile, masculine nature of the monarch. In "Lim(b)inal Images: 'Betwixt and Between' Louis XIV's Martial and Marital Bodies," Abby Zanger focuses on the "preliminary stage in the performance of Bourbon absolutism," the years 1658 and 1659 when the young king had triumphed in Flanders and made a politically advantageous marriage to a Spanish princess. At this time, Zanger reminds us, Louis's rule was still "unstable"; as a remedy, his propaganda apparatus strove to create images of virility. This visual strategy, however, created its own instability, as Zanger shows, by evoking the very thing it sought to dispel: disrupted female passions or sexuality.

Mark Franko's essay, "The King Cross-Dressed: Power and Force in Royal Ballets," also analyzes the gendering of the royal person, this time in dance. Between 1651 and 1668 Louis performed regularly as an androgynous figure. One might assume that these cross-dressed performances would subvert the royal person, but Franko demonstrates that in fact just the opposite occurred: this open androgyny dramatized the self-

17. For insights into how Louis XIV manipulated his physical image, see Louis Marin, *Portrait of the King* (Minneapolis: University of Minnesota Press, 1982); Apostolidès, *Roi-machine;* and, most recently, Peter Burke, *The Fabrication of Louis XIV* (New Haven: Yale University Press, 1992).

sufficiency of the king's body. Moreover, it reasserted one of the key tenets of Bourbon absolutism, the duality of the king's body.

Like dance, music also promoted the state's agenda. In "Unruly Passions and Courtly Dances: Technologies of the Body in Baroque Music," Susan McClary argues that music constituted a key "technology of the body," able to colonize interiority and harness the flesh to its rhythms. Because music risked unleashing the passions, and with it rebellion, McClary argues, the French state sought to censor the unruly rhythms of Italian music and replace them with the cultivated Platonic order and strict detachment of the French idiom. In this way music was made to serve the state—but always at some risk, for although the passionate nature of music could be shunted aside, it could not be obliterated.

In "Body of Law: The Sun King and the Code Noir," Joseph Roach also analyzes the effects—some unintended—of the performing arts cultivated at Versailles. Roach shows how Louis XIV sought to "extend his body" to the black slaves in Louisiana, who were subject to his patriarchal rule as defined in the Code Noir, a body of law "Concerning the Discipline and the Commerce of Negro Slaves of the Islands of French America." As Roach shows, one of the means for effecting this "transatlantic incorporation" was through enactment of such spectacles as *Les Plaisirs de l'île enchantée* (1664). However, certain provisions of the Code Noir also left the door open to Senegambian rituals of celebration and performance that cemented African-American identity. In this way, the Sun King fostered subversion and helped create a body that did not dance to his rhythms.

The essays in the second half of the volume describe how the eighteenth-century monarchs lost control not only of their subjects' bodies, but of their own as well. Antoine de Baecque's question "How did the King lose his body?"[18] is not merely facetious, for if we can understand how the king's body became desacralized, we can understand why Louis XVI lost his head. Thomas Kaiser's essay "Louis *le Bien-Aimé* and the Rhetoric of the Royal Body" locates the crucial moment in the demystification of the royal body in August 1744. At that time, royal image makers dubbed Louis "the well-loved," a public relations ploy that backfired almost from the start. First, it made royal legitimacy dangerously dependent on popularity. Was the king head of state only because he was loved? Second, it proved immediately ironic as Louis returned to his philandering ways, sparking stories of self-indulgence and indecision that only fu-

18. De Baecque, *Corps de l'histoire*, 45.

eled a growing *un*popularity. If Louis XV could not govern his own body, how could he rule the body politic?

Just as notions of the king's sacred body were being undermined, so was the old aristocratic comportment promoted at Versailles disappearing. With Susan Leigh Foster's "Dancing the Body Politic: Manner and Mimesis in Eighteenth-Century Ballet" we return to that crucial site of body politics, the dance. Foster describes the birth of a new dance genre in 1734, when ballerina Marie Sallé danced the story of Pygmalion without either corset or mask. Using pantomime, Sallé developed a vocabulary of gesture based not on social status but on personal identity. "Pantomime ballets," Susan Foster argues, "embodied a new conception of individuality as discrete and bounded by individuated bodies." Bodies previously "enmeshed . . . in social protocol" were now freed to express "an autonomous identity." Drawn from performances at "fair theaters," which arose in opposition to the three authorized theatrical establishments of Paris, Sallé's ballet reflected a "new social world," one in which individuals —not kings—would call the tune.

If on the dance stage bodies were beginning to move autonomously and take on meanings outside the great royal themes, a new drama was emerging in the courtroom as well. In "The Theater of Punishment: Melodrama and Judicial Reform in Prerevolutionary France," Sarah Maza shows how the authors of judicial briefs, or *mémoires judiciaires*, of the 1780s employed the same conventions—pathos and melodramatic expression—as the playwrights working within the *genre sérieux* or bourgeois drama. Both groups sought to make their audience—whether readers of briefs or viewers of plays—into active spectators of the events described. Their aim was to reflect the moral dilemma of ordinary people, not some "eternal truth" of a transcendent monarchical order. In both kinds of drama, then, individuals became the visual embodiment of the secular ideals of the Enlightenment.

To a certain degree, bourgeois theater was a forerunner of the great revolutionary pageants staged during the Terror and the Directory.[19] The festivals of Federation (1790–92) and of Reason (1793) were in effect morality plays, where the drama of the revolution was acted out for a popular audience. Here, abstract moral principles like reason, equality, and fraternity found bodily expression in the form of bare-chested goddesses or hardy *féderés*. As de Baecque right observes, we are wrong to consider the revolutionaries highly abstract or legalistic thinkers.[20] The new regime,

19. Ozouf, *Fête révolutionnaire*, 118–21.
20. De Baecque, *Corps de l'histoire*, 12.

like the old one, needed to manifest power in a physical, bodily form; it therefore chose Hercules and Marianne to represent the invisible "nation."[21] Such embodiment of the abstract and new was a necessity in the first republic, but it also posed a terrible problem, for it raised the most bothersome question of the time: precisely which bodies would be included in the renewed body politic? We know how the revolutionaries answered this question when it came to gender: women would not be full participants in the new democracy. But the issue of race has been much less clearly delineated.

In her essay "Sex, Savagery, and Slavery in the Shaping of the French Body Politic," Elizabeth Colwill explores this neglected aspect of the revolution and shows how feminism and abolitionism entered into the revolutionaries' definition of the new body politic. "Sexual hierarchy and the slave regime," she argues, "posed interrelated moral and practical dilemmas for the revolutionaries," bringing "the promise of universal rights into conflict with the Republicans' struggle to obtain political legitimacy at home and retain control of their empire abroad." Misogyny further complicated their response, for any discussion of political participation in the new body politic inevitably raised the issue of women's enfranchisement. As late as 1794, the question of which bodies—male or female, white or black—would be included in the new body politic remained unresolved.

Equally charged for the revolutionaries was the question of dress. Indeed, argues Lynn Hunt in her essay "Freedom of Dress in Revolutionary France," it was one of the "most hotly contested arenas" of the revolution, for it raised the question of what the body would signify in the new political order, and how. Certainly the revolutionaries were united when it came to condemning the old sumptuary legislation. No distinctions in dress, like the noble sword or the clerical collar, would be allowed to undermine the equality of men. But "dressing for equality" foundered in practice, first on gender and then on politics. Revolutionaries never really wanted to sweep away *all* distinction of dress. Bodies, they believed, needed to bear visible signs that conveyed political allegiance. Bodies without signs were unreadable and therefore suspect or dangerous.

The political pressures of the revolution made such signs imperative. With democracy the concept of the nation replaced the monarch and sovereignty was dispersed from the king's body to all bodies. Suddenly every

21. On body metaphors in revolutionary France, see ibid., 99–161. On Hercules and the Marianne, see Lynn Hunt, *Politics, Culture, and Class in the French Revolution* (Berkeley: University of California Press, 1984).

body bore political weight; clear, visible codes were more necessary than ever before. This transparency was difficult to achieve, however, for a new kind of body had emerged in the eighteenth century as well. On the stage, bodies wept, gestured, and declaimed in ways that revealed personality and expressed individuality. In dance and in fashion, bodies became more individualistic and idiosyncratic. With the old sartorial and behavioral codes gone, bodies were less legible, and a person's place in the nation was unclear.

The task of developing a new relationship between the body and the state fell now to the revolutionaries.[22] Just how they envisioned the political role of the body is beyond the scope of this volume. Suffice it to say that power would henceforth be embodied differently: the body would cease to bear the signs of absolutism and would assume new forms and roles.

This collection of essays is drawn from the papers presented at a series of conferences, "Constructing the Body," organized by Anne Mellor, Sara Melzer, and Kathryn Norberg at UCLA in 1992–93, sponsored by UCLA's William Andrews Clark Memorial Library and the Center for Seventeenth- and Eighteenth-Century Studies. Peter Reill, director of the Center, and Lori Stein, assistant director, helped inspire us to create a new, interdisciplinary vision and to make that vision a reality. At every step of the conference and publication process they were our steady support. We also wish to thank the Center's staff for their masterful organizational skills. Debbie Handren was a wizard at coordinating all the details of the conferences; Marina Romani and Candis Snowddy were the backbone of the sturdy support staff. We are particularly grateful to the Center for providing funds for illustrations and clerical costs.

We were most fortunate to have as our trusty editor Sheila Levine, whose knowledge of French culture and history helped shape the body of the text.

22. On the revolutionary body, see Outram, *The Body and the French Revolution*.

1

The Body Politics of French Absolutism

JEFFREY MERRICK

During his childhood Valentin Jamerey, born into a peasant family in 1695, heard fantastic stories about the city of Paris, which reportedly had paved streets lined with houses almost as big as the church in his village. He assumed that the people who lived in these oversized dwellings were larger than his own neighbors. He also assumed that the king, who was responsible for the administration of justice throughout the country, was even taller than the local judge, who was himself noticeably taller than the villagers under his jurisdiction. The child knew that the judge had an imposing voice, so he imagined that the king, who exercised "absolute power," commanded respect by means of his thunderous speech. He wondered, furthermore, if the monarch was invisible and immortal, like the Divinity, or in fact accessible to ordinary subjects.[1] No matter what peasants like Jamerey might have suspected, Louis XIV was no giant or god. Heels and wigs made him look taller than he really was. He outlived most of his contemporaries, not to mention his own son and grandson, but he eventually died from gangrene, after having survived smallpox, scarlet fever, measles, blennorrhagia, dysentery, intestinal parasites, respiratory infections, gravel, gout, rheumatism, skin diseases, oral abscesses, and the celebrated anal fistula. During his seventy years on the throne the Sun King, like other mortals, suffered from headaches, dizziness, palpitations, indigestion, flatulence, and nightmares.[2]

1. Valentin Jamerey-Duval, *Mémoires: Enfance et éducation d'un paysan au XVIIIe siècle*, ed. Jean-Marie Goulemot (Paris: Sycomore, 1981), 117.

2. See Michelle Caroly, *Le Corps du roi-soleil: Grandeurs et misères de Sa Majesté Louis*

The young Jamerey made sense of the concept of sovereignty by projecting suitable physical characteristics onto the person of the sovereign he had never seen with his own eyes or heard with his own ears. The doctors who scrutinized Louis XIV's flesh and feces day after day periodically attempted to discipline his gargantuan appetite and tactfully refrained from documenting his sexual athletics. They recorded his numerous afflictions in private journals and used their limited skills to help him preserve public appearances. The material body of the king, which hungered, lusted, and suffered, was connected with the figurative body of the kingdom through ritual, representation, and rhetoric. State ceremonies transformed the monarch, outfitted with all the trappings of majesty, into the visible image of monarchy. Writers and artists camouflaged his foibles and failures by clothing him, with Olympian or imperial apparel, in heroic style. The metaphorical traditions of the French crown, elaborated and emended over the course of centuries, structured the political culture of the kingdom around the sacralized and symbolized body of the king. The Bourbons did not simply ride the juggernaut constructed by apologists of absolutism across the country, which resisted centralization in many ways. The principles of absolutism, by the same token, did not constitute an inflexible ideology that precluded opposition, because they remained susceptible to conflicting interpretations throughout the ancien régime. This essay outlines the ways in which the sovereign embodied these principles and, like those by Abby Zanger and Thomas Kaiser in this volume, explores the tensions within the body politics of French absolutism.

Rituals and Representations

The French monarch, according to generations of jurists and clerics who stated and restated the tenets of absolutism under the Bourbon dynasty, inherited his crown from his predecessor and derived his authority from the Deity, not from the people. He was therefore ac-

XIV (Paris: Imago, 1991). On the physical and psychological history of his predecessor, documented in the remarkable journal of Jean Héroard, see Elizabeth Wirth Marvick, *Louis XIII: The Making of a King* (New Haven: Yale University Press, 1986); A. Lloyd Moote, *Louis XIII, the Just* (Berkeley: University of California Press, 1988); and Madeleine Foisil, "Le Corps de l'adolescent royal," in *Le Corps à la Renaissance: Actes du XXXe Colloque de Tours 1987*, ed. Jean Céard, Marie-Madeleine Fontaine, and Jean-Claude Margolin (Paris: Aux Amateurs de Livres, 1990), 309–20.

countable only to God, who commanded the heterogeneous population entrusted to his care to obey him but also charged him to rule them justly. Differentiated, like the organs and limbs that composed the human body, by the distinctive but complementary functions assigned to them by the Creator, subjects were subordinated, for their own good as well as the general welfare, to their divinely ordained ruler. Divided by their disparate loyalties as members of multitudinous and contentious corporate groups, they were united by their common allegiance to the sovereign, who, unlike them, had no selfish interests of his own and recognized the needs of the realm as a whole. He maintained public order by adjudicating conflicts and restoring harmony among the various parts of the body politic, which could not collaborate or survive without a head to direct them or, for that matter, with more than one head in charge. The king and the kingdom were distinguished in principle, because the one effectively limited the prerogatives and inevitably outlasted the reign of the other, but they could not be separated in practice, because the state had no other collective incarnation and no constitutional initiative of its own.

Apologists of absolutism characterized the king as "the head of his state" and the state as "the body of its king."[3] The monarch, also described as the soul, mind, heart, or spirit that animated and sustained the people, ruled his subjects in the way a responsible father ruled children connected to him through love, as opposed to the way an irresponsible despot ruled slaves alienated from him through fear. In dispensing royal justice and promulgating royal declarations, the king used his authority to secure the general welfare without misusing it in an arbitrary or tyrannical manner. He was not restricted by contractual obligations or restrained by institutionalized checks and balances, but he respected the precepts of divine and natural law, the fundamental laws of the realm, and the customary privileges of estates, provinces, cities, professions, guilds, and so forth. The sovereign did not share the plenitude of power annexed to the hereditary crown, but he necessarily relied on the services of administrative agents and willingly listened to the grievances of corporate groups. With the example of his ancestors in mind and the advice of his counselors in hand, he fulfilled the mission of the monarchy, in theory at least, by preserving the established order of things. In reality, of course, the Bourbons tampered with the religious, social, and political structures of the ancien régime. They routinely found themselves involved in negotiations as well as contestations with their unruly subjects,

3. Jean-François Senault, *Le Monarque, ou les devoirs du souverain* (Paris, 1661), 250.

and they regularly exercised their prerogatives in ways that belied their fatherly pretensions.

The king, needless to say, played the starring role in the state rituals that embodied the principles of the unwritten constitution of the kingdom.[4] During the royal coronation ceremony at Reims he was anointed in several locations, including the head and hands, with the miraculous oil conserved in the Holy Ampulla. Following this consecration of wisdom and strength, he was invested with the glorious regalia accumulated by his predecessors. Visibly ordained by God, visibly identified with Clovis, Charlemagne, and Saint Louis, he released prisoners, distributed alms, and cured scrofulous men and women with his thaumaturgic touch, subsequently exercised on major religious holidays. Having vowed at Reims to defend orthodoxy and punish iniquity, the sovereign traditionally confirmed the privileges of the corporate groups that acted out their submission by parading before his person during royal *entrées* in the capital and the provinces. Municipalities extolled his virtues and celebrated his victories in his presence, and eulogists remembered them after his death. The royal funeral ceremony, as elaborated during the sixteenth century, involved a life-size and lifelike effigy of the deceased monarch, which effectively prolonged his reign until the next coronation and thereby ensured the corporeal and juridical continuity of the monarchy. The individual, physical, and mortal body of the king ended up in the ancestral crypt at

4. See Ralph E. Giesey, *Cérémonial et puissance souveraine: France, XVe–XVIIe siècles* (Paris: Armand Colin, 1987); Alain Boureau, *Le Simple Corps du roi: L'Impossible Sacralité des souverains français* (Paris: Editions de Paris, 1989). On the coronation, see Richard A. Jackson, *Vive le Roi! A History of the French Coronation from Charles V to Charles X* (Chapel Hill: University of North Carolina Press, 1984); and Marina Valensise, "Le Sacre du roi: Stratégie symbolique et doctrine politique de la monarchie française," *Annales E.S.C.* 41 (1986): 543–78. On the entry, see Lawrence M. Bryant, *The King and the City in the Parisian Royal Entry Ceremony: Politics, Ritual, and Art in the Renaissance* (Geneva: Librairie Droz, 1986); idem, "Politics, Ceremonies, and Embodiments of Majesty in Henry II's France," in *European Monarchy: Its Evolution and Practice from Roman Antiquity to Modern Times*, ed. Heinz Duchhardt, Richard A. Jackson, and David Sturdy (Stuttgart: Franz Steiner Verlag, 1992), 127–54; and François Moureau, "Les Entrées royales ou le plaisir du prince," *XVIIIe Siècle* 17 (1985): 195–208. On the funeral, see Ralph E. Giesey, *The Royal Funeral Ceremony in Renaissance France* (Geneva: Librairie Droz, 1960); and Robert N. Nicolich, "Sunset: The Spectacle of the Royal Funeral and Memorial Services at the End of the Reign of Louis XIV," in *Sun King: The Ascendancy of French Culture During the Reign of Louis XIV*, ed. David Lee Rubin (Washington, D.C.: Folger Shakespeare Library, 1992), 45–72. On the *lit de justice*, see Sarah Hanley, *The Lit de Justice of the Kings of France: Constitutional Ideology in Legend, Ritual, and Discourse* (Princeton: Princeton University Press, 1983); Mack P. Holt, "The King in Parlement: The Problem of the *Lit de Justice* in Sixteenth-Century France," *Historical Journal* 31 (1988): 507–23; and Elizabeth A. R. Brown and Richard C. Famiglietti, *The Lit de Justice: Semantics, Ceremonial, and the Parlement of Paris, 1300–1600* (Sigmaringen: J. Thorbecke, 1994).

Saint-Denis (except for the heart and bowels, consigned as a matter of course to various Parisian churches), but the collective, intangible, and immortal body of kingship lived on in the person of his successor.

The programs and meanings of these rituals changed after 1610, when Henry IV was assassinated by Ravaillac and the underage dauphin was recognized as king by the Parlement of Paris during a *lit de justice*. This unprecedented method of inauguration, replayed when five-year-olds inherited the crown in 1643 and 1715, eclipsed the constitutional significance of the funeral and coronation ceremonies. The effigy of the deceased monarch disappeared from the funeral because it was no longer necessary for the purpose of assuring dynastic succession. The popular acclamation preceding the royal oaths disappeared from the coronation because it suggested a measure of popular consent incompatible with absolutist ideology. Intent on consolidating royal sovereignty over their realm, still divided by countless legal and fiscal distinctions, the Bourbons reworked the ritualistic resources of the monarchy. They downplayed the practice of collaboration between ruler and ruled and emphasized the principle of the concentration of authority in their own hands. By the time of Louis XIV they used *entrées*, staged less frequently than before, to promote royal power at the expense of local privileges. By the time of Louis XV they used *lits de justice*, staged more frequently than before, to force registration of royal declarations by the troublesome parlementaires, who led the resistance to absolutism in the eighteenth century. They largely abandoned journeys through the provinces, undertaken by their predecessors to pacify or unify the country, and constructed a microcosmic model of religious, social, and political order around themselves at Versailles.[5]

Louis XIV, who traveled through the Midi after the conclusion of the prolonged war with Spain and entered Paris triumphantly with his bride in 1660, settled at Versailles some two decades later.[6] The elaborate etiquette regulating language, gestures, and conduct demonstrated his sovereignty more effectively than impressive but infrequent rituals invested with constitutional significance. The theatrical life of the French court collapsed the mystical into the physical body of the king, who played the role

5. On royal journeys, see Jean Boutier, Alain Dewerpe, and Daniel Nordman, *Un Tour de France royal: Le Voyage de Charles IX, 1564–1566* (Paris: Aubier, 1984).

6. On the Parisian entry, see Karl Mösender, *Zeremoniell und monumentale Poesie: Die Entrée solonnelle Ludwigs IV. 1600 in Paris* (Berlin: Gebrüder Mann, 1983). On the royal court, see Giesey, *Cérémonial et puissance souveraine;* Norbert Elias, *The Court Society*, trans. Edmund Jephcott (New York: Pantheon Books, 1983); and Jean-François Solnon, *La Cour de France* (Paris: Fayard, 1987).

of the sun not only when costumed as such in allegorical ballets but also during the daily cycle from *lever* to *coucher*. The palace and gardens, decorated with Apollonian imagery, manifested and reinforced his authority. They provided a stage for plays and pageants that celebrated his mastery over self and subjects as well as external enemies and forces of disorder in the natural and human worlds.[7] Quotidian routines and extravagant spectacles focused the attention of the domesticated aristocracy—and by extension, the corporate kingdom as a whole—on the figure of the monarch, who dispensed sinecures and pensions to the courtiers congregated around him and distributed favors by controlling proximity to his person.[8] Louis XIV, who distinguished France from servile countries in which rulers assumed that majesty required them to conceal themselves from their people, dressed, dined, and even defecated with an audience.[9] He generally avoided Paris, which had rebelled against the regency government during his childhood, but did make himself accessible to ordinary subjects at times during the regular course of events at Versailles.

The Bourbon withdrawal from public view accelerated during the reign of Louis XV, who frequented the private quarters of his mistresses and stopped exercising the royal touch on religious holidays.[10] Parisians acclaimed him as Louis "the Beloved" after his miraculous recovery from an illness at Metz and his glorious victory on the battlefield at Fontenoy in 1744.[11] They shouted "Long live the king!" when he laid the cornerstone of the church of Saint Geneviève and kneeled in the mud before the holy sacrament on the Pont Neuf.[12] More detached from this less vis-

7. See Abby Zanger's essay in this volume, as well as her "Making Sweat: Sex and the Gender of National Reproduction in the Marriage of Louis XIII," *Yale French Studies* 86 (1994): 187–205.

8. On festivals, see Robert M. Isherwood, *Music in the Service of the King: France in the Seventeenth Century* (Ithaca: Cornell University Press, 1973); Jean-Marie Apostolidès, *Le Roi-machine: Spectacle et politique au temps de Louis XIV* (Paris: Editions de Minuit, 1981); Marie-Christine Moine, *Les Fêtes à la cour du Roi-soleil, 1653–1715* (Paris: Editions Fernand Lanore, 1984); and Orest Ranum, "Islands and the Self in a Ludovican Fête," and Régine Astier, "Louis XIV, 'Premier Danseur,'" in Rubin (ed.), *Sun King*, 17–34 and 73–102, respectively.

9. *Mémoires de Louis XIV*, ed. Jean Longnon, rev. and corrected ed. (Paris: Librairie Jean Tallandier, 1978), 133.

10. See Jean de Viguerie, "Le Roi et le public: L'Exemple de Louis XV," *Revue d'histoire moderne et contemporaine* 34 (1987): 23–35.

11. See Thomas Kaiser's essay in this volume, as well as his "Madame de Pompadour and the Theaters of Power," *French Historical Studies* 19 (1996): 1025–44.

12. Siméon-Prosper Hardy, "Mes Loisirs, ou journal des événements tels qu'ils parviennent à ma connaissance," Bibliothèque Nationale, MS. fonds français 6680, fol. 52; Anne-Emmanuel-Ferdinand-François de Croy, *Journal inédit*, ed. Emmanuel-Henry de Grouchy and Paul Cottin, 4 vols. (Paris: Flammarion, 1906), 2:227.

ible sovereign, they confronted him with damning silence on many other occasions, especially when he traversed the capital in order to discipline the popular parlementaires, widely regarded as defenders of liberty against despotism. The royal body, in the spotlight during the *lit de justice*, projected not health, courage, or piety, but rather brutality. It was reported that Louis XV not only "sat down" on the bed of Lady Justice but also "raped" her.[13] Prolonged conflicts concerning religious, fiscal, and administrative issues during the 1750s suggested that the king, apparently blind to the misery of his people and deaf to the protests of his magistrates, did not have the interests of the kingdom at heart or in mind.[14] These conflicts motivated Damiens to strike the sacred person of the monarch—who seemed figuratively, if not literally, inaccessible—in the courtyard at Versailles in 1757. The public executioners dismembered this regicide, like Ravaillac before him, for attacking the divinely ordained sovereign and thereby endangering the body politic as a whole.[15]

The parlementaires, who claimed to speak for the body politic, had already staked out more independence for it, and for themselves, than absolutist ideology allowed. During the so-called session of the flagellation in 1766, the king had to remind them that "the public order as a whole" emanated from his person and that "the interests of the nation," which they had dared to describe as a corporate body differentiated from the crown, remained inseparable from his own and rested in his hands alone.[16] The increasingly unpopular Louis XV exerted royal authority in a patriarchal manner by suppressing the parlements, and the initially popular Louis XVI exercised royal prerogatives in a paternalistic style by recalling them. As late as 1786, when he made his only substantial trip away from Versailles, ordinary people flocked to see him. He allowed his "children," as he called them, to approach his unguarded person and did not take offense when one woman spontaneously kissed him "like a

13. *Correspondance secrète, politique, et littéraire*, 18 vols. (London, 1787–90), 1:69.

14. On public opinion, see Roger Chartier, *The Cultural Origins of the French Revolution*, trans. Lydia G. Cochrane (Durham, N.C.: Duke University Press, 1991); and Arlette Farge, *Dire et mal dire: L'Opinion publique au XVIIIe siècle* (Paris: Editions du Seuil, 1992).

15. See Dale K. Van Kley, *The Damiens Affair and the Unraveling of the Ancien Régime, 1750–1770* (Princeton: Princeton University Press, 1984); and Pierre Rétat, ed., *L'Attentat de Damiens: Discours sur l'événement au XVIIIe siècle* (Paris: Editions du CNRS; Lyon: Presses Universitaires de Lyon, 1979). On regicide more generally, see also Roland Mousnier, *L'Assassinat d'Henri IV, 14 mai 1610* (Paris: Gallimard, 1964); Jacques Hennequin, *Henri IV dans ses oraisons funèbres, ou la naissance d'une légende* (Paris: Klincksieck, 1977); and Pierre Chevallier, *Les Régicides: Clément, Ravaillac, Damiens* (Paris: Fayard, 1989).

16. *Les Remontrances du parlement de Paris au XVIIIe siecle*, ed. Jules Flammermont, 3 vols. (Paris: Imprimerie Nationale, 1888–98), 2:558.

father."[17] He distinguished himself, during this voyage "in the midst of his family," from "despots" who "hide in the depths of their palaces," and many of the *cahiers de doléances* drafted in 1789 addressed him in affectionate and respectful terms.[18] By that time, however, the monarchy had lost control of its ritualistic and representational resources, as well as political culture more generally. The "nation," more disengaged from the royal body and less infantilized by the royal father, expressed its sentiments on the occasion of the funeral of Louis XV in 1774 and the coronation of Louis XVI in 1775, not to mention the *lits de justice* of 1787–88 and the ceremonies culminating in the royal excursion to Paris just days after the assault on the Bastille.[19]

French sovereigns may have confined themselves more and more to Versailles, but they dispatched representatives and disseminated representations throughout the country. The royal name, inscribed on laws and invoked in public prayers, and the royal image, stamped on coins and sculpted in public squares, identified the largely invisible king as the embodiment of the kingdom and gave kingship real presence in the daily lives of his subjects, who celebrated the births of his children and the victories of his armies.[20] Writers and artists commonly described and depicted the monarch in stylized form by glorifying his piety, prowess, prudence, and patronage. They disguised, or at least embellished, his person with classical, Christian, and historical references and symbols that illuminated his royal mission and illustrated his royal virtues.[21] They regularly asso-

17. *Le Voyage de Louis XVI en Normandie, 21–29 juin 1786*, ed. Jeanne-Marie Gaudillot (Caen: Société d'Impression Caron, 1967), 50, 35.

18. *L'Espion anglais, ou correspondance secrète entre Milord All'Eye et Milord All'Ear*, 10 vols. (London, 1784–86), 2:54. On the *cahiers*, see John Markoff, "Images du roi au début de la Révolution," in *L'Image de la Révolution française*, ed. Michel Vovelle, 4 vols. (New York: Pergamon Press, 1990), 1:237–45.

19. See Jeffrey Merrick, "Politics in the Pulpit: Ecclesiastical Discourse on the Death of Louis XV," *History of European Ideas* 7 (1988): 149–60; Martin Papenheim, *Erinnerung und Unsterblichkeit: Semantische Studien zum Totenkult in Frankreich, 1715–1794* (Stuttgart: Klett-Cotta, 1992); Alain-Charles Gruber, *Les Grandes Fêtes et leurs décors à l'époque de Louis XVI* (Paris: Librairie Droz, 1972); Hermann Weber, "Das Sacre Ludwigs XVI. vom 11. Juni 1775 und die Krise des Ancien Regime," in *Vom Ancien Regime zum Französischen Revolution: Forschungen und Perspektiven*, ed. Ernst Hinrichs, Eberhard Schmitt, and Rudolf Vierhaus (Göttingen: Vandenhoeck & Ruprecht, 1978), 539–65; and Lawrence M. Bryant, "Royal Ceremony and the Revolutionary Strategies of the Third Estate," *Eighteenth-Century Studies* 22 (1989): 413–50.

20. On the diffusion of royal news, see Michèle Fogel, *Les Cérémonies de l'information dans la France du XVIe au XVIIIe siècle* (Paris: Fayard, 1989).

21. On royal symbolism in general, see Jean Céard, "Les Visages de la royauté en France à la Renaissance," in *Les Monarchies*, ed. Emmanuel LeRoy Ladurie (Paris: Presses Universitaires de France, 1986), 73–90; Anne-Marie Lecoq, "La Symbolique de l'état: Les Images de la monarchie des premiers Valois à Louis XIV," in *Les Lieux de mémoire*, ed. Pierre Nora,

ciated him with Hebrew kings and Roman emperors, as well as with Hercules, Apollo, and Jupiter. Representations of monarchy repeated traditional themes but also reflected changing sensibilities. In the second half of the eighteenth century, for example, royal monuments shed some of their mythological and military attributes and emphasized the ruler's fatherly concern for the welfare of his people. Subjects applauded the installation of the monuments but sometimes desecrated these surrogate figures of Louis XV that reigned over urban spaces. Defamatory placards deposited on the pedestals rewrote effusive inscriptions in much less flattering terms. The menacing stick planted in the outstretched hand of the Pigalle statue in Reims one night in 1772, a year after the suppression of the parlements, made the bronze body of the sovereign reveal the despotic sentiments attributed to him by "patriotic" critics.[22] Images, as well as ceremonies, registered the impact of prolonged political conflicts by the time of Louis XVI, who was portrayed in prints not only as the worthy descendant of Henry IV but also as a pig.[23]

Rhetoric and Resistance

The rituals of the French monarchy and representations of French monarchs employed verbal and visual versions of a conventional rhetoric of order and disorder. This rhetoric located the crown within con-

2 vols. in 4 (Paris: Gallimard, 1984–86), 2/2:145–92; Gérard Sabatier, "Les Rois de représentation: Image et pouvoir (XVIe–XVIIe siècle)," *Revue de synthèse*, 4th ser., 3–4 (1991): 387–422. On representations of Louis XIV in particular, see Nicole Ferrier-Caverivière, *L'Image de Louis XIV dans la littérature française de 1660 à 1715* (Paris: Presses Universitaires de France, 1981); Louis Marin, *Portrait of the King*, trans. Martha M. Houle (Minneapolis: University of Minnesota Press, 1988); Michel Martin, *Les Monuments équestres de Louis XIV: Une Grande Entreprise de propagande monarchique* (Paris: Picard, 1986); Jean-Pierre Néradeau, *L'Olympe du roi-soleil: Mythologie et idéologie royale au XVIIe siècle* (Paris: Les Belles Lettres, 1986); Guy Walton, *Louis XIV's Versailles* (Chicago: University of Chicago Press, 1986); Chantall Grell and Christian Michel, *L'Ecole des princes ou Alexandre disgracié: Essai sur la mythologie monarchique de la France absolue* (Paris: Les Belles Lettres, 1988); Peter Burke, *The Fabrication of Louis XIV* (New Haven: Yale University Press, 1992); Robert W. Berger, *The Palace of the Sun: The Louvre of Louis XIV* (University Park: Pennsylvania State University Press, 1993); and idem, *A Royal Passion: Louis XIV as Patron of Architecture* (Cambridge: Cambridge University Press, 1994).

22. See Jeffrey Merrick, "Politics on Pedestals: Royal Monuments in Eighteenth-Century France," *French History* 5 (1991): 234–64.

23. See Annie Duprat, "La Dégradation de l'image royale dans la caricature révolutionnaire," in *Les Images de la Révolution française*, ed. Michel Vovelle (Paris: Publications de la Sorbonne, 1988), 168–75; and idem, "Du 'roi-père' au 'roi-cochon,'" in *Saint-Denis ou le dernier jugement des rois* (La Garenne-Colombes: Editions de l'Espace Européen, 1992), 81–90.

centric structures of authority and subordination, routinely embodied by cosmological, familial, and corporeal metaphors that naturalized politics and politicized nature.[24] Like the sun in the heavens, the father in the household, and the mind in the self, the sovereign unified, guided, and disciplined the country. In principle, at least, the sun did not scorch the planets, the father did not abuse his wife or children, the mind did not endanger the limbs, and the sovereign did not misuse his prerogatives, intended to preserve the privileges of his subjects and secure the welfare of the realm as a whole. The corporate kingdom, insofar as it resembled the human body, was composed of a multitude of interdependent parts with a variety of functions to perform. Some texts worked out the comparison in detail, for example by identifying magistrates, soldiers, and artisans and peasants as eyes and ears, arms and hands, and legs and feet, respectively.[25] As long as all of its parts, including its figurative head, cooperated, the body politic remained healthy. If the organs and limbs rebelled—as they did in La Fontaine's fable about the stomach—or if the head ignored their needs, the state fell sick.[26] If not cured, through purgation or some other appropriate treatment, it eventually perished.

According to the natural order of things, the mind, which associated humans with the suprahuman Creator and entitled them to dominion over the earth, ruled, or at least should rule, the body, which associated humans with the subhuman animals and involved them in disruptive misconduct. Husbands, fathers, and kings, by the same token, were supposed to rule wives, children, and subjects, all of whom were ruled by their instincts and therefore incapable of ruling themselves.[27] Endowed with ra-

24. On political metaphors in general, see James Daly, *Cosmic Harmony and Political Thinking in Early Stuart England* (Philadelphia: American Philosophical Society, 1979); George Armstrong Kelly, "Mortal Man, Immortal Society: Political Metaphors in Eighteenth-Century France," *Political Theory* 14 (1986): 5–29; Otto Mayr, *Authority, Liberty, and Automatic Machinery in Early Modern Europe* (Baltimore: Johns Hopkins University Press, 1986); and Stephen L. Collins, *From Divine Cosmos to Sovereign State: An Intellectual History of Consciousness and the Idea of Order in Renaissance England* (Oxford: Oxford University Press, 1989).

25. François de Gravelle, *Politiques royales* (Lyon, 1596), 118. On the body and the state, see Paul Archambault, "The Analogy of the Body in Renaissance Political Literature," *Bibliothèque d'humanisme et renaissance* 29 (1967): 21–53; D. G. Hale, *The Body Politic: A Political Metaphor in Renaissance English Literature* (Hague: Mouton, 1971); and Anne-Marie Brenot, "Le Corps pour royaume: Le Langage politique de la fin du XVIe siècle et du début du XVIIe," *Histoire, Economie, Société* 10 (1991): 441–66.

26. Jean de La Fontaine, "Les Membres et l'estomac," in *Oeuvres complètes*, ed. René Groos and Jacques Schiffrin, 2 vols. (Paris: Gallimard, 1954), 1:74–5.

27. On the household and the state, see Natalie Zemon Davis, "Women on Top," in *Society and Culture in Early Modern France* (Stanford: Stanford University Press, 1973), 134–51;

tionality and invested with authority, patriarchal figures preserved domestic and public order by correcting the errors and curbing the passions of the unreasoning and unruly characters subordinated to them. Thanks to the progress of reformed Catholicism and royal absolutism, they consolidated their disciplinary powers over the disorderly bodies of their dependents.[28] The crown regulated female waywardness by punishing illegitimacy and adultery, checked youthful recklessness by strengthening paternal control of marriage, and bridled popular forwardness by suppressing rural and urban rebellions.[29] Bodily and familial metaphors provided a way of describing, connecting, and maintaining social and political order. These familiar but versatile tropes, at the same time, did not have just one fixed configuration or one fixed signification during the period from the Renaissance to the Revolution. At different times, in different circumstances, jurists and pamphleteers used them in different ways for different purposes, not only to justify but also to challenge the official version of absolutism.

In their classic expositions of the principles of French absolutism, written in the 1570s, 1670s, and 1770s, respectively, Jean Bodin, Jacques-Bénigne Bossuet, and Jacob-Nicolas Moreau linked order in the kingdom with order in the cosmos, the family, and the self. Bodin subordinated kings to God, magistrates to kings, subjects to magistrates, wives to husbands, children to fathers, servants to masters, and "bestial" appetites to

---

Pierre Ronzeaud, "La Femme au pouvoir ou le monde à l'envers," *XVIIe siècle*, no. 108 (1975): 9–33; Gordon J. Schochet, *Patriarchalism in Political Thought: The Authoritarian Family and Political Speculation and Attitudes, Especially in Seventeenth-Century England* (New York: Basic Books, 1975); Susan Dwyer Amussen, *An Ordered Society: Gender and Class in Early Modern England* (Oxford: Basil Blackwell, 1988); Sarah Hanley, "Engendering the State: Family Formation and State Building in Early Modern France," *French Historical Studies* 16 (1989): 4–27; idem, "The Monarchic State in Early Modern France: Marital Regime, Government, and Male Right," in *Politics, Ideology, and Law in Early Modern Europe: Essays in Honor of J.H.M. Salmon*, ed. Adrianna Bakos (Rochester, N.Y.: University of Rochester Press, 1994), 107–26; Robert Descimon, "Les Fonctions de la métaphore du mariage politique du roi et de la république: France, XVe–XVIIIe siècles," *Annales E.S.C.* 47 (1992): 1127–47; and Lynn Hunt, *The Family Romance of the French Revolution* (Berkeley: University of California Press, 1992).

28. See Robert Muchembled, *Culture populaire et culture des élites, XVe–XVIIIe siècles* (Paris: Flammarion, 1978); idem, *L'Invention de l'homme moderne: Sensibilités, moeurs, et comportements collectifs sous l'ancien régime* (Paris: Fayard, 1988); and James R. Farr, *Authority and Sexuality in Early Modern Burgundy, 1550–1730* (New York: Oxford University Press, 1995).

29. On "the people," see Pierre Ronzeaud, *Peuple et représentations sous le règne de Louis XIV: Les Représentations du peuple dans la littérature politique en France sous le règne de Louis XIV* (Aix: Université de Provence, 1988); and Benoît Garnot, *Le Peuple au siècle des lumières: Echec d'un dressage culturel* (Paris: Imago, 1990).

"divine" reason.[30] The members of the household and the population of the realm obeyed their superiors, just as organs and limbs obeyed the head, because they embodied the dictates of reason, "always in conformity with the will of God."[31] These superiors, who deserved to rule others because they managed to rule themselves, restrained the cupidity of women, curbed the excesses of sons and daughters, and repressed the license of the populace, described as an unreasoning "beast with several heads."[32] They ruled their subordinates, of course, justly and not despotically. Bodin distinguished the "royal" monarch, devoted to public welfare and visible to subjects who loved him, from the "tyrannical" monarch, preoccupied with selfish pleasures and inaccessible to subjects who feared him.[33] Against the background of the civil wars, which he compared to self-destructive fighting among parts of the human body, he condemned rebellion within the body politic, but he also qualified the obligations of subordinates.[34] Wives did not have to comply with "illicit" orders of their spouses. Fathers who squandered their estates, abused their children, or lost their senses deserved to be deprived of their powers over others, "inasmuch as they have none over themselves."[35] Subjects were not obliged to obey their sovereign in things "contrary to the law of God or nature."[36] Bodin scorned unmanly husbands dominated by their wives and effeminate monarchs dominated by their passions (like Sardanapalus, who spent more time "among women than among men") because they betrayed the standard of reason and degraded the authority entrusted to them.[37]

Bossuet excluded planets, climates, and humors from his analysis of politics, based on "the very words of Holy Scripture" alone, but he endorsed the patriarchal vision of the interconnected state, household, and body outlined by Bodin. In the 1670s, as in the 1570s, the Creator invested husbands, fathers, and kings with authority over various categories of irrational subordinates identified with the passions that disrupted human society. "The whole state exists in the person of the ruler," according to Bossuet, because "the reason that guides the state" resided only in the ruler,

30. Jean Bodin, *Les Six Livres de la république*, 6 vols. (Lyon, 1593; repr. Paris: Fayard, 1986), 1:34.

31. Ibid., 52.

32. Ibid., 6:149.

33. Ibid., 2:35.

34. Ibid., 1:54.

35. Ibid., 75.

36. Ibid., 2:80.

37. Ibid., 4:17.

who embodied and administered justice.[38] The divinely ordained sovereign, with "eyes and hands everywhere," preserved order throughout the body politic by restraining the "natural indocility" of the people, who were obligated to obey his commands provided "they contain nothing contrary to the commands of God."[39] He respected the lives and property of his subjects, whom he treated like children, not slaves, and they, in return, loved him like a solicitous father instead of hating him like "a ferocious beast."[40] The paternalistic monarch, whose mastery of the realm depended on his mastery of the self, "the foundation of all authority," did not allow whims, resentments, or desires to confound his intelligence or weaken his resolve.[41] In this regard at least, he shunned the Old Testament examples of David, who, despite his prowess, failed to discipline his own children, and Solomon, who, despite his wisdom, surrendered to slackness and dissipation.[42]

Moreau, who, like Bossuet, composed his text at the behest of the crown for the instruction of the dauphin, restated many of the same lessons a century later, in more modern and less metaphorical language. He attributed the authority of husbands over wives, which supposedly ensured the preservation of morals in most countries, to the laws of nature and the difference established by the Creator between the "strengths" (presumably in multiple senses of the word—physical, mental, and moral) of the two sexes.[43] He described the family as the foundation of the state because it inculcated "domestic docility," "the model for political subordination," among the younger generation.[44] Nature, according to Moreau, made humans sociable, by making them dependent upon each other for the satisfaction of their needs, and also made them something other than animals, by giving them the faculty of reason to regulate their conduct. Nature granted rights but also imposed obligations, which the multitude, inclined "to let itself be led astray" by unruly passions, could

38. Jacques-Bénigne Bossuet, *Politique tirée des propres paroles de l'Ecriture sainte*, ed. Jacques Le Brun (Geneva: Librairie Droz, 1967), 185.

39. Ibid., 170, 99, 194.

40. Ibid., 90.

41. Ibid., 111.

42. On the shortcomings of these kings, see ibid., 429 and 435, respectively.

43. Jacob-Nicolas Moreau, *Les Devoirs du prince réduits à un seul principe* (Versailles, 1775), 312. On Moreau, see Dieter Gembecki, *Histoire et politique à la fin de l'ancien régime: Jacob-Nicolas Moreau, 1717–1803* (Paris: Librairie A.-G. Nizet, 1979); and Keith Michael Baker, "Controlling French History: The Ideological Arsenal of Jacob-Nicolas Moreau," in *Inventing the French Revolution: Essays on French Political Culture in the Eighteenth Century* (Cambridge: Cambridge University Press, 1990), 59–85.

44. Moreau, *Devoirs du prince*, 313

not fulfill unless coerced into doing so.[45] The royal father, responsible for "protecting us against our own license," subjected "all our passions and all our interests" to the rule of justice, without translating all of his own desires into decrees.[46] He was not required to negotiate with his people, but he was expected to promulgate reasonable laws, after consultation and deliberation, that served the collective welfare.

Bodin, Bossuet, and Moreau, writing in different centuries and different circumstances, explicated the body politics of French absolutism in somewhat different terms. They agreed, nevertheless, that husbands, fathers, and especially kings, in order to prevent the blindness and brutality of their ignorant and irresponsible dependents from turning the world upside down, must, in their persons and their policies, embody the dominance of reason over the passions. Richelieu incorporated this exhortation into his political testament, addressed to the temperamental Louis XIII. He declared that humans, as a species, should obey the faculty that distinguished them from beasts and specified that kings "more than all others should be motivated by reason," both because God made them responsible for enforcing its authority and because subjects automatically loved rulers who were guided by its dictates.[47] Women were excluded from government, he explained, because "the disorderly ascendency of their emotions" deprived them of "the masculine virtue of making decisions rationally" along with "the masculine vigor necessary to public administration."[48] The cardinal warned the monarch against the weakness and indolence characteristic of women, which disposed them to injustice and cruelty. He urged Louis XIII to exercise foresight, avoid precipitousness, weigh the judicious advice of male counselors, and shun the destructive influence of female favorites, who inevitably subordinated "public interest" to "private affections."[49]

The masculinist myth of royal rationality, like other types of gendered discourse identified by Joan Scott, articulated relationships of power.[50] Given its mixed or at least multiple messages, which were acknowledged by exponents of the official version of absolutism, this myth turned out

45. Ibid., 36.

46. Ibid., xvii, 63.

47. *The Political Testament of Cardinal Richelieu: The Significant Chapters and Supporting Selections*, ed. Henry Bertram Hill (Madison: University of Wisconsin Press, 1961), 39 (excerpted and translated from the French edition of Louis André [Paris, 1947]).

48. Richelieu, *Political Testament*, 75, 45.

49. Ibid., 108.

50. See Joan Wallach Scott, "Gender: A Useful Category of Historical Analysis," in *Gender and the Politics of History* (New York: Columbia University Press, 1988), 28–50.

to be one of several ideological sites in which debates about the unwritten constitution were played out in figurative form. Bodin, Bossuet, Moreau, and Richelieu all supported royal authority in prescriptive literature by linking personal order in the male self with public order in the lawful state, which was peopled by infantilized subjects. They insisted that kings, like husbands and fathers, must discipline themselves, as well as their subordinates, because they recognized that the passions of these patriarchal figures, if not carefully regulated, might cause injustice and legitimize disobedience. Critics of royal policies throughout the early modern period fixated on the dangerous consequences of the fallibility of ministers and monarchs. They challenged royal authority, or at least abuses of royal authority, in polemical literature by linking personal disorder in the feminized and animalized self with public disorder in the lawless state, which was reduced to slavery or even savagery. During the sixteenth-century civil wars, for example, pamphleteers accused Catherine de Medici and Henry III of tyranny not only by cataloguing their misdeeds but also by characterizing them as diseased, depraved, and diabolical.[51]

During the Fronde critics of the regency government denounced Anne of Austria and, even more aggressively, Jules Mazarin for mismanaging their own bodies as well as the body politic.[52] The authors of the Mazarinades (some five thousand tracts published between 1648 and 1653) made extensive use of cosmological, familial, and corporeal rhetoric in condemning Louis XIII's widow and minister for ruling the country in an ungodly and unjust manner. Working within the flexible framework of conventional principles outlined above, pamphleteers blamed misrule on the disruptive passions of the Spanish queen, who corroborated traditional stereotypes about female indiscipline, and the Italian cardinal, who betrayed traditional expectations about male discipline. The disorderly couple, allegedly obsessed with the pleasures of the flesh, effectively repudi-

51. See David L. Teasley, "Legends of the Last Valois: A New Look at Propaganda Attacking the French Monarchs During the Wars of Religion, 1559–1589," Ph.D. diss., Georgetown University, 1985; and idem, "The Charge of Sodomy as a Political Weapon in Early Modern France: The Case of Henry III in Catholic League Polemics, 1585–1589," *Maryland Historian* 18 (1987): 17–30.

52. On the Mazarinades, see Marie-Noëlle Grand-Mesnil, *Mazarin, la Fronde, et la presse, 1647–49* (Paris: Armand Colin, 1967); Christian Jouhaud, *Mazarinades: La Fronde des mots* (Paris: Aubier, 1985); and Hubert Carrier, *La Presse de la Fronde, 1648–1653: Les Mazarinades*, 2 vols. (Geneva: Librairie Droz, 1989–91). On the theme of the undisciplined body in these texts, see Jeffrey Merrick, "The Cardinal and the Queen: Sexual and Political Disorders in the Mazarinades," *French Historical Studies* 18 (1994): 667–99; and Lewis C. Seifert, "Eroticizing the Fronde: Sexual Deviance and Political Disorder in the Mazarinades," *L'Esprit Créateur* 35 (1995): 22–36.

ated the young Louis XIV's fatherly obligation to defend the persons, property, and privileges of the men and women entrusted to his care. Instead of preserving "the legitimate liberty that makes kings reign in the hearts of the people," they surrendered themselves to debased and despotic appetites that degraded the monarchy and alienated the affections of the population.[53] Instead of consulting the faculty of reason, which should have guided their policies, and cultivating the spirit of love, which should have united the country, the selfish and licentious foreigners spread discord, violence, and fear throughout the realm.

Pamphleteers, who blamed Mazarin, more often than not, for the misgovernment of the country, inscribed his many offenses on his disfigured body and in his perverted biography. One of them anatomized his monstrous person, described as a sewer full of refuse, from head to foot—or rather, the other way around. His feet guided him into "sordid places" and directed him toward prey and booty. His hands, "completely crooked," were suitable only for grabbing and pillaging. His stomach consumed "enough food to provision a well-ordered kingdom." His liver produced an overabundance of bile that fueled his rage. His lungs filled him with pride and presumption that choked his heart, which engendered thoughts "darker than hell." His tongue pronounced nothing but contradictions and curses. His eyes, like those of the legendary basilisk, emitted deadly vapors. His physiognomy, marked by ferocious veins, revealed his tyrannical disposition. His head, full of devious and malicious spirits, plotted the despoliation of the French people and misled all the other parts of his body into "the most enormous crimes."[54] Another pamphleteer, recounting one of the king's nightmares, represented the rapacious cardinal as a snarling monster with huge teeth and a body composed of vermin and vultures.[55] The Mazarinades condemned "this animal who is the cause of our problems" by describing him as a veritable menagerie of parasitic and predatory creatures: leech, serpent, wolf, panther, tiger, dragon, harpy.[56]

The diabolical minister, animalized or at least feminized by his destructive and debilitating appetites, disrupted and disintegrated the state. In his case the body, which should have been the "slave," instead usurped the role of "master," such that he spent his entire life in the state of sat-

53. *Journal de ce qui s'est fait ès assemblées du Parlement* (Paris, 1649), 28.
54. *L'Effroyable Accouchement d'un monstre dans Paris* (Paris, 1649).
55. *Songe du roi admirable et prophétique pour la consolation de la France* (Paris, 1649).
56. *Recueil général de toutes les chansons mazarinistes* (Paris, 1649), 6.

urnalian disorder that the Romans celebrated only once a year.[57] Wallowing in sensory pandemonium, the "Sardanapalian" cardinal squandered royal revenues, extorted from overtaxed and oppressed subjects, on expensive perfumes, exquisite sauces, and exotic pets.[58] Addicted to "the most immoderate pleasures," he used or rather misused his genitals, like his prerogatives, in a lawless and unnatural manner, by committing sodomy throughout his meteoric career.[59] During his adolescent years in Rome, the effeminate Mazarin adopted the passive role in anal intercourse in order to manipulate his superiors and advance his fortunes. He graduated to the active role, without losing his feminine characteristics, by the time he settled in Paris, where he reportedly buggered numberless pages and priests, as well as Anne of Austria herself, who was quickly seduced by and completely infatuated with him. Enslaved by "the passion that tyrannizes her," she allowed him to enslave the country.[60] Since his ministry supplied the realm with "so much p[rick] and so little cash," the devious and dissolute cardinal had the perverse satisfaction of sodomizing and dominating the entire French population as well as the regent herself.[61] His oversized and undisciplined penis, the synecdochical "tool that makes its master rule," not only degraded her but also disordered the kingdom as a whole.[62]

By exposing his grotesque body and carnivalesque biography, the Mazarinades condemned "the Italian sausage" for inverting and corrupting the divine and natural order of things in the cosmos, household, self, and state.[63] He gained rank and wealth incommensurate with his lowly antecedents and meager talents, they charged, through collusion with Satan, whose rebellion against God he reenacted. He ran away from home to escape the beneficial discipline imposed by his father and later disunited households throughout France by turning "the father against the son, the brother against the sister, the uncle against the nephew, the wife against the husband, and the servant against the master."[64] He "kidnapped" Louis XIV from the capital, thereby depriving the realm of its figurative sun, father, and head, and did his best to deaden the young king's

57. *Apparition du cardinal de Saint-Cécile à Jules Mazarin* (Paris, 1649), 3.

58. *La Mazarinade* (Brussels, 1651), 10.

59. *Requête civil contre la conclusion de la paix* (n.p., 1649), 3.

60. *L'Admirable Harmonie des perfections, qualités et reproches de Mazarin* (Paris, 1649), 4.

61. *La Pure Vérité cachée* (n.p., n.d.), 4.

62. *Satire ou imprécation contre l'engin du surnommé Mazarin* (n.p., 1652), 4.

63. *Les Logements de la cour à Saint-Germain-en-Laye* (n.p., 1649), reprinted in *Choix des Mazarinades*, ed. Célestin Moreau, 2 vols. (Paris, 1853), 1:173.

64. *Le Flambeau d'état* (n.p., n.d.), 14

solicitude for the extended family composed of French subjects. He renounced the rule of reason, identified with men, and embraced the yoke of passion, associated with women and animals. Having acquired unnatural authority through unnatural means, the minister ruled his ruler but not himself. Out of place and out of control, he could not embody royal rationality or dispense royal justice. In doing "whatever he wants with his body," he left the country littered with the bodies of his victims.[65] Emasculated by his appetites, the deformed, depraved, and despotic foreigner prolonged the dissension that poisoned and plagued the body politic. Some pamphleteers, speaking like doctors, prescribed purgation to cure the sickness caused by the kingdom's ingestion of "abominable monsters," one of which, "all red with her blood" (a reference to the sanguinary cardinal's scarlet robes), lacerated her entrails.[66] Others, speaking like magistrates, prescribed corporal punishments, including dismemberment and castration, to make Mazarin's body expiate his sexual and political transgressions.

The Mazarinades projected the disobedience of the Frondeurs as well as the chaos of the Fronde onto the fictionalized figure of their namesake ("you who govern yourself according to your passions"), whose unruly genitals broke down the distinctions between law and license that regulated both sexuality and politics.[67] Unlike attacks on Henry III, who was allegedly ruled by his minions, and Louis XV, who was allegedly ruled by his mistresses, they did not incriminate the sovereign himself, who was too young, after all, to rule or misrule in his own name. In denouncing the heartless and mindless cardinal, whose body was not, of course, linked with the body politic through ceremonial and symbolic traditions, they nevertheless articulated standards of accountability for monarchs as well as ministers. Mazarin's critics reminded Louis XIV that he must regard his people as "the members of the body of which he is the head" and that he, unlike Mazarin, must subordinate his own desires to the collective welfare.[68] He must not have "any greater passion" than that of ruling the population "with every kind of justice."[69] He must not, in fact, have any "passions that are not thoroughly just," because unjust

65. *Le Gouvernement présent ou éloge de Son Eminence* (n.p., 1649), 5.

66. *Consultation et ordonnance des médecins de l'état pour la purgation de la France malade* (Paris, 1649), 5.

67. *Fiction: L'Heureux Succès du voyage que le cardinal Mazarin a fait aux enfers* (Paris, 1649), 7.

68. *Le Zèle et l'amour des parisiens envers leur roi* (Paris, 1649), 2.

69. *Instruction royale ou paradoxe sur le gouvernement de l'état* (n.p., n.d.), 3.

passions like greed, anger, and lust caused not only misconduct at court but also misfortune throughout the kingdom.[70] According to one pamphleteer, who stated the point more bluntly than Bodin, Bossuet, or Moreau, subjects did not have to obey kings who were themselves "subject to their passions," because passions made kings forget their divine, natural, and constitutional obligations.[71]

Having rebelled against the monstrous minister who embodied rebellion in so many ways, French men and women clamored for the underage monarch to restore the health of the metaphorical body and the unity of the metaphorical family. Their sovereign, moved by his "paternal affection" for the people subjected to him by God, chastised and then forgave them. As the head of the figurative body and the collective household, he also instructed them to obey him unconditionally in the future.[72] In the wake of the Fronde, jurists, clerics, writers, and artists systematically distanced Louis XIV from the sexual and political irregularities associated with the Rabelaisian villain of the Mazarinades. They turned the world right side up again by reasserting the authority of the crown and repossessing the rhetoric of cosmological, familial, and corporeal order. They represented the Sun King, on paper and canvas, as the incarnation of "masculine" virtues, as opposed to "feminine" vices. The royal Apollo included many of their lessons, which he could not have learned from the Mazarin portrayed by the pamphleteers, in memoirs addressed to his son. He condemned rebellion in no uncertain terms but denied that divine ordination, which exempted the sovereign from accountability to his subjects, entitled him to conduct his life "in a more disorderly way."[73] As "the head of a body of which they are the members," the king must master himself and never let himself be mastered by passions, women, or ministers.[74] In governing the people, who could not govern themselves, he must shun both unmanly indolence and unseemly agitations and also stifle or at least conceal "vulgar feelings," "as soon as they cause harm to public welfare."[75]

Through ritual, representation, and rhetoric, the Bourbon monarchy reaffirmed the principle that the head of the monarch, who served as the

70. *La Prospérité malheureuse ou le parfait abrégé de l'histoire du cardinal Mazarin* (Paris, 1652), 13.

71. *Ambassadeur extraordinaire apportant à la reine des nouvelles certaines de son royaume et de ce qui s'y passe* (Paris, 1649), 5.

72. *Lettre du roi écrite à son parlement de Paris sur les affaires présentes, le 11 février 1652* (Paris, 1652), 4.

73. *Mémoires de Louis XIV*, 256.

74. Ibid., 90.

75. Ibid., 159.

head of the body politic, must rule the royal body in order to prevent any divergence between the interests of the king and the kingdom. Louis XIV, perpetually on stage at Versailles, subjected himself, as well as his entourage, to rules and routines intended to promote and preserve religious, social, and political order at court and throughout the country. He disciplined parlementaires, peasants, and Protestants but failed, at least according to domestic and foreign critics, to live up to his own prescriptions. Unlike poets and painters in the service of the crown, these critics did not disguise or decorate the mortal body of the Sun King with classical, Christian, and historical trappings. They portrayed him, on the contrary, as debauched, diseased, defeated, and despotic.[76] The authors of slanderous texts published during the eighteenth century recycled the charges about sexual and political disorders against his successors. They defamed the profligate Louis XV, who evidently could not control his unruly libido, and the impotent Louis XVI, who apparently could not control his unruly wife.[77] Both kings, dominated by women, betrayed "the spirit of counsel, justice, and reason" that supposedly distinguished "the sovereign power" residing in the person of the male sovereign.[78] Royal ideology itself, which connected order in the royal body with order in the body politic, supplied much of the raw material for gendered accusations about the disruptive effects of royal sexuality on royal rationality and, by extension, the welfare of the French people.

In the eighteenth century, as during the Fronde, critics of royal policies reprimanded ministers and monarchs for violating in practice obligations that apologists of absolutism like Bodin, Bossuet, and Moreau acknowledged in principle. Parlementaires legitimized resistance by expropriating the religious and familial language deployed by the monar-

76. See Ferrier-Caverivière, *Image de Louis XIV*, pt. 2, chap. 5; and Burke, *Fabrication of Louis XIV*, chap. 10.

77. On criticism of Louis XV (and his mistresses), Louis XVI (and Marie Antoinette), and the privileged orders in general, see Jean-Pierre Guicciardi, "Between the Licit and the Illicit: The Sexuality of the King," in *'Tis Nature's Fault: Unauthorized Sexuality During the Enlightenment*, ed. Robert Purks Maccubbin (Cambridge: Cambridge University Press, 1985), 88–97; Antoine de Baecque, "Pamphlets: Libel and Political Mythology," in *Revolution in Print: The Press in France, 1775–1800*, ed. Robert Darnton and Daniel Roche (Berkeley: University of California Press, 1989), 165–76; Chantal Thomas, *La Reine scélérate: Marie-Antoinette dans les pamphlets* (Paris: Editions du Seuil, 1989); Jeffrey Merrick, "Sexual Politics and Public Order in Late-Eighteenth-Century France: The *Mémoires Secrets* and the *Correspondance Secrète*," *Journal of the History of Sexuality* 1 (1990): 68–84; Hunt, *Family Romance;* Antoine de Baecque, *Le Corps de l'histoire: Métaphores et politique, 1770–1800* (Paris: Calmann-Lévy, 1993); and Robert Darnton, *The Forbidden Books of Pre-Revolutionary France* (New York: W. W. Norton, 1995).

78. *Remontrances du Parlement de Paris*, 2:557.

chy to consolidate the sovereignty of the crown.[79] They not only reminded the king that he must rule in a godly and fatherly manner, as he himself claimed to do, but also deplored and even denounced departures from the standards of godliness and fatherliness. These standards turned out to be much more ambiguous and flexible than they looked in prescriptive sources, especially during constitutional conflicts, when the deceptive consensus about figurative ways of describing relations of authority and subordination broke down. The magistrates generally interpreted them in such a way as to justify their own political pretensions, without discarding the traditional metaphorology and reconstructing the state in disembodied style as some of their "patriotic" and "philosophic" contemporaries did. Pamphleteers, meanwhile, supported parlementary opposition to despotism by exposing and exaggerating depravity at court and throughout French society. They suggested that the bodies of Louis XV and his grandson, who seemed less visible and also less reliable than their predecessors, actually endangered the realm, instead of unifying, guiding, and disciplining it. Lawyers reinforced the message by publicizing the sexual politics of dissension within households during the last decades of the ancien régime.[80] As long as kingship remained entangled with corporeal order, as well as divine purposes and domestic authority, kings remained vulnerable to charges formulated within the framework of traditional principles. The conventional rhetoric, in the last analysis, was largely reversible, and critics of the official version of absolutism, even before 1789, manipulated it more effectively than the monarchy itself did.

79. See Jeffrey Merrick, *The Desacralization of the French Monarchy in the Eighteenth Century* (Baton Rouge: Louisiana State University Press, 1990); and idem "Fathers and Kings: Patriarchalism and Absolutism in Eighteenth-Century French Politics," *Studies on Voltaire and the Eighteenth Century*, no. 308 (1993): 281–303.

80. See Sarah Maza, *Private Lives and Public Affairs: The Causes Célèbres of Prerevolutionary France* (Berkeley: University of California Press, 1993); Jeffrey Merrick, "Domestic Politics: Divorce and Despotism in Eighteenth-Century France," in *The Past as Prologue: Essays to Celebrate the Twenty-fifth Anniversary of ASECS*, ed. Carla Hay and Syndy Conger (New York: AMS Press, 1995), 373–86; and idem, "Impotence in Court and at Court," *Studies in Eighteenth-Century Culture* 25 (1995): 199–215.

2

Lim(b)inal Images

"Betwixt and Between" Louis XIV's Martial and Marital Bodies

ABBY ZANGER

Most studies of the representation of Louis XIV focus on the absolutist king at the height of his power, portraying a king who was largely autonomous.[1] This essay examines images of Louis XIV from an earlier, more tentative moment in his reign, before his *prise de pouvoir* or personal rule: the period following France's successful military campaigns in Spanish-occupied Flanders in 1657 and 1658.[2] At this point in his reign the king was still under the tutelage of Mazarin, and his portrayal reflects his connection both to the minister and to the players in the larger political arena. Indeed, portraits of the king that were associated with military triumph relied heavily on the depiction of other bodies: his ministers and generals, his family, French soldiers, and the allegories of vanquished disorder. As a marriage treaty was negotiated, and images of kingship moved toward what Thomas Kaiser describes in this volume as "the pastoral image of monarchy based on love, harmony, and

1. See, for example, Louis Marin, *The Portrait of the King*, trans. Martha M. Houle (Minneapolis: University of Minnesota Press, 1988); and Jean-Marie Apostolidès, *Le Roi-machine: Spectacle et politique au temps de Louis XIV* (Paris: Editions de Minuit, 1981). Consider as well Roberto Rossellini's *The Rise to Power of Louis XIV*, a film that has served to anchor many clichés, true and false, about the symbolic power of Louis XIV.

2. This preliminary stage in the performance of Bourbon absolutism was a period of military victories in which the French conquest of territory in Spanish-Hapsburg–occupied Flanders provided the French minister Mazarin with the leverage to negotiate a treaty, the Treaty of the Pyrenees, that turned the balance of power in Europe away from Spain and toward France. The main clauses of this treaty forged a marital alliance that reflected the larger political issues in its terms for the exchange of territory, the infanta's dowry, her rights of succession to the Spanish throne, and the repatriation of the Fronde rebel Prince of Condé.

peace," Louis XIV's power was promoted by displaying his marital (and hence mortal qua sexual) body. In this shift, Louis XIV's political body was further framed and complemented by supporting characters and props.

It is important to note that the images of the young Louis XIV examined in this essay emerged from a period of transition and flux. Even though it is accepted today that the events in Flanders in 1657 and 1658 occasioned the marriage of Louis XIV and lay the groundwork for the political stability on which Louis XIV would begin his personal rule after the death of Mazarin, during the campaigns proper the outcome of the military engagements was of course an unknown. As late as early 1659 the treaty marriage, with its attendant political triumphs, was only a goal coming into view, a fantasy of the fixed, socially and politically stable state to which the French aspired. Images of the king's body produced during this transitional time differ significantly from the now canonical fictions of "the king's two bodies" elucidated by Ernst Kantorowicz and Ralph Giesey.[3] Such fictions of a body split between mortality and divinity arose in response to a specific political crisis: the death of the monarch. It was the aim of these conceptions of sovereignty to attenuate that crisis by downplaying the importance of the king's mortal body and by creating the conditions in which one ruler's body could be substituted for another. It was the aim of these conceptions to reduce multiplicity (multiple bodies or rulers) to divine unity.

Fictions of the king's body produced during the period between war and marriage were not primarily a response to the threat of a monarch's death. They arose out of the activity of diplomatic interaction and emphasized how adjudication of territorial disputes and the exchange of kin could stabilize power in a period of change. Representations of the king during such flux depended on his interaction with other bodies—courtiers, generals, the queen mother, the minister, a future queen—and with the props of sovereign performance—clothing, royal limbs, even the frames that surround and highlight such performances or representations. These images of sovereignty relied heavily on the perception that the king's mortal body was vigorous, not to counter fears of his death, but to counter questions about his viril-

3. Ernst H. Kantorowicz, *The King's Two Bodies: A Study in Mediaeval Political Theology* (Princeton: Princeton University Press, 1957); and Ralph E. Giesey, *The Royal Funerary Ceremony in Renaissance France* (Geneva: Librairie Droz, 1960). For a more specific critique of the paradigm of the "king's two bodies," see Abby Zanger, "Making Sweat: Sex and the Gender of National Reproduction in the Marriage of Louis XIII," *Yale French Studies* 86 (1994): 187–205.

ity. Born under the cloud of Louis XIII's impotency, Louis XIV would have had to demonstrate his own sexual potency to project the strength of his political body. Indeed, in the years before he took power, images of the king's virile—hence mortal—body were fundamental to relaying the potential strength of his rule. It was thus that in the period before his *prise de pouvoir*, the king's sexual body was not seen as detrimental to displays of his power, but as constitutive of it. The representation of other bodies around him was necessary to drive home that potency.

Almanac engravings from 1658 and 1659 depicting the king's military triumphs and suggesting the possibility of royal military and matrimonial success provide an example of the visual and rhetorical strategies of representing kingship (and its bodies) on the as yet unstabilized stage of Louis XIV's absolutist reign. Projecting images of long-desired peace and prosperity, the almanacs shift between visions of war and marriage. Their fictions emerge from what the anthropologist Victor Turner termed the "betwixt and between," the liminal, the neither here nor there: undefinable and uncontrollable, often chaotic, moments of transition, becoming, or transformation.[4] According to Turner, such periods have "cultural properties" that are distinct from those that characterize definable states such as marriage; for Turner, liminal periods are transforming, whereas states are confirmatory. As such, liminal periods are often marked by ambiguity and paradox, by a confusion of customary categories and divisions and by the unknown, unbounded, limitless. In such moments of flux, many fixed ideas are open to interrogation, oppositions—such as high/low, history/allegory, divine body/mortal body, male/female, and war/marriage—tend to dissolve and collapse, and liminal persons or phenomena tend toward structural invisibility. Despite this general tendency toward disorder and dissolution, it must be understood that liminality is linked to reordering. Preceding or bordering stable, familiar states, liminal periods help transform and reformulate old elements into new patterns. As Turner noted, if "liminality may perhaps be regarded as the Nay to all positive structural assertions," it must also be seen as, "in some sense, the source of them all, and more than that, as a realm of pure possibility whence novel configurations of ideas and relations may arise."[5]

4. In "Betwixt and Between: The Liminal Periods in *Rites de Passage*," in *The Forest of Symbols* (Ithaca: Cornell University Press, 1967), Turner focuses on other writings about liminality: Mary Douglas's *Purity and Danger: An Analysis of Concepts of Pollution and Taboo* (1966; reprint, London: ARK, 1988); and Arnold Van Gennep's *The Rites of Passage* (Chicago: The University of Chicago Press, 1960).

5. Turner, "Betwixt and Between," 97.

It is the uneasy yet productive relation between the flux of liminality and the fixity of established, stable, recurrent states or conditions that is of particular interest for this discussion. For such images of military triumph that point toward the dream of a stable state emerging out of military victory and out of the empire building of royal marriage were efforts on the part of the representational apparatus of the absolutist state under Mazarin to freeze the flux of historic events, to contain their unknowns and uncertainties and reestablish the fundamental oppositions and hierarchies on which the performance of sovereign power rested. These images thus offer a unique glimpse into the struggle of representational forms to maintain fixity in a situation of liminality or flux, of betwixt and between. This struggle is especially evident in an iconography whose two most salient images are of legs and frames—most particularly, but not exclusively, of the king's legs, and most particularly, but also not exclusively, of frames that contain cameo images of potential queens.

The play between the visual role of the leg or limb as a space of demarcation, a limit (indeed *limb* and *liminal* share a common etymology in the Latin *limes*, limit, and *limen*, threshold), on the one hand, and the nature of what is being demarcated, limited, encircled, and framed (i.e., ordered), on the other, illustrates in particular the dialectic between disorder and containment so characteristic of the fictions from this period. For limits and frames appear in these almanac images precisely where fixed boundaries (and the order they imply) are threatened, that is, at the meeting of the liminal and the fixed, what Turner characterized as "that realm of pure possibility." This realm is also, paradoxically, the place where boundaries and order may be fixed. It is precisely that play between fixing and unfixing evidenced on the microscopic level of iconography and reproducing the larger historic movement from war (before marriage) to marriage (after war) that is pertinent to an analysis of these almanac images. The properties of the representation of this "realm of pure possibility," a realm stirred up and constructed from this encounter, differ significantly from the characteristics of the portrait of the mature king.

Before examining the almanac images, it is important to note that the genre of almanac engravings itself engages in the mediation of flux and stability on two levels. Almanacs incarnated both the transitory nature of time and the attempt to foretell and fix that ephemerality. They encapsulated both recovery and anticipation, insofar as their upper register recaptures and freezes images of a year recently completed, while their lower half lays out and projects the as yet unknown year ahead in a grid of numbers and lines. Often almanacs made elaborate observations about planets and such conditions as their eclipses,[6] although the almanacs studied here simply list saints' days or predict the weather. The first set examined, produced to mark the year 1658, refers to events that occurred during the summer of 1657: the battles between Turenne and Condé that resulted in French victories at St. Venant, Montmédy, and Mardyck, and the first rumors of a possible marriage for the king. The second set, produced to mark the year 1659, pertains to events from 1658: the French victories at Dunes, Dunkerque, Gravelines, and Ypres that culminated in the Peace of the Pyrenees. They also allude to the agreement of nonintervention negotiated with the Electors of the Austrian Hapsburg Empire, the king's recovery from a near-fatal illness contracted while on a military campaign in July, and again—much more specifically this time—to the possibility of a marriage match for the young monarch. Looking back, they also look toward and claim to predict the future.

This play between past and future (as well as the condensation of several events from throughout the year into one image) that seems to freeze the flux of time may also be seen to function more generally for the status of the almanac in the larger sphere of print culture. These one-page broadsides covered with visual images and numbers were in fact a particularly potent medium for fixing ideas in the public imagination.[7] As almanac specialist Geneviève Bollême has noted, the mission of historic almanacs in particular was not to give facts to their "readers," but to form their opinions (122). Produced by engravers according to a system of permissions, or *privilèges*, like that which organized the print trade more generally, and sold in shops and by peddlers (*colporteurs*) on the streets of Paris and the provinces, such broadsides widely and easily disseminated authorized (legitimized) images to the largest public possible, one made up of both readers and nonreaders. Bollême gives impressive figures for the

6. One example of such an almanac is the often-reproduced *Le Jansénisme foudroyé*, Bibliothèque Nationale [hereafter cited as BN], Cabinet des Estampes, Qb[5]P68493.

7. All the almanac engravings discussed in this section can be found in the Bibliothèque Nationale's Cabinet des Estampes. For information on the commerce of engravings in the seventeenth century, and in particular for a discussion of almanacs, see Marianne Grivel, *Le Commerce de l'estampe à Paris au XVIIe siècle* (Geneva: Librairie Droz, 1986). For general information about almanacs, see Victor Champier, *Les Anciens Almanachs illustrés* (Paris: Bibliothèque des Deux Mondes, 1886); G. Saffoy, *Bibliographie des almanachs et annuaires* (Paris: Librairie G. Saffoy, 1959); John Grand-Carteret, *Les Almanachs français* (Paris: J. Alisié, 1896); Jean Adhémar, Michèle Hébert, J. P. Seguin, Elise Seguin, and Philippe Siguret, *Imagerie populaire française* (Milan: Electa, 1968); and Geneviève Bollême, *Les Almanachs populaires aux XVIIe et XVIIIe siècles: Essaie d'histoire sociale* (Paris: Mouton, 1969) [subsequent page references in the text are to this last book].

numbers of almanacs published and their broad social reach (13–17), calling them "the books of people who hardly read" (les livres des gens qui lisent peu; 16).

Seen in this light, almanacs participated in the very flux of events; by anchoring these events in the French field of vision, that is, by moving the stage of the king's out-of-sight battlefield activities onto the streets and into the households of the kingdom, they served the machinery of symbolic power. The term *stage* is used literally here, because the various scenes shown in the almanacs are often depicted on the Italian proscenium-arch stage. Richelieu had promoted this design in a rationalization of the space of illusion that is now understood as founding the performance of absolutist power by organizing and controlling the gaze of the spectator. With their combination of iconography, information, prognostication, and political allegory, these 50-by-80-centimeter sheets cut a broad swath across a large audience of viewers and readers. It is perhaps for this reason that the French historian of publishing, Henri-Jean Martin, echoes the 1690 *Dictionnaire universel* of Antoine Furetière in referring to these almanacs as *feuilles volantes*—loose or, more exactly, flying sheets, because they were able to literally fly in and out of the public eye, fixing images, then disappearing when they were no longer timely.[8]

1658: Lim(b)inal Images

The first almanac image considered here, *The Magnificent Triumph* (fig. 2.1), does not broach the issue of an upcoming marriage but refers only to the king's military victories. It presents a topos common to military triumph: a monarch in his chariot crushing what is out of control or disorderly, here represented by the allegorical images of Rage, Envy, and Sedition.[9] The engraving's depiction of these passions

8. Henri-Jean Martin, "Information et actualité: De la feuille volante au journal," in *Livre, pouvoirs, et société à Paris au XVIIe siècle, 1598–1701* (Geneva: Librairie Droz, 1969), 1:253–75. Martin uses the term *feuille volante* to refer to broadsides as well as short *livrets* such as *factums*, occasional pamphlets reporting on natural wonders, and almanacs. He thus uses the term as it was defined by Antoine Furetière in his *Dictionnaire universel* (The Hague: Arnout & Renier Leers, 1690).

9. The image of the king in his chariot is a common topos linked to triumph and peace, as, for example, in the Belgian painter Pierre Claeissens Le Jeune's 1577 *Allégorie de la paix aux Pays-Bas* (Groeninge Museum, Bruges, Belgium). Dating from the period of Philip II's occupation of Flanders, the painting features a chariot (of allegorical women) crushing Envy. This imagery is also available in images from the marriage of Louis XIII such as the engraving

Figure 2.1 *The Magnificent Triumph*, 1658. By permission of the Bibliothèque Nationale.

is traditional, based on widely accepted images from the manuals of iconology.[10] Barely visible, Rage, Envy, and Sedition are reduced largely to sinewy limbs (arms and legs) wrapped with equally powerful serpents emerging from under the wheels of the chariot that is crushing them, as well as from under the hooves of the horses pulling that chariot. These limbs and snakes suggest the powerful and predatory nature of passions. They are sexualized images of potency and penetration, the kind Jeffrey Merrick links to personal disorder and state lawlessness in the political pamphlets of the Fronde he discusses in this volume. It is not surprising that the king is figured above these problematic passions. He is placed on a higher plane, surrounded by higher-order images, the historical figures of the court situated behind him to the right and the other trophies of his victories off to the left. These trophies are to be contrasted with Rage, Sedition, and Envy; they are not invidious limbs being crushed, but cities, controlled not by dismemberment but by containment. Put into relief, they are miniaturized, immobilized, and placed on a portable surface carried high above the heads of the soldiers in the fashion of a Roman triumph. If disorder and movement mark the limbs of Rage, Envy, and Sedition, the cities are the model of civic order and constraint, as are the neatly covered limbs of the soldiers who carry them.

The prose text at the top center of the engraving offers further indices for reading the figures below. Interestingly, the prose does not open with a reference to the moral victory over the disorderly allegorical limbs. Nor does it refer to the military victory over the now ordered, contained cities. Instead the text speaks of another kind of triumph, one not figured visually in the engraving: the celebration of the king's own self-mastery, his triumph over *his* (disorderly) passion. It announces:

THE MAGNIFICENT TRIUMPH

Where our august monarch is seen mastering himself and his enemies because he places his passions among his war trophies.

"Le Roi conduit par les vertus terrasse la discorde et l'envie de ceux qui avoient traversé son Mariage" (BN, Cabinet des Estampes, Qb¹M89113). It can also be found in images from after the marriage of Louis XIV, such as in the engraving "Le Triomphe de la Paix et du Mariage" (Qb⁴P69268), as well as throughout the preceding battles in such engravings as "Le Triomphe royal de la Victoire obtenue par les armes de sa Majesté à la Bataille de lens" (Qb¹M91723).

10. Cesare Ripa, *Iconologia in Baroque and Rococo Pictorial Imagery*, trans. and ed. Edward A. Maser (New York: Dover, 1971).

LE TRIOMPHE MAGNIFIQUE

Ou l'on voit Nostre Auguste Monarque triomphant de soi mesme et de ses ennemis puis qu'il met ses passions au nombre de ses Trophées.[11]

Invoking a king's self-mastery is not an unusual rhetorical move in this sort of celebratory material.[12] Such stoic self-control was a desirable trait in a king, and lack of royal self-control was, as Jeffrey Merrick points out,

11. The full text is as follows:

> Where our august monarch is seen mastering himself and his enemies because he places his passions among his war trophies. The duke of Anjou his brother, the prince of Conti, his eminence, Monsieur de Turenne and Monsieur de la Ferté increase the brilliance of this triumph by their presence. One sees as well the soldiers who march in front, laden with the spoils of the enemies and carrying on their shoulders in the Roman manner the cities of Montmedy, St. Venant, Bourbourg, and Mardic represented in relief, which has been conquered by the very great king with all the [military] standards carried off in the various battles with the Spaniards as well as their shameful retreat from Ardre.
>
> Ou l'on voit Nostre Auguste Monarque triomphant de soi mesme et de ses ennemis puis qu'il met ses passions au nombre de ses Trophées. Le duc d'Anjou son frere, Le Prince de Conty, Son Eminence, Mr de Turenne et le Mr de la Ferté augmentent de leur presence l'eclat de ce Triomphe. on y voit en suite les Soldats qui marchent devant, chargez des depouilles des ennemis, et portant sur leurs espaules à la maniere des Romains, les Villes de Montmedy, St Venant, Bourbourg, et Mardic representées en relief, qui ont esté la conqueste de Trẽ grand Roy avec tous les estandars remportez en divers combatz sur les Espagnols comme aussi leur hont^{se} retraite devant Ardre.

All translations of texts in engravings are by the author of this essay. Original French spelling, punctuation, and capitalization are retained throughout.

12. The topos appears, for example, in Puget de la Serre's *Panégyrique de Louis Quartième, Roy de France et de Navarre* (n.p., n.d.), a pamphlet that, judging by references in the text, probably dates to the same period as the almanac. The text's frontispiece is an engraving in which the king's portrait in a medallion is held by an angel in a chariot. The third engraving in the text shows the king on a throne and is accompanied by the following verse:

> Who would be able to oppose the illustrious projects
> Of a Prince to whom heaven has promised all glory:
> He prevails over himself [in] his first victory,
> And devotes his passions to his subjects.
>
> Qui pourroit s'opposer aux Illustres projets
> D'un Prince à qui le ciel a promis tout le gloire:
> Il emporte sur luy la première victoire,
> Et met ses passions au rang de ses sujets.

In reading the text, it seems that this verse refers to the king's tireless military endeavors. See, for example, page 19 of the *Panégyrique*: "Et certes ce grand Roy nous fit bien connoistre qu'il preferoit le repos de ses peuples au sien, puis que dés le lendemain de son arrivée dans son Louvre il prefere les fatigues d'un nouveau voyage, aux delices de sa Cour sans considerer l'incomodité qu'il pourroit courre" (And certainly this great king has made us understand that he would prefer the repose of his people to his own, because since the day after his arrival in the Louvre he prefers the fatigues of a new voyage to the pleasures of his court without considering the inconvenience that he could risk).

often cited as a reason for civil disobedience.[13] The implication of the statement in the almanac is that the king's visible mastery over others is causally related to his unseen and perhaps unrepresentable mastery over himself. It seems a bit paradoxical, however, to draw attention to an invisible kind of mastery in the heading over an image that is meant to make the king's authority visible. It also seems paradoxical to attempt to make authority visible by drawing attention to the king's mastery over passions he should not have. Suggesting that the king may have had uncontrollable urges would, one might think, only emphasize his humanness. As the work of Ernst Kantorowicz has demonstrated, an early modern European king's constitutional entitlement rested largely on his ability to repress the fact of his humanness via elaborately ritualized fictions of his divine status. It would seem that underlining a dimension of the king such as his passions—a dimension he is not supposed to have—might serve not only to fit the king into a traditional stoic framework, but also to arouse the viewer's curiosity by drawing him or her outside the fixed moral and military boundaries to reflect on the passions and personal disorder edging those boundaries, in particular a king's own potentially disordering passions: the unspoken, liminal, disorderly, invisible side of monarchy. The prose text thus invites the viewer to comb the image for residues of such disarray emerging from the vision of domination and reordering. And indeed, if the dismembered limbs of Rage, Envy, and Sedition suggest a world of such lawlessness, the curious viewer can also find traces of the potentially unfixed passions of the king by easily matching the limbs of defeated passions first to those of the horses, and then, moving higher, to those of the king, as muscled and sinewy as the legs of the animals.

Of course, all limbs in the picture are always lower-order members. One goal of the image seems to be to reprocess lower-order images into containable trophies. The diorama as trophy epitomizes this movement, for, as the text notes, the king placed his passions "among his war trophies." Reading these images after the age of Freud, it is easy to recognize both the repression and condensation at work in the image. The work of Michel Foucault has made critics aware, furthermore, that exclusion and policing, framing sexuality out of the picture (which is what often happens in the representation of a monarch's body), are methods for deal-

13. Merrick, in his essay in this volume, cites Bodin, Bossuet, and Moreau, as well as a 1649 Mazarinade, *Ambassadeur extraordinaire apportant à la reine des nouvelles certaines de son royaume et de ce qui s'y passe*.

ing with the sticky issues of sexuality.[14] But Foucault also characterized such an exclusion as a manner of keeping *jouissance*—gratuitous, ephemeral, nonutilitarian pleasure—and the power that contains it, in the picture.[15] This play between exclusion and exhibition is evident in the treatment of Rage, Sedition, and Envy. Although in pieces, these figures, objects to be crushed by military and visual mastery, are nonetheless always hovering at the edge, as if it is their energy that keeps the wheels of the king's machinery of domination moving forward. Like the burlesque king discussed by Mark Franko in this volume, the king mastering these liminal forces makes royal power, both political and personal, visible.

If *The Magnificent Triumph* leaves the viewer more interested in the king's disorderly and uncontrolled ephemeral passions than in the parading of his permanent military control, other almanac images from the same year bring these passions into relief, containing them in a manner that makes them more visually available, if perhaps less powerful and interesting. Consider, for example, another 1658 almanac engraving, *The Legitimate Wishes of Victorious France for the Marriage of the King* (fig. 2.2). This image more overtly organizes the relation between disorderly affairs of passion and the (ideally) more stable affairs of state, legitimizing the king's passions, which had been, so to speak, rolled under the bed—or under the triumphal chariot of the previous image. Indeed, "legitimation" is the first modifier in the descriptive heading:

THE LEGITIMATE WISHES OF VICTORIOUS FRANCE FOR THE MARRIAGE OF THE KING, dedicated and presented by the love of virtue and by that of France itself to our invincible monarch Louis XIIII.

LES JUSTES SOUHAITS DE LA FRANCE VICTORIEUSE POUR LE MARIAGE DU ROY, dedies et presentes par l'amour de la vertu et par celui de la France mesme a nostre invincible monarque Louis XIIII.[16]

14. Michel Foucault, *The History of Sexuality*, vol. 1: *An Introduction* (New York: Vintage Books, 1990).

15. Michel Foucault, "Power and Sex," an interview from the *Nouvel Observateur*, 12 March 1977, translated and republished in *Michel Foucault: Politics, Philosophy, Culture, Interviews, and Other Writings, 1977–1984*, ed. Lawrence Kritzman (London: Routledge, 1988), 110–124.

16. The full text is as follows:

The legitimate wishes of France for the marriage of the king, dedicated and presented by the love of virtue and by that of France itself to our invincible monarch Louis XIIII followed by the joy of the people, the desires for peace, and the wishes of renown, one in the hope of one day seeing a dauphin born, the other of soon seeing the Christian princes in perfect harmony, and the third the empire united to the crown of France; and below, the conquests of Monmedie, Mardic, St. Venant, the shameful flight of the

Figure 2.2 *The Legitimate Wishes of Victorious France for the Marriage of the King*, 1658. By permission of the Bibliothèque Nationale.

As the prose text states, the legitimized wishes or hopes for (the legitimate passion of) marriage are placed center-stage in this engraving, displayed in the middle of the image in a framed picture of the king holding out his hand to a woman dressed in the French queen's traditional wedding garb. A banner inside this interior image reads, "Great King place

---

Spaniards from Ardres with the representation and victory, firm and solid support of the French monarchy.

LES JUSTES SOUHAITS DE LA FRANCE VICTORIEUSE POUR LE MARIAGE DU ROY, dedies et presentes par l'amour de la vertu et par celui de la France mesme a nostre invincible monarque Louis XIIII suivis de la Joye des peuples des desires de la paix et des voeux de la Renommee, l'une dans lesperance de voir un jour naistre un dauphin l'autre de voir bien tost les princes chrestiens dans une parfaitte concorde Et celle cy lempyre unie a la couronne DE FRANCE et plus bas les conquestes de MONMEDY MARDIC ST VENANT la fuitte honteuse des Espagnoles de devant ARDRES avec la representation de labondance et la victoire fermes et solides appuye de la monarchie françoise.

On the term *appuye*, see note 19 below.

yourself henceforth under Hymen / Upon this sacred bond depends the holy bond of peace" (Grand Roy dessouz hymen metez vous desormais / De ce saint noeud Depend le sainct noeud de la paix). Note as well that the interior picture is being presented to the king by the allegorical figure France, and that each of the two central figures, France and the king, is surrounded by similar characters: grouped around France on the left are the three (actually four) allegorical female figures, the Joy of the People, the Desires for Peace, and the Wishes of Renown (the fourth figure, barely seen, is not referred to), and grouped around the king on the right are five historical persons, the king's brother, his mother Anne of Austria, the minister Mazarin, and two other figures, perhaps Le Tellier and Le Marechal de Créqui.[17]

This combination of right and left imagery (allegorical and historical) echoes the visual play seen in *The Magnificent Triumph* (see fig. 2.1) between the domain of unregulated allegory as passion and that of regulating military victory. Here, however, the allegorical emerges not as dismembered Rage, Sedition, and Envy, but as full-bodied Peace, Joy, and Renown, legitimate passions carrying legitimate wishes for a Bourbon heir, for reconciliation between Philip IV and Louis XIV, and for an agreement with the Electors not to interfere in the events in Flanders. As such, these allegorical figures and their passions can be revealed and advertised. Particularly important is how this meeting of now-legitimated allegorical figures and the historical personages allows the entry of the king's passion into the scenario. Or rather, how it allows the emergence of a legitimated and civilized form of the king's passion, the royal and regulated (productive, heterosocial) marriage represented within the framed image as if in an equation: Wishes (Allegory) + Royal Family (History) = The Scene of Marriage.

To understand more fully how this equation factors passion into the scenario (albeit now a stable and contained passion because set apart, legitimized and sanitized), it is necessary to find a way to re-bisect this image, shifting from the grid set out to frame our gaze, that is the division between left (allegory) and right (history), to a different split between top and bottom (high and low). To do so, one must resist the temptations of the framing scene and look at details or limits—in this case, limbs.

17. I thank my research assistant Elizabeth Hyde for helping to speculate on who the other two courtiers might be. Despite examining a large number of engraved images, however, we found it difficult to be sure of exactly who is in the picture. Note, as well, the addition of Anne of Austria to the group. She was not present in the battle scene of *Le Triomphe Magnifique*.

In adopting this perspective, it is evident that even legitimized sexuality (that is, the framed image) is a lower-order member, occupying the domain of the king's own lower-order member, his iconic leg.[18] Visually positioned at the same level as the picture, the leg seems to counterbalance or suggest the limit of the interior image's framed, legitimized sexuality. A similar tension can be seen between the king's regal upper body, draped in, or framed by, formal robes, and the lower, more functional part of himself that is involved in the less regal but equally important (and tempting) aspects of kingship, not just walking, but coming together in a "holy bond/*saint noeud*" to make babies (indeed, one definition of the word *noeud* is erect phallus). The idea that procreation, and therefore sexual bodies (erect penises or women), are a necessary if knotty (or naughty) aspect of monarchy is also reinforced by the fact that the king's limb is situated opposite the medallion held by the Wishes of the people: an iconic scene of Anne of Austria invoking God's help to become pregnant after nearly two decades of childlessness. The restrained, legitimized, framed scenario of heterosociality that the allegorical figure France offers the king thus plays off the less restrained sexuality of the leg. Both elements work together, however, to reinforce what is announced in the last line of the heading, that "abundance and victory"—in bed and on the battlefield—are "the firm and solid support of the French monarchy" (labondance [*sic*] et la victoire fermes et solides appuye de la monarchie françoise).[19] This description—actually of two caryatids in the bottom, missing half of the engraving—suggests once again that the monarchical body rests on the lower order, either in its liminal (unstable and ephemeral) form or in its framed (fixed and monumental) form . . . or as the two work together.

The status of framed images as a basis or limb of the monarch's power can be more fully examined in another almanac engraving in which the king is being shown a collection of portraits of potential queens (fig. 2.3). In this image, where the issue of marriage takes center stage, the passion eliminated from (or crushed in) *The Magnificent Triumph* and allowed,

18. Simon Schama, *The Embarrassment of Riches: An Interpretation of Dutch Culture in the Golden Age* (New York: Alfred A. Knopf, 1987), 433–34. Schama notes that legs are seen as lower order, a sign of a fallen woman and wantonness in Dutch painting of the period.

19. The term *appuye* may be a misprint and should be in the plural like *fermes* and *solides*, because I suspect the two allegorical figures Abundance and Victory were caryatids, holding up the bottom portion of the image. Misprints are not uncommon in these images, and, of course, the rules of grammar were not conventionally followed or even in existence as we know them today.

Figure 2.3 *The Gifts Offered to the Very Christian King Louis XIV by All the Virtues*, 1659. By permission of the Bibliothèque Nationale.

framed, into *The Legitimate Wishes* as a necessary component has exploded and multiplied to assert its presence more fully in the king's scenario. The history/allegory division now corresponds to that between upper and lower, with historical figures—the king, his family, and his advisors—situated on the top of the image, and allegorical ones—Virtues holding portraits of potential candidates for queen—situated below.[20] The occasion of this display is given in the title of the almanac, *The Gifts Offered to the Very Christian King Louis XIV by All the Virtues* (Les Estrennes presentees au Roy tres Chrestien Louis 14e Par touttes les Vertus). The gifts (*estrennes*) are probably those given on the New Year, a theme in keeping with the almanac, although a second possibility might be that these are gifts offered at the beginning of a new undertaking, a foretaste of things to come. As such they would mark the king's maturity and potential entry into matrimony upon the successful completion of the military campaigns. The latter, figured in the top corners of the graphic, recede into the margins or frame of the page, acting as pendants to the cameos below depicting the king's new field of action. The banner above focuses exclusively on the field of the portraits, the scene within the proscenium arch, emphasizing that the king will make a choice from among the offered gifts, women chosen by the Virtues from "all the provinces of Europe." According to the text, the king will make a "happy choice which will raise to the height of the highest grandeur . . . the one his Majesty will wish to honor with his love":

The virtues, charmed by the merit of our great monarch, after having chosen from all the provinces of Europe, those they found the most perfect and accomplished, come to present to him whom they consider their protector, ex-

20. There has not been a great deal of work done on portraits of this period. Perhaps the most useful overview of the genre of the portrait-within-an-engraving is the chapter on portraiture in Erica Harth's *Ideology and Culture in Seventeenth-Century France* (Ithaca: Cornell University Press, 1983). For an interesting discussion of the nature of portraits of women in Renaissance Italy, see Patricia Simons, "Women in Frames: The Gaze, the Eye, and the Profile in Renaissance Portraiture," *History Workshop*, no. 25 (1988): 4–30. Although it is disappointing that Simons does not actually fulfill her proposed agenda to offer not only a social and historical analysis of the female gaze but also a psycho-sexual one, her readings of portraits of women, particularly her analysis of the use of such portraits for dynastic purposes (marriage, displaying riches) and of the way women were positioned within the portraits, are quite suggestive for understanding the portraits within almanac engravings. For information on portraiture in classical France that is not specifically concerned with the issue of portraying women, see Francis Dowley, "French Portraits of Ladies as Minerva," *Gazette des beaux arts*, May–June 1955, 261–86; and Lorne Campbell, *Renaissance Portraits: European Portrait Painting in the Fourteenth, Fifteenth, and Sixteenth Centuries* (New Haven: Yale University Press, 1990).

pecting this happy choice which will raise to the height of the highest grandeur and the most charming fidelity, the one His Majesty will wish to honor with his love.

Les vertus charmées du merite de nostre grand Monarque apres avoir choisi dans touttes les Provinces de l'Europe, ce qu'elles ont peu trouver de plus parfait et de plus accompli, le viennent presenter a celuy quelles [*sic*] regardent comme leur Protecteur, attendant ce choix heureux qui doit eslever au comble de la plus haute grand et de la plus charmante fidelité, celle que sa Majesté voudra honorer de son amour.

The emphasis on choice here is important and can be understood in terms of the framework provided by Marcel Mauss's observations about the activity of gift exchange as a practice in which relations of submission transform the physical violence of the battlefield into symbolic interaction.[21] In exchanging gifts, the recipient, and not the giver of the gift, ultimately finds himself in a position of submission, since he is the one who will have to reciprocate. One possible action, albeit a dangerous one, is for the recipient to choose not to reply with a gift in turn. According to Mauss, such behavior is the strongest possible response, for it is a display of independence (and this is the sovereign position). Here the king adopts a version of that posture by not accepting just any gift, but by choosing among gifts, in a kind of fairy-tale fantasy of the king choosing from the fairest in the land. Thus, if there is a veritable explosion of choice in this image, that multiplicity does not privilege the possibility of royal disorder because of either submission, sexual excess, or polygamy. Rather, it offers the king the possibility of displaying his power over his passions and over the allegorical women who present him with gifts, in that it shows him exercising his power to make "a happy choice."

Looking at the image, one cannot help but recognize that a choice has already been made. Only one of the five cameos is completely visible, the one suggestively situated to the right of the king's leg, as if ready to slide up along the limb—the limit separating the allegorical and historical registers—to join the royal family. Even if the king does not look directly at his chosen princess, she is the choice displayed for the viewer

21. Marcel Mauss, *The Gift*, trans. Ian Cunnison (New York: W. W. Norton, 1967). For Mauss, gift exchange functions similarly to kinship exchange as presented by Claude Lévi-Strauss in *The Elementary Structures of Kinship*, trans. and ed. James H. Bell, John R. Von Sturmer, and Rodney Needham (Boston: Beacon Press, 1969).

of the almanac. Situated diagonally opposite an unframed image of her predecessor, Louis XIV's mother, Anne of Austria, the cameo is the only image that might compete with the king's for the viewer's interest. The other portraits are partly obscured by plants and by the bodies of the Virtues holding them. Something is also missing from the portrait of the chosen princess: her body. Indeed, the dissonance between the king's full body and the truncated, framed, cameo image of the queen is striking. Her body seems to be another version of the truncated historical figures surrounding the king, although in the case of the queen the truncation echoes the tension of the gift-exchange paradigm. Just as gift exchange abbreviates and reprocesses potential social violence into a containable, symbolic activity, so too does the cameo "police" the potentially disruptive parts of the woman. If an unmarried woman has been allowed to enter into the picture, it is only insofar as she is framed and contained in a form as easily distributed among the courts of Europe as the almanac engraving could have been passed around among the streets of the realm. There is no danger of this female image walking around: she has been crippled, desexualized, cut in pieces like the disorderly Rage, Envy, and Sedition seen in *The Magnificent Triumph*.[22] But there is no denying that her excluded parts (breasts, womb, and so on) will be the origin of the dynastic continuity, just as the gift-exchange dynamic is the foundation of social interaction, or, on another level, just as kinship exchange, the paradigmatic model of gift exchange for Lévi-Strauss, serves as a basis for civil accord. In both cases (gift exchange and kinship exchange), tension over the unseen (social aggression) does not disappear; it is simply policed by the structure. So, too, the almanac engraving has found a way to circumscribe the necessity of the limbs (sexual body parts) supporting the sovereign performance by making them at once visible and invisible.

22. In this light it is interesting to consider a contrasting image of woman circulating in France in roughly the same period, that is, the illustration of a proverb about a woman without a head. This image was brought to my attention in a talk by Sarah Hanley given at Harvard in March 1993. She showed several images illustrating the adage "femme sans teste tout en est bon," including one by Jacques Lagnet that dates to 1657 (BN, Cabinet des Estampes, Collection Hennin, no. 3819), discussed by Roger-Armand Weigert in *Inventaire du fonds français, graveurs du XVIIe siècle* (Paris: Bibliothèque Nationale, 1939), 55. The illustrated proverb seems to suggest that if you can separate women's bodies from their heads they will be rendered harmless. In the image, however, the idea seems to be to get rid of the head. In the almanacs it is the bodies that are missing. Since no other information is available about this proverb, it is impossible to comment further except to suggest that the contrast merits further consideration.

1659: Framing the Body's Politics

The iconographic topoi of *The Gifts* are not new to the marriage of Louis XIV, but actually repeat and popularize an image predicated on many of the same dynamics between war and marriage, framing and curiosity, politics and sexuality, seen in the almanac images: Rubens's painting of Henri IV receiving the portrait of his intended bride (fig. 2.4), produced approximately thirty-five years earlier in a series depicting the life of Marie de Médicis. In the Rubens image, illustrated here by an eighteenth-century engraved reproduction, Henri IV has discarded the trappings of war at the sight of his intended wife. In *The Gifts* of 1659 (see fig. 2.3), while there are wishes for peace, the process of marriage is one not of playful relaxation, but of herculean labor. Is it possible that *The Gifts* makes a subtle pun on Rubens's painting by replacing the cheerful cherubs at the bottom with two caryatid-like figures straining to support the proscenium arch? The lion's skin between them underlines their herculean effort, reminding the viewer of at least two forms of labor behind making a royal alliance: that of skinning the Spaniards in Flanders (the lion being the symbol of Flanders), and that of holding up (and together) the stage of the king's passions.[23] There are also cherubs in the almanac engraving, but they are located at the top, not the bottom, of the visual field. And they are not playing with the trappings of war, but seriously displaying them, exhibiting the lion's head-helmet on the right and tail-helmet on the left along with the medallions of the battlefield. Rubens's image also includes the battlefield in the distance, evaporating in a wisp of smoke.[24] Finally, in Rubens's painting, the allegorical and the historical figures mingle; they are not separated. Indeed, in the Rubens it seems as if there is no need for any boundary between the allegorical and the historical images. Likewise, there seems to be no need to place the object of desire (the framed image) on a lower register than the king.

Of course, Rubens's painting and the almanac engraving are different genres with different formats. The first is a large, 3.94-by-2.95-meter history painting done in oils and meant to be hung in the palace, while the second is an 80-by-50-centimeter engraving intended for popular circu-

23. See Schama, *Embarrassment of Riches*, 52 and 55, for examples of the iconography of Flanders.

24. Ronald Rofsyth Millen and Robert Erich Wolf, *Heroic Deeds and Mystic Figures: A New Reading of Rubens' Life of Maria de Medicis* (Princeton: Princeton University Press, 1989), offers the most recent, comprehensive study of Rubens's Médicis cycle.

Figure 2.4 *Henri IV Deliberating on His Future Marriage*, after Rubens, eighteenth century. By permission of the Bibliothèque Nationale.

lation. The works are also the product of two distinct historical moments: Rubens's piece was painted in the 1620s to describe earlier events, and the almanacs were printed in the late 1650s contemporaneous with the events they depict. One might, nonetheless, pause over the way sexuality seems less fraught, more noble, in the portrayal of Henri IV looking at Marie de Médicis. Perhaps that is because the image was painted after the king's death and his establishment as the virile *Roi vert gallant*. Another reason for the elevation of the queen might be that Rubens's painting was not underwritten by the king but by Marie de Médicis herself, who emerged full-bodied in the ensuing paintings in the series. María Teresa also emerged full-bodied onto the scene of the almanacs, but not until after her marriage. It seems as if queens are allowed out of their frame only after the consummation of marriage and of the accords on which it was founded.[25]

The relation between the full-bodied king and framed queen is clarified when Rubens's painting is juxtaposed with another almanac from the year 1659, "The Celebrated Assembly of the Court." In it, Rubens's iconographic topoi are once again reworked (fig. 2.5). This engraving illustrates both the similarities with and differences from Rubens's image, most particularly in the position of the cameo portrait as it is being shown to the king, but also in the relation between the registers of history and allegory and in the juxtaposition of the images of war and passion, all of which affect the presentation of the potentially disorderly political bodies' roles in the (it is to be hoped) more ordered affairs of the body politic.

Once again, it is the banner over the image that guides our reading: "THE CELEBRATED ASSEMBLY OF THE COURT UPON THE CONVALESCENCE OF HIS MAJESTY AND UPON THE SUCCESSFUL OUTCOME OF HIS ARMS" (LA CELEBRE ASSEMBLEE DE LA COUR SUR LA CONVALESCENCE DE SA MAJESTE ET L'HEUREUX SUCCEZ DE SES ARMES). A new element in the staging of the period between war and marriage appears in this heading: the acknowledgment (after the fact, of course) of the king's near-fatal illness in late June 1658 just after the surrender of the Spanish at Dunes that turned the tide of the war irrevocably toward the French triumph and occasioned the marriage. He had fallen victim to what his own physician Vallot characterized as "a hidden venom" (un venin caché) caused by "the corruption of the Air, the infection of waters, and the large number of ill people, of several dead bodies, and many other circumstances" (la corruption de l'Air, de l'infection des eaux, du grand nombre des malades, de plusieurs corps morts sur la place, et de mille autres circonstances).[26] If the king is shown to be convalescing in this image, it is because his ill-

25. See images of the king and queen during the marriage from the Qb[1] series in BN, Cabinet des Estampes.

26. *Journal de la santé du roi Louis XIV de l'année 1647 à l'année 1711 écrit par Vallot, D'Acquin, et Fagon*, ed. J.-A. Le Roi (Paris: Auguste Durand, 1862), 52.

Figure 2.5 *The Celebrated Assembly of the Court*, 1659.
By permission of the Bibliothèque Nationale.

ness was so serious that even though it occurred in Calais, outside the French field of vision, it could not help but occupy the French imaginary. During the course of the illness, the king almost died: his physicians recorded that the king's body was purple and swollen, he was feverish and convulsive, and, at one moment of crisis, the king was unable to breathe.[27] According to Madame de Montpensier, Louis XIV was even given last rites in the expectation of his death.[28] It is not surprising, therefore, that in announcing the king's convalescence, the *Gazette* acknowledged that

27. Ibid., 54–57.
28. Madame de Montpensier, *Mémoires*, vol. 2 (Paris: Librairie Fontaine, 1985), 53.

the illness "appeared to threaten France with the most noticeable and distressing loss possible" (semblait ménacer la France de la plus sensible et de la plus désolante perte qu'elle ait pût faire). Of course, in recording the progression of the ailment, the king's physician Vallot was understandably reluctant to suggest that the illness was in any way connected to the monarch's being a weak physical specimen. Indeed, Vallot's notes underline that it was the king's own courage, the "too great impatience and keenness that he had to be present at opportunities, without sparing his life or health" (trop grande impatience et âpreté qu'il avait de se trouver aux occasions, sans ménager ni sa vie ni sa santé), and not any bodily weakness, that caused his malady.[29] Despite these gestures to the immortal body of the king, however, Vallot's journal, Montpensier's memoirs, the *Gazette*, and even popular almanac engravings all leave no doubt that the illness that threatened the king's body in the summer of 1658 also threatened the body politic.[30]

Concern expressed for the young king during the crisis and convalescence was, therefore, also concern expressed for the health of the Bourbon dynasty. Less than a decade after the crises of the Fronde, and in the midst of victories against the long-time enemy, Hapsburg Spain, the tide seemed to be turning in favor of the Bourbon dynasty, which could at last look forward to the assumption of power by a young and virile king. Were Louis XIV to have succumbed to his illness in July 1658, the vigor of the body politic would have been far less certain. For the crown would have passed to his younger brother, the duke of Anjou. He would have been a less compelling monarch in the French imaginary, since there were already grave reservations about his ability to procreate, let alone rule. It was apparently no secret that the duke of Anjou took after his father, Louis XIII, a king more interested in the bodies of other men than in the more manly affairs of the body politic or state.[31] Indeed, Louis XIII's lack of interest in women had left his marriage barren for many years, underlining the dynasty's dependence on mortal urges for its continuity: if a king sired no heirs to the throne, succession would move laterally to the monarch's brother.

29. *La Gazette,* no. 82: 642; *Journal de la santé du roi*, 52.

30. For a more complete analysis of the passages about the 1658 illness, see Abby Zanger and Elizabeth Goldsmith, "The Politics and Poetics of the Mancini Romance: Visions and Revisions of the Life of Louis XIV," in *The Rhetorics of Life-Writing in Early Modern Europe: Forms of Biography from Casssandra Fedele to Louis XIV*, ed. Thomas F. Mayer and D. R. Woolf (Ann Arbor: University of Michigan Press, 1995), 341–72.

31. Jean-Claude Pascal, *L'Amant du roi* (Paris: Editions du Rocher, 1991).

In this context it seems likely that Louis XIV's "scandalous" romance with Marie Mancini, begun during the king's convalescence and coming to an end only with his marriage in 1660, may have been utilized or even staged by Mazarin to demonstrate to the country that the king's body was once again in good working order after his brush with death.[32] With broadside almanacs widely circulating grim images in late 1658 and early 1659—for example, "FRANCE RESUSCITATED by the remedy sent from the heavens to the greatest monarch in the world for the peace of his people and the confusion of his enemies" (LA FRANCE RESSUCITEE par le remede Envoyé du Ciel au plus grand monarque de la terre pour la paix de son peuple et la confusion de ses ennemis; fig. 2.6)—the idea of a young king giving into passion, that is, lusting after a politically inappropriate or even potentially threatening consort, may have offered an indication of the king's (and France's) ability to erect himself (itself) from the sick bed (or the turmoil of civil war), escaping the shadow or frame of Thanatos to move into the full, fertile field of Eros. Note how, in figure 2.6, the king himself has been relegated to a cameo image, framed by the bed, in a representation resembling the kind of portrait-within-a-portrait noted earlier as a form of containment. Such usage is not surprising in a genre popular in this period not only as a way to introduce potential queens, but also as a way to memorialize dead persons.[33]

In the face of such dire events, it is not surprising that the king's mortal body, framed (or missing) in *France Resuscitated*, is the very first focus of *The Celebrated Assembly* (see fig. 2.5). There the descriptive banner that tells the reader/viewer:

> Our august monarch is admired on his throne, adorned only by his healthy appearance, because the brilliance of it is so beautiful that it takes away the luster of the richest clothing that he wears. The queen his mother, the duke of Anjou his brother, the duke of Orleans, and the prince of Conty are regarded with the respect owed to the Majesty of one and the conditions of the others. His Eminence the chancellor, Messieurs Turraine, La Ferté, Grammont, Villeroi, augment by their presence the pomp of this assembly, where France is seen presenting the king with the portrait of a princess, who is unnamed, as a certain omen of his future marriage. Flanders, reduced to his mercy, expresses simultaneously by her silence both her admiration and astonishment,

32. This is the argument I make in "The Politics and Poetics of the Mancini Romance."

33. The ill king's image, however, is placed in a masculine square frame, which should be contrasted to the round cameo in which the living queen candidates were portrayed. On the commemorative convention of portraits within portraits, see Erica Harth, *Ideology and Culture in Seventeenth-Century France* (Ithaca: Cornell University Press, 1983), 83.

Figure 2.6 *France Resuscitated by the Remedy Sent from the Heavens*, 1659. By permission of the Bibliothèque Nationale.

not being able to comprehend the wonders that this great monarch performed in his last campaign, and by the sound of his renown and by the force of his arms, the four elements represented at the four corners, the four successful battles, the great victories of this young conqueror, and the taking of the cities with the ceremonies of the alliance of France with the Elector princes of the empire, as well as the actions of thanks rendered by his majesty upon his convalescence in order to move his people to follow his example.

Nostre Auguste MONARQUE s'y fait admirer sur son Trosne Paré de sa bonne mine Seulement, puis que l'eclat en est si beau qu'il oste le lustre aux Plus Riches habits qu'il porte. la Reyne Sa Mere, le Duc d'anjou son Frere, le Duc D'orleans, et le Prince de Conty, s'y font considerer avec le respect Qu'on doit a la Majeste de l'Une et aux conditions des autres. Son Eminence, le Chancelier, les M.aux de Turaine, de la Ferté, de Grammont, et de Villeroy augmentent de leur Presence la Pompe de Cette ASSEMBLEE, Ou la France se fait Voir en Action de Presenter au ROY le Portrait d'une Princesse qui na point de Nom, Pour un presage certain de son future Himenée. La FLANDRE, Reduitte a sa mercy, Exprime tout a la fois par son Silence, et son admiration, et son Estonnement, ne pouvant comprendre les Merveilles que ce Grand MONARQUE a faittes dans cette derniere Campaigne, et par le bruit de son Renom et par la force de ses Armes, les quatres Elemens Representent aux quatre coings les heureux Combats, les Grandes Victoires de ce Jeune Conquerant et les prises des villes, avec les Ceremonies des Alliances de la France et les Princes Electeurs de Lempire, Comme aussy les Actions de graces Rendues par sa Majesté de sa Convalescence afin d'animer ses peuples a suivre son Exemple.

This image and its prose heading underscore the relation between the health of the king's body and that of the state; in so doing, they legitimize curiosity about the king's mortal body. Indeed, in its insistence that the king is adorned only by his healthy appearance (*bonne mine*), the heading focuses attention on the monarch's mortal body. But although the king's power or health is supposed to be discerned by looking at his body alone, a large number of accouterments establish his power qua health in the picture more forcefully. In fact, one perceives the king's "bonne mine" (meaning not just face, but countenance or bearing) in large part from what drapes it, since most of the healthy body is obliterated by clothing. Only the face, the hands, and a leg are visible. The last item, the leg, is actually covered by a silk stocking, although its contour is emphasized, not effaced, by that clinging material. And yet, despite the encasing garments, the eye is drawn to the royal body not just because of the words over the image but because of what one is supposed to admire. The real object of our interest, while covered over, is also exposed, or signified by the leg and scepter rising from it, both now clearly identified with power, sexual as well as political. The phallic dimension of that martial/marital power is underscored by a new addition to the iconography: the fashionably wide petticoat breeches (wide enough to contain the master's absolutist genitalia) and even the fleur-de-lys motif strewn over the royal robes (the fleur-de-lys being not only the royal emblem of France, but also the emblem of male genitalia and semen).[34]

The healthy appearance that indicates the victory over the disorder of disease is thus a celebration of successful arms (or legs)—or rather tools—the most successful of all being the king's sexual potency (his ability to stay erect) on the battlefield, in his sickbed, and in the marital chamber. In it, the king's mortal-sexual body is an asset to state-building and not the liability it has been too often categorically deemed when evaluated within the framework of constitutional fictions of monarchy generated around funerary symbolism. It may not be the king's sexuality that is a problem in this image, but rather the fact that displaying sexuality requires other images and props (stockings, women, and so on). Indeed, in later representations of Louis XIV the king's sexual power would be one of his icons, as for example in Hyacinthe Rigaud's 1701 *Louis XIV en habit de sacré* (fig. 2.7), which displays the sixty-two-year-old king as still virile. Louis Marin and Claude Reichler both note the tension in this painting between the sexuality of Louis XIV's leg and the aging face, a tension they argue undermines the power of the image. Their interpretations are clearly inspired by the Kantorowicz-Giesey paradigm, internalizing the funeral ritual's (logical) lack of focus on the king's sexuality. Indeed, in their analyses of this painting both Marin and Reichler focus on sexuality only in terms of decay, the dissonance between Louis XIV's iconic leg and his aging face as portrayed in the painting.[35] Looking at figure 2.7 in terms of the

34. For information on the petticoat breech and other aspects of men's fashions, see François Boucher, *2000 Years of Fashion: The History of Costume and Personal Adornment* (New York: Harry N. Abrams, 1967). One important point to make here is that although this costuming may seem quite effeminate by our standards, silk stockings and high-heeled shoes were the norm at Louis XIV's court. It is generally accepted that the adoption of such excessive style helped Louis XIV to transform his noble class into a court society (from a warrior class).

35. Claude Reichler, "La Jambe du roi," in *L'Age libertin* (Paris: Editions de Minuit, 1987); and Louis Marin, "Le Corps glorieux du roi et son portrait," in *La Parole mangée et autres essais théologico-politiques* (Paris: Klincksieck, 1986). In both cases the critics follow Kantorowicz's formula, focusing on the tension between the king's aging upper body and the iconic sexuality of the leg. Marin has also written on the rhetoric of the king's physicians in discussing his mortal body, in "Le Corps pathétique et son médecin: Sur le *Journal de santé de Louis XIV*," in *La Parole mangée;* also published in a slightly different version in 1985 in *Revue des sciences humaines*, no. 198. Again, Marin focuses on the mortal body as decaying, not victorious.

Figure 2.7 Hyacinthe Rigaud, *Louis XIV en habit de sacré*, 1701. By permission of the Bibliothèque Nationale.

images discussed in this essay, however, it is particularly striking that the king is the only human figure on the canvas. Portrayed alone, it is as if Louis XIV's potency were innate and eternal, rising like the phoenix out of its own ashes in a vision of absolute, onanistic masculinity. Therefore, as Marin and Reichler suggest, the image *is* ultimately about decay, for the king alone is sterile. In *The Celebrated Assembly*, however, as well as in the other almanac engravings considered here, the young virile king is posed (or framed) not just by his royal robes and by the usual lines of the architectural backdrop or stage, but by the group setting that includes those with whom he still shares the spotlight: in the upper register, his mother, his brother, and the duke, and in the lower register, the now legitimate allegorical female supporters, the conquered and awed Flanders and France, seen offering what the prose text refers to as the portrait of an unnamed princess as a sure omen of his marriage, an object labeled in the actual image as "the picture of his desires" (le tableau de ses souhaits).

The dichotomy between allegorical figures paying tribute to historical ones, the gift-exchange model, the equation between submissive cities and submissive women, the unnamed, framed princess, the leg leading to her portrait as libido or drive to its object, Mazarin's hand pointing out and legitimizing his protégé's leg, and the opposition between high and low can now be read as familiar elements of the iconography that merged images of war with those of marriage. Here, however, the potential threats to the king's power—ill health, sexuality, military insubordination—are contained by the various enclosures, of which frames and clothing are two examples. The display of the king's healthy body as evidence of his military/sexual prowess is always dependent on these framing images. As such, the process of celebrating the king is that of celebrating the assembly around him as well as the assembled images and objects. This process plays out the etymological meaning of allegory: from *allos*, meaning other, and *agorein*, to speak publicly, as well as *agora*, assembly, which can be combined, meaning to speak of the other in public assembly. Here the figurative other is not just the king's masculine power or his prospective bride, but also his dependence on other *limen*: the limbs of the royal entourage—the celebrated assembly of the court, an assemblage of family, courtiers, a cameo female, conquered territories, an implied viewing public, frames, and so forth. Without these elements, would the king's power be secure? Such dependence is nowhere to be seen in Riguad's image of the mature, well-ensconced Sun King.

Indeed, it is the other assembled "bodies," liminal to the king's centering image, that finally attract the viewer's attention in a picture where passion has been enrobed, conquered, framed, and stabilized for display. These other bodies highlight this passion and offer an acceptable field on which to display or stand the king's desires. Just as the drape of clothing serves to enhance interest in the real site of his male power, so too do modestly dressed and submissive allegorical figures and cameo images with missing bodies (Rage, Envy, and Sedition's limbs amputated and framed into submission) also safely pique our interest first in the king's own well-wrapped limb, and then in the process of peace. But this process of allegoresis, or speaking of the (unspeakable) other in a manner suitable to public assembly, is more complex. For if the unspeakable urges are wrapped up, might they not reemerge in the engraving to disrupt the happy family picture of the successful, virile, and healthy king on his throne, a king with appropriate political and sexual fantasies? Indeed, could not some alternate, competitive desires lurk in the hearts of those happily assembled family members and courtiers? Could disordering fantasies or bodies transgress this scene of family romance?

Answers to these questions may be found by considering the figure on the far left edge of *The Celebrated Assembly*, the king's younger brother, the duke of Anjou. As previously noted, he was next in line for the throne should Louis XIV die or his projected marriage prove sterile. This potential pretender is the only member of the assembly whose full body is portrayed in the upright position. Interestingly, the frame around the image cuts off the duke's right leg, the very member so prominently displayed by the king on his throne. Does the duke's walking stick, an object longer than the king's scepter, compensate for the elimination of his leg? Note as well that although it totters at the edge of the focal field, the body of the duke of Anjou nonetheless occupies a unique position or site: he straddles the two registers of the engraving, the upper zone of mimetic portrayal of historical characters and the lower, allegorical field of women. Is it perhaps because of the brother's own liminal position that he, like the potential queen, stands in the register of the king's limb? For in 1658 he was the least significant (smallest and youngest) in the royal family, but also crucial because next in line for the throne. Or might his position be, rather, a function of his well-known effeminate tendencies, an urge apparently encouraged in order to further enhance the power of Louis XIV and yet also elided when the duke was married off twice to safeguard the continuity of the Bourbon dynasty. The duke's position is parallel to that of the "imagined" queen who is also necessary yet peripheral, hopefully fertile yet visually castrated. In the engraving, Louis XIV seems to cast his glance more in his brother's direction than in that of the "picture of his desires," suggesting that in this scenario of precarious health the duke may be a source of anxiety about the virility and power of members or limbs supporting the Bourbon family and thus about the permanence of the titular monarch. As the king recovers his health and the marriage treaty is negotiated and signed, the new queen will replace the prince as the object of such anxiety, being seen in contemporary terms as the vessel necessary for the Bourbon dynastic procreation, but also invoking the memory of the enemy, Philip IV, her father, and his coveted Spanish-Hapsburg throne. It is at this point that she will become the central propping (and anxiety-provoking) image of the fictions generated on the eve of the treaty marriage.[36]

In 1659, however, it is another female figure who visually mediates such unspeakable fantasies, again in the form of a disembodied female head, this time of another former Spanish infanta who became a French queen, Louis XIV's mother, Anne of Austria, a woman intimately acquainted with all sorts of disorders or liminal phenomena: the vagaries of Bourbon homosexuality from her years of marriage to Louis XIII, the nature of competition among the blood princes from her experiences during the Fronde uprisings in the late 1640s and early 1650s, as well as the necessity of the female liminal position to the representation of sovereign masculinity within those dynamics.[37] Positioned unframed between her two sons, she is a reminder that liminality is always lurking at the edge of the absolutist state, since it is, so to speak, the limbs on which the monarchy rests, or the female body that breeds and bears those limbs. As a still-present trace of such liminality, however, she is also the visual proof that if disorderly, ephemeral passions (or props) cannot be fully contained by representational frames, they can at least be utilized and fashioned—shaped—to fit into the larger image of, or frame for, a stable, absolutist, body politic.

In recognizing the role of such liminal images in state-building, one begins to recognize how such fictions have been groomed out of the picture by scholars who examine the portrayal of the king's body solely from the perspective of the political fiction of "the king's two bodies." That

36. These fictions are the subject of my book *Scenes from the Marriage of Louis XV: Nuptial Fictions and the Making of Absolutist Power* (Stanford: Stanford University Press, 1997).

37. Sarah Hanley describes the ritual of the *lit de justice* ceremony in which, upon the king's death and in the case of a regency, the young minor king took the throne publicly in Parlement. Hanley's discussion of Anne of Austria's transgressive role in Louis XIV's own *lit de justice* is particularly interesting in light of the idea that she understood the possible symbolic impact she could have on legitimizing her son's ritual activities. See Sarah Hanley, *The Lit de Justice of the Kings of France: Constitutional Ideology in Legend, Ritual, and Discourse* (Princeton: Princeton University Press, 1983).

paradigm, rooted in the discourses and rituals of death, can account better for the decay of the king's mortal body than for its sexuality. The images examined in this essay were not generated from the funereal model, but were created out of the fictions of marriage. In such a context, highlighting the king's mortality would not be detrimental to, but rather fundamental to, making the ruler (and his rule) seem strong. In the almanac images considered here, display of the king's mortal body as healthy and virile plays a crucial role in state-building, as do all the props and players—persons, limbs, and frames—that work with him to project his (and the state's) vitality. Of course, as the king moves beyond the liminal period between war and marriage, such props and bodies may no longer profitably serve to structure his image. Rather, they become distractions, *divertissements*, in a symbolic logic predicated on promoting his divine autonomy and authority. The representations of this later period have been productively accounted for by scholars working from the Kantorowicz paradigm precisely because these images do not contain and display liminal passions, but rather battle against them to produce a portrait of the king alone on his stage, staving off death (real or political) in a struggle to obliterate the many frames and limbs supporting him, to move beyond the liminal moment and toward (the fantasy of) absolute unity and stability.

3

The King Cross-Dressed

Power and Force in Royal Ballets

MARK FRANKO

Gender studies frequently identify *travesti* with deviations from patriarchal dominance in Western society or as a form of masculine anxiety. It is thus surprising to encounter cross-dressing as a spectacular element in the theatrics of French patriarchal rule, indeed even as a royal performance practice. Considering the period just prior to and including the first decade of Louis XIV's personal reign, one may wonder why the monarch played an impressive number of burlesque and, particularly, cross-dressed roles between 1651 and 1668.[1] To what purpose—strategic, semiotic, ideological—could his theatrical androgyny correspond in productions containing but shadows of burlesque indeterminacy and no apparent satire? More pressing still, to what end—sociosexual, anthropological, iconographic—could the absolute monarch be said to appropriate burlesque cross-dressing in the light of his implicit yet irrevocable interdiction of burlesque ballets in his founding doctrine of dance pedagogy, the *Letters Patent*?[2] To begin to answer some of these questions, I situate

1. For a general discussion of the roles played by Louis XIV in court ballets, see Philippe Hourcade, "Louis XIV travesti," *Cahiers de littérature du XVIIe siècle* 6 (1984): 257–71. The author views the evidence as inconclusive and partial but notes that the king's cross-dressed roles included a Bacchante, a Muse, an Hour, a Fury, a Dryad, Jupiter disguised as Diane, Ceres, a village girl, and a nymph on two separate occasions. For an overview of Louis's dancing career, see Régine Astier, "Louis XIV, 'Premier Danseur,'" in *Sun King: The Ascendency of French Culture During the Reign of Louis XIV*, ed. David Lee Rubin (Washington: Folger Shakespeare Library, 1992), 73–102.

2. The original text of the *Letters Patent* and an English translation can be found in Mark Franko, *Dance as Text: Ideologies of the Baroque Body* (Cambridge: Cambridge University Press, 1993), app. 3, pp. 166–85.

royal cross-dressing in the larger historical context of French court ballet. I ask what political goals cross-dressing may have served under Louis XIII, and then compare those earlier examples with later instances of Louis XIV's cross-dressing.

Given the central place of ballet in ancien régime cultural politics, one might assume dance historians to be among those most likely to formulate challenging approaches to "performing the body" in seventeenth-century French culture. That this has not been the case is due in part to absorption in preliminary work by a myriad of details that yield little cohesiveness. Moreover, further facts may still emerge. But there is no reason to forestall interpretation indefinitely. Traditionally, dance scholarship has restricted its efforts to the compiling and collating of evidence as if the supposed sensory status of this evidence were sufficient for dance. This was merely a way to postpone the encounter of dance and critical theory. I do not shun the facts I can muster, but they frequently have to be wrested from a dense yet fragmentary textual network. That is, they are in part based on the evidence organized by earlier scholarship, and in part the effect of a process of reading. The ensuing discussion of cross-dressing will draw on bits of information and innuendo culled from ballet libretti, costume drawings, and scripted dance scenes (*entrées*) for which there is little corroborative choreographic or performative data. I examine these fragments of evidence, however, not only to engage with the historical density of their factual status, but also to ask how royal performance and royal ideology fashioned one another. This relationship is intrinsic to dance studies in that what was performed was chosen equally for ideological and aesthetic reasons. Above all, an understanding of royal cross-dressing is vital to any reassessment of power and representation in the seventeenth century, if only because of its problematic relationship to propaganda.[3]

One cannot place the issues raised by royal cross-dressing in the perspective of power and representation without invoking the groundbreaking work of Louis Marin and Jean-Marie Apostolidès.[4] Both historian/theorists deemphasized personal agency (the king's or anyone else's) to focus on the ideologies subtending royal representations. Instead they

3. The relationship of performance to power was a central theme to emerge in the conference "Performing the Body" and remains preponderant in the present volume.

4. See Louis Marin, *Le Portrait du roi* (Paris: Editions de Minuit, 1981), translated as *Portrait of the King* by Martha M. Houle (Minneapolis: University of Minnesota Press, 1988); and Jean-Marie Apostolidès, *Le Roi-machine: Spectacle et politique au temps de Louis XIV* (Paris: Editions de Minuit, 1981).

privileged the behind-the-scenes calculations by which the king's image was fashioned. The monarch's appearances or representations were thus studied as the outcome of others' calculations rather than as the personal expression of his own political acumen. Agency, in other words, becomes an effect of representation, and power is a term for disembodied agency exerted by representations of the king.

In Marin's account, power exerts a certain performativity: its skillful representation makes us mindful of power's presence to itself, of a self-consciousness with regard to its potential, and, thus, of an ability to predict its effects on the unsuspecting spectator. The representation of power brings with it a certain self-assurance. For a representation to be *of power*, it must simulate power's own effects in the viewer. It achieves this by causing itself to be doubly felt, as if self-confirming. Marin deduced this seventeenth-century strategy from analyses of maps, medals, portraits, and historical narratives. More precisely, all such media employed in the seventeenth century to disseminate the king's prestige presuppose that the visible is governed by a reading and, reciprocally, that what is read produces an image.[5] The supplementary text brought to mind by the image—or image brought to mind by the text—constitutes simulated reception, or what he calls the "presencing effect" (*effet de présence*). In Marin's terms, absolutism is a semiotic system in which the visible and the legible become each other's confirming context. Through such incursions of the descriptive into the narrative and of the narrative into the descriptive, reception becomes predetermined, if not overdetermined. In other words, a kind of agency is lent to representation.[6]

This aesthetic of self-confirmation could be applied equally well to the king's roles in court ballets and their accompanying verse, which, spoken to the action, serves as "legend" to the performance's "image."[7] When it comes to the king's cross-dressed roles, however, there is a problem. Ironies between the visible and the verbal in *travesti* roles are not self-confirming. When a role ironizes on its verse text, mutual reinforcement is stymied. Alternatively, if there indeed is a presencing effect, it acts to impose a multiple and decentered royal subject. That is, it confirms only the simulacral part of Marin's formula: power is (only) representation,

5. Marin, *Portrait du roi*, 231.

6. "Power is, first, to have the ability to exert an action on something or someone, not to act or to do but to have the potential of doing so, *to have* the force to do or to act" (ibid., 6).

7. The texts of libretti are made up chiefly of such verse, more rarely of notations of the physical action. Consequently, cues as to action must be surmised from the verse itself, unless one derives help from costume or scene sketches.

where the emphasis is on effect and not on presence. In all the other official arts, the king's body is portrayed—made present—as the "presencing effect," but in burlesque style self-confirmation is troubled.

Despite the most specialized skills, performance always entails physical risks that place the perfect symmetry of power and representation at risk. Dance in particular is founded on an inherently fallible, even if dependably virtuosic, human performance before onlookers. When it comes down to the body, court ballet offers resistances to the larger project of royal portraiture. How, for example, does a body mythically identified with the state—at its center, so to speak—represent power while remaining perpetually at risk and in danger of losing face? If dancing in royal ballets constitutes the property and propriety of the king's physical performance—the aesthetic glue of the body natural to the body politic—how is the ideology of absolutism furthered in the transgression of its aesthetics of reception by the cross-dressed king?[8]

The Dance-Historical Context

Cross-dressing was a regular feature of burlesque ballets, a court ballet genre that contested monarchical power by satirizing its most political performances. Burlesque works, especially between 1624 and 1627, were formally self-conscious, structurally open ended, and politically allusive, and, as such, they disrupted prior court ballet traditions such as the centrality of a spoken or sung text, the human figure's recognizably noble status, and its erect and staid dancerly demeanor, all of which had characterized composite spectacle.[9] Yet the burlesque moment was short lived. The most virulent burlesque works of the 1620s satirized the melodramatic ballets sponsored by Richelieu to glorify Louis XIII. At the time of Louis XIV's productions, there were no longer any obviously burlesque ballets, only scattered burlesque roles. A muted burlesque survived into

8. The terms *body politic* and *body natural* are central to Kantorowicz's study of kingship as political theology, and will be referred to later in this discussion. See Ernst H. Kantorowicz, *The King's Two Bodies: A Study in Mediaeval Political Theology* (Princeton: Princeton University Press, 1957).

9. Composite spectacle was so called because it blended a variety of genres into one totality: dance, music, song, stage design. See Franko, *Dance as Text*, 32–51. The stated goal of such performances was frequently the harmonization of the genres whose most patent demonstration occurred in the geometrical dance itself.

the 1630s, whereas only stylistic remnants of it endured in Benserade's ballets of the 1650s.

In 1662, Louis XIV founded the Royal Dance Academy with the *Lettres patentes du roy pour l'etablissement de l'Academie royale de danse en la ville de Paris*. This document reveals how the monarch proposed to and did extend his control over oppositional choreographic initiatives by usurping and regulating dance pedagogy. The *Letters Patent* do not treat the creation of ballets, addressing instead the more fundamental pedagogical issue of how people should be trained to move. They undergird the institution of dance as an art under royal surveillance. I interpret the institutionalization of dance as a preventive measure, as insurance against the unsettling return of burlesque performance.[10] A structural comparison between geometrical or horizontal dance prevalent in composite spectacles of the Valois court (1573–82) with burlesque ballets of the 1620s and 1630s will permit us to ascertain the key aesthetic components of the burlesque trend within which cross-dressing emerged as a theatrical activity.[11]

In geometrical dance, bodies were given over to the strategic project of royal self-representation, their movements organized to spell the monarch's name or visually to symbolize his presence. Such "figures" were composed by group patterns within which the body lost its distinctively individual traits. Dancers performed geopolitical configurations of the *king's* space—the provinces, for example, whose cooperative spatial arrangement produced the nation. Composite spectacle was thus a spectacle of the power in the spatial coordination of bodies, and geometrical dance was its choreographic realization.[12] The dancers' discipline addressed a highly coordinated "division of the terrain" according to which certain points in space were to be marked and occupied with an acute awareness of proportionate spatial relationships and the timing necessary to assure each figure's visual coherence.

Approximately thirty years after the cultural dominant of composite spectacle, but within a still-evolving ballet culture, burlesque works challenged the structural, kinesthetic, and generic expectations of what court

10. Ibid., 109–12.

11. For an extended study of these contrasts, see ibid., 15–31, 63–107.

12. The performance of geometrical dance was an analog for the performance of social and political harmony, furthered by state-sponsored spectacle. Composite spectacle was dominated by the workings of proportion, generically, musically, and spatially. Although he did not specifically address performance, Michel Foucault's comment on the role of geometry in absolutism seems uncannily apt in this context: "Geometry belongs to oligarchy since it demonstrates proportion through inequality" (*L'Ordre du discours* [Paris: Gallimard, 1971], 20; my translation).

ballet had until then been. In the face of ballet's hegemonic image as an official celebration of monarchical legitimacy and might, translated into terms of overwhelming aesthetic opulence, burlesque works must have appeared outwardly transgressive, from both the aesthetic and the political perspectives, although burlesque works were also, in their own way, quite opulent.[13]

By displacing previous emphasis on spatial patterning, this new burlesque genre appears to have contradicted the venerable choreographic tradition of geometrical dance. Frequently grotesque individuals or groups drew attention to their own peculiarities in costume and movement. Burlesque works were not populated by delicately suspended and uncannily immobilized dancers tacitly complying with one another's mapping of a harmonious state. Rather, burlesque figures danced unpredictable gestures, their bodies writhing and twisting downward or propelled precipitously into the air. These were certainly not "noble" figures in ways earlier defined, and their choreography was not the measured and expansive one of courtly social dance, as adapted for geometrical patterning. Burlesque bodies assumed singular if fanciful attributes, angular attitudes, abruptness of attack, and postural contortions, as we can surmise from extant illustrations. These initiatives, although not fully without precedent, were potentially experimental and surely broadened the choreographic lexicon, especially with regard to airborne steps. Burlesque dancing also heralded the beginning of a theatrical dance of character that was to develop in the eighteenth century.

Excursus on Time and Space

This paradigm shift in choreographic values could be summed up by proposing that an art of spatial arrangement and coordination for large groups presided over by the king had given way to an art of physiognomy and time in which the king himself performed. The lack of pattern in burlesque-style works necessarily introduced time as a new dimension within which danced ideas evolved. This new dimension lack-

13. Their opulence is much more related to the individually costumed figure than to the organization of space, the ornamentation of the spatial surround, or the machinic animation of decor. See Margaret M. McGowan, *The Court Ballet of Louis XIII: A Collection of Working Designs for Costumes, 1615–33* (London: Victoria & Albert Museum, 1986).

ing tested formal structures to justify it must have destabilized the old cohesion of aesthetics and ideology in pattern making. Following upon a diminution of hieratic visual effects, the new sensation of time connoted a new sensibility with respect to duration. Burlesque works may even have induced some visual fatigue for the sensation they permitted of letting time drag on. This is less an indication of poor craftsmanship than the inevitable consequence of a new choreographic premise: to allow moving bodies to define space in terms of what they do and who they pretend to be.

The older understanding of spatial arrangement as constitutive of choreographic structure was connected to the expression of political theology. Bodies expressed grace (a power not directly their own) through their physical alignment with spatial pattern. Ernst Kantorowicz reminds us that divine grace and human nature were unified only in *potestas*.[14] The doctrine of the king's two bodies otherwise held them distinct, as a godly but incorporeal and a natural because corporeal presence. In its performative union of the corporeal and the incorporeal, power was potentially unlimited. Thus the juridical necessity for a two-body doctrine, both to ensure royal succession and to circumscribe the power accruing to an individual as ruler. The abandonment of spatial aesthetics for the exploration of individual languages of character—among them the king's character—heralded a different orientation to the ritualizing of *potestas* by bodies. The new emphasis on the time taken to perform individual actions rather than on the measured time of spectacular patterning suggests a potential splintering of grace and nature. Spectacular bodies, the king's body being no exception, were becoming "real" in the sense intended by Kantorowicz's term *nature*. They were being placed within a mortal and fallible frame inhabited equally by the king and his subjects. Time, as Kantorowicz also reminds us, falls outside of eternity.[15] Time is the dimension not of power (a union of grace and nature), but of human mortality. Yet it is equally a dimension of wild power, that is, of force. Dancing bodies governed only by their own character(s) suggests the raw physical potential of force.

In composite spectacle of the late sixteenth century, the monarch presided over the ballet from his conspicuous position in the audience. By the early decades of the seventeenth century, however, the king's own physical movement was staged within the spectacle. The decision that the

14. Kantorowicz, *King's Two Bodies*, 48.
15. Ibid., 49.

king himself perform as a solo figure was not due entirely to the emergence of burlesque trends. An intervening form of ballet, called melodramatic by dance historian Margaret M. McGowan, also staged the king as a dramatic figure in an allegorical plot.[16] My point, however, is that with the burlesque focus on bodies rather than on patterns or narratives as a structural rationale, a brave new world of theatrical risk-taking unknown to earlier decades emerged. The sorts of risks involved in performances of character—wherein the king was no longer a prominent spectator but a player—was in some perplexing ways the very antithesis of contemporaneous royal image management. It was within this context that the cross-dressed king initially appeared.

Does choreographic logic help us to perceive how differential emphases on space and time can alter the relationship of dance to power? Yes, but even so, aesthetics do not transparently reveal what has been added to, what subtracted from, an ideological imperative. Military theory can help elucidate dance theory at this juncture.

The switch from space to time is one from a choreographically centered practice to a dance-technical practice. Choreography, in other words, as exemplified by pattern making, is a plan or a strategy. Dance itself, when considered in isolation from the dictates of choreography, is more intrinsically burlesque in its tactical skirmishes with choreography's plan, its attempts to realize, approximate, or ironize choreography. Military theorist Carl von Clausewitz's concept of strategy seems applicable to baroque geometrical dance where the unified body of the group is deployed simultaneously in a project aiming for maximum *spatial* impact: "Strategy," notes Clausewitz, "knows only the simultaneous use of force." For Clausewitz, space is the most rational of physical coordinates, whereas time is the most aleatory. He associates tactics with time because their duration is unpredictable. Tactics call for the pragmatic and "successive use of force" over time, the use of forces in "disarray and weakness" rather than as planned and concentrated. Tactics, in short, imply "strategic uncertainty."[17] They are not a project but a resistance to failure, a way to re-

16. See Margaret M. McGowan, *L'Art du ballet de cour en France, 1581–1643* (Paris: CNRS, 1963), 72. McGowan situates melodramatic ballets predominantly between 1610 and 1620. For a discussion of gender ambiguities in melodramatic ballet, see my "Jouer avec le feu: la subjectivité du roi dans *La Déliverance de Renault*," in *Gestes d'amour et de guerre: "La Jérusalem délivrée" du Tasse*, ed. Giovanni Careri (Paris: Editions du Louvre, forthcoming).

17. Carl von Clausewitz, *On War*, ed. and trans. Michael Howard and Peter Paret (Princeton: Princeton University Press, 1984), 206, 210–11. For further elaboration on strategy and tactics, see Michel de Certeau, *The Practice of Everyday Life*, trans. Steven F. Rendall (Berkeley: University of California Press, 1984), 34–39.

coup failed strategy. Burlesque dance was tactical, whereas composite spectacle was strategic. We are able to grasp this distinction based on a merging of aesthetic and ideological criteria only thanks to the preceding critical analysis of space and time in these two performance genres.

We should not limit our consideration of this new performative body natural of burlesque to the risks it runs of confirming its own mortality. In the ritual context of ballet, the king's sexual ambiguity was doubtless performed to reassert agency as a personal trait. In its very ambiguity or doubleness this personal trait can reestablish a sensation of what Victor Turner called "communitas with one's peers." "Communitas," notes Turner, "is a relationship between concrete, historical, idiosyncratic individuals."[18] The king's cross-dressing thus opens up the realms of his physical and sexual force, even potential violence. Being performative and only "of the now" (antistructural in Turner's sense) makes royal cross-dressing all the more terrible in that it announces the threat of a return to structure. I will develop these ideas later with particular reference to Marin's distinction between power and force. Let us turn now, however, to that apparently paradoxical situation in which the king's connection to androgynous theatrical traits enhances aspects of his institutional strength.

Androgyny and Succession

Consider first an example of balletic androgyny prior to the reign of Louis XIV in *Le Ballet de Madame* (1615), an unusual work in several respects. Although occasioned to celebrate the marriage of Elizabeth, daughter of Marie de Médicis, with a Spanish prince—and therefore a controversial union between France and Spain—it also necessarily commemorated the recent assassination of Henri IV and the succession of his son, Louis XIII. Although the main focus of the ballet is Elizabeth, "Madame," who also plays Minerva, the ballet celebrates the project of a controversial political alliance contravening the wishes of the late king. Thus, in an atmosphere of controversy, it could not but refer to succession. And although it performs the political aspirations of the Bourbon dynasty, it does so without the composite spectacle format. Stylistically, *Le Ballet de Madame* is a transitional work in which allegory is no longer

18. Victor Turner, *The Ritual Process: Structure and Anti-Structure* (New York: Walter de Gruyter, 1995), 131.

supported by narrative but appears instead embedded in a series of apparently disconnected tableaux suggesting the expansion of the interlude typical of later burlesque works.[19] In a section of *Le Ballet de Madame* entitled "Ballet des Androgynes," the body politic under Louis XIII was portrayed by male nobles as androgynous, that is, as sexually ambiguous or doubled. The libretto's verse for this ballet announces the ritual of royal succession and continuity from Henri IV to Louis XIII as one in which the people of France are "celestes Androgynes."

Puis, comme si un noeud les mariast ensemble,
A mesme temps ce zele en un corps les assemble
Pres le Ciel ou souloit luire son beau Soleil.
La, chacune, à l'envi, promptement se vient rendre,
Pour garder le phenix qu'avoit produit sa cendre
En courage à son pere, et en vertus pareil.[20]

Then, as if drawn together in one knot [erection],
This zeal unites them in a single body
Near the heaven where his Sun was wont to shine.
Each hastened there to see
This phoenix rising from its ashes
Equal in courage and virtue to his father.

In this reference to succession from Henri IV to Louis XIII when the monarchical phoenix is reborn from it ashes, warrior nobles personify the nation as a multiplicitous body unified in its love of Louis ("this zeal unites them in one body"). The *noeud* (knot) that draws them together is also the seventeenth-century French term for the erect male member. The nation is a troop of androgynes receiving and multiplying "his happy seed" (*son heureuse semence*). They do this among themselves, as per their verses, as they swarm about Louis like bees, watch him like sentinels, nurture the flame of love in their hearts, and spread his seed with their hands.[21]

A clear distinction between the androgyne's sexual indeterminacy and the hermaphrodite's sexual doubleness does not appear operative in seventeenth-century French usage. Furetière, for example, defines the

19. *Le Ballet de Madame* is also unusual because a separate publication exists to explain its allegorical intricacies. See McGowan, *L'Art du ballet*, 85–99; and Elie Garel, *Les Oracles françois, ou explication allegorique du Balet de madame, soeur aisnee du roy* (Paris: P. Chevalier, 1615).

20. Paul Lacroix, *Ballets et mascarades de cour de Henri III à Louis XIV (1581–1652)*, 6 vols. (Geneva: Slatkine, 1968), 2:83; the translation that follows is mine.

21. Ibid., 82–83.

term androgyne as "Hermaphrodite qui a les deux natures, qui est masle et femelle tout ensemble."[22] Being "both together" is being both indeterminate (ambiguous) and overdetermined (double). It would therefore seem that the king's body politic is drawn into such a hermaphroditic union with the nation, with royal succession being staged by the ballet as sexual submissiveness of the people and hermaphroditic reproduction of the body politic. Inasmuch as the nation is represented by the king's immediate male entourage, there is also the implication of same-sex object choice. Although we could imagine some reference to the sexual preferences of Louis XIII in *Le Ballet de Madame*, he was only nine years old at the time of its performance. The hermaphrodite's ability to reproduce itself, however, may be a way to allay anxieties about a succession to which policy changes offensive to the memory of the father are attached. A rapprochement with Spain, signified by a marriage that is in turn fêted by a ballet during a time of mourning, might well necessitate a self-sufficient image of royal succession, one insulated from both political and sexual conventions. Nevertheless, this succession is performed as male parthenogenesis.

The mystical distinction between the king's mortal and immortal body (the "body natural" and the "body politic" in Kantorowicz's terms) has sometimes taken the form of a horizontal anatomical split.[23] In iconography of the High Middle Ages the king's material body—especially his feet and lower body—could emblematize the bodies of his subjects as the nation, whereas his head figured the body politic. In *Le Ballet de Madame*, it is as though the nation's cohesiveness—its willingness to "band together" (*bander* also being a possible contemporary French pun on *noeud*) and assure royal succession—constitutes his erection as well as their "knot," their allegorical and performative togetherness. In the verse just cited, the (male) nation gathers at the site of the king's sexual organ in order to demonstrate the monarchy's self-procreating power. The nonreproductive aspects of this political sex are in their turn textually desexualized, or at least attenuated in that the androgynes are called "celestial." The ballet's verses present many production possibilities, none of which can be historically documented in the work's mise-en-scène except inasmuch as their recitation suggested unrealizable images a public could

22. Antoine Furetière, *Dictionnaire universel* (Rotterdam, 1690), s.v. "androgyne."

23. This iconography is proper to the "God-man" or liturgical version of kingship in which the monarch is an impersonator of Christ or "christomimetes." See Kantorowicz, *King's Two Bodies*, 61–78.

nonetheless not disregard. They remain, however, a commentary whose ironic collision or collusion with the actual event is more certain than the form of that event itself.

The anthropological concept of ritual, particularly Victor Turner's use of liminality as a ritual phase, offers further interpretive nuance to this situation. According to Turner, who bases his thinking on van Gennep's notion of rites of passage, any change of status or transition from one state to another is necessarily accompanied by a ritual period of withdrawal whose characteristics are ambiguous. The ritual subject "passes through a cultural realm that has few or none of the attributes of the past or coming state."[24] The plausibility of Turner's liminality resides for me in his view that all status quo reversals of this sort are temporary and tend on the whole to reinforce structure. There are other manifestations of cross-dressing in court ballets, however, that are less reassuring with regard to structure.

Androgyny and Discord

The figure of the androgyne populates burlesque ballets as well, although there cross-dressing bears none of the sexual-political links that enable it to speak for royal legitimacy in official contexts. In burlesque, the androgyne appears frequently in the locus of, or even as a substitute for, vanquished or deprecated and colonized peoples, particularly Africans and native Americans. For example, in the noted burlesque work *Le Grand Bal de la douairière de Billebahaut* (1626), androgynes appear in America following a scene that caricatures that land's native inhabitants.[25] Even in *Le Ballet de Madame*, the same "Machlyenes" who portrayed the androgynous nation in the *entrée* discussed above appear also as female companions of a girl dressed "à l'antique Africaine" and serenading attending royalty.[26] Burlesque androgyny is not figured in a horizontal, but rather in a vertical split (fig. 3.1). This is consonant with Aristophanes' speech in Plato's *Symposium* on androgynes as split entities seeking their other halves. Androgynous figures, however, are also implied in the frequent mise-en-scène of individuals mirroring one another, and who are frequently

24. Turner, *Ritual Process*, 94.
25. For more details on this work, see Franko, *Dance as Text*, 186–90.
26. Lacroix, *Ballets et mascarades*, 2:65.

Figure 3.1 Androgynous figure from *Le Grand Bal de la douairière de Billebahaut*, 1626. Courtesy of the Board of Trustees of the Victoria and Albert Museum.

"doubled" by apes or bears. Such scenes are always related to either status reversals or racial depictions of Moors, Jews, Amerindians, and other reviled outsiders.

The impact of these figures is tied to their critical import, which is evanescent by design. Burlesque techniques included verbal opacity through punning and burlesque verse, constructed shapes in costuming, and physical twisting on the ground as well as experimentation with aerial virtuosity, all of which were, as previously stated, programmatic critiques of composite spectacle. Along with an increased range of movement vocabulary, burlesque works employed carnivalesque techniques of character reversal, obscenity, and sexual, racial, or class cross-dressing, the most emblematic figure of which was the androgyne. Thus, as I have argued elsewhere, an economically and politically besieged nobility placed the monarchy in symbolic jeopardy by creating and performing "burla" (mystifications) in which nobles identified themselves with persecuted groups. The motif of androgyny as employed in many burlesque ballets no longer conveyed assurances of political stability and continuity but presaged instead veiled threats of discontinuity or radical change.[27]

Given this state of affairs, the androgyne is paradigmatic for its indeterminacy. Despite the suggestions of cross-dressing, the cross is always ambiguous, or rather, it is anchored in the action of the crossing itself. The intermediary status of the androgyne thus becomes emblematic of an enterprise whose criticism is liminoid in Victor Turner's sense. "Liminoid phenomena," remarks Turner, "develop apart from the central economic and political processes, along the margins, in the interfaces and interstices of central and servicing institutions—they are plural, fragmentary, and experimental in character."[28] Thus, burlesque androgyny implies a more disturbing dislocation of masculine heterosexual identity, a rendering liminoid of royal ritual. Liminoid phenomena derive from individuals, have commodity value, and enable social critique.

What this explanation of the political tendencies of the burlesque enables us to understand is the historical significance of its disappearance. Thirty years after the fact, memory of the burlesque was still sufficiently threatening for Louis XIV to interdict its performance in his *Letters Patent*, a document that simultaneously founded the Royal Dance Academy.

The Return of Force: Toward a Performative Two-Body Theory

It should be clear by now that we are talking about the king's two bodies in a very performative sense. But the ramifications of Kantorowicz's dyad in such fully material terms need further clarification.[29] The king's body politic is performed via Apollo or the sun, his

27. See Franko, *Dance as Text*, 63–107.

28. Victor Turner, "Liminal to Liminoid," in *From Ritual to Theatre: The Human Seriousness of Play* (New York: PAJ, 1982), 54. I would argue that burlesque ballet, although clearly marginal, occurs remarkably close to the economic and political center, frequently even with the king's personal participation.

29. The two-body doctrine is one of juridical separation, making it particularly applicable to the English monarchy. As Thomas Hobbes stated: "In a Body Politique, if the Representative be one man, whatever he does in the person of the Body, which is not warranted

Figure 3.2 Louis XIV as Apollo in *Les Noces de Pelée et de Thétis*, 1654. Reproduced by permission.

body natural via a fury. What does this mean for our understanding of power and representation in royal spectacle? Are they both equally powerful representations? How can we apprehend them in their hypothetical complementarity?

Let us consider for a moment Marin's analysis of sacrament and its

in his Letters, nor by the Lawes, is his own act, and not the act of the Body, nor of any other Member thereof besides himselfe" (*Leviathan* [1651; New York: Washington Square Press, 1964], 159). Regarding the place of kingship in French culture, Roger Chartier has discussed the merging of the two bodies into one as initiated by Louis XIII and sustained by Louis XIV; see his *Cultural Origins of the French Revolution*, trans. Lydia G. Cochrane (Durham: Duke University Press, 1991), 124–25.

links to the power of representations. He gives as an example the body of Christ, present yet, in the language of the sacrament, invisible ("This is my body"); absent despite its symbolic visibility in the wafer whose materiality is consumed to produce presence as an idea (properly, to *represent* presence).[30] By extension, when Louis XIV performs the role of rising sun in *Ballet de la nuit* (1653), his natural body offers itself for visual consumption in a political sacrament of monarchical power as illuminating, but also blinding, radiance. The role of rising sun is, like the wafer, the visible talisman of an absence (a sign) producing the idea (representation) of body politic in the mind. When Louis XIV dances Apollo, there is royal sacrament. His glorious roles evidence the transubstantiation of body natural into body politic. Yet, what ramifications ensue for the two-body theory when he dances a coquette, a nymph, or a fury?

If an androgynous appearance marked the self-sufficiency of rulership in balletic terms, it is not surprising that Louis XIV should have presented a feminized appearance in his 1654 performance of Apollo, for it was as Apollo that he symbolized most unambiguously his rulership (fig. 3.2). Nevertheless, this monarch said to be enamored of ballet inherited androgyny stemming from two divergent courtly traditions: the official and the burlesque. The performance of androgyny had one leg, so to speak, in legitimacy and the other in irony or resistance. How did Louis XIV negotiate the cultural memory of this dual performance tradition in roles not otherwise associated with his ceremonious royal identity?

Consider his role as a Fury in *Les Noces de Pelée et Thétis* (1654).[31] In this work, as in many other ballets, the king plays more than one role. He first appears, in fact, as Apollo surrounded by his Muses. In the third scene, however, he plays one of nine furies of jealousy vomited from a sea monster's mouth. The monster has been called forth by Juno to prevent

30. Louis Marin, *La Critique du discours: Sur la "Logique de Port-Royal" et les "Pensées" de Pascal* (Paris: Editions de Minuit, 1975), 254–55.

31. The libretto, originally printed by Robert Ballard, has not been reprinted in any collection. The text is at the Bibliothèque Nationale [hereafter cited as BN]: In-8 BN Rés. Yf 1460. Ballard also published a synopsis of the ballet, reprinted in Marie Françose Christout, *Le Ballet de cour de Louis XIV, 1643–1672* (Paris: A. & J. Picard, 1967), 205–11. Some of the costume studies for *Les Noces* are housed in the Musée Carnavalet; see Laurence Guilmard-Geddes, "'Les Noces de Pélée et Thétis': Costumes de Ballet," in *Dons et achats récents: Bulletin du Musée Carnavalet* 30, no. 2 (1977): 5–9. See also Marie-Françoise Christout, "'Les Noces de Pelée et Thétis': Comédie italienne en musique entremêlée d'un ballet dansé par le roi (1654)," *Baroque* 5 (1972): 55–62; Charles I. Silin, *Benserade and His Ballets de Cour* (Baltimore: Johns Hopkins University Press, 1940), 232–38; and Christout, *Ballet de cour de Louis XIV*, 72–77.

Jupiter's abduction of Thetis. The king's presence in this *entrée* might seem unremarkable in that he is one among nine other performers. Special verses that single him out are, however, attributed to the king as Fury.

Et suis si tu peux cette jeune Furie,
Espagne, dont l'orgueil est trop long-temps debout,
Elle te va dompter d'une force aguerrie,
Et la torche à la main s'en va de bout en bout
Mettre le feu par tout.

Elle suit les meschans, les presse, les opprime,
Leur fait dans ses regards lire un sanglant decret,
Et dans le mesme instant qu'ils commettent le crime
Leur glisse dans le coeur un eternel regret,
Comme un serpent secret.

Que je voy de Beautez dont la rigueur extresme
A plus de mille Amans a causé le trepas,
Qui voudroient tout le jour, et toute la nuict mesme
Avoir cette Furie attachée à leurs pas,
Et qui ne l'auront pas.[32]

And follow if you can this young Fury,
Spain, whose pride has been too long afoot,
She will tame you with a warrior's seasoned force,
And torch in hand she will pass from end to end,
Setting fire everywhere.

She pursues the wicked, presses and oppresses them,
Has them read in her expression a bloody decree,
And in the very moment they commit their crime
Slips into their heart an eternal regret,
Like a secret serpent.

How many beauties I see whose extreme rigor
Caused the death of a thousand lovers,
Who would like to have all day, and all night,
This Fury behind them,
But who won't have her.

The king's verse introduces a triple scenario in which the Fury's pursuit of Jupiter, who is himself in pursuit of Thetis, is manipulated in several disconcerting ways. First, the political context of Spain in its relationship to France is foregrounded when the audience is asked to reposition the cross-dressed king ("that young Fury") as ostensible prey of

32. Ballard, *Les Noces*, 21 (In-8 BN Rés. Yf 1460).

the Spanish. Yet the Fury is herself in pursuit of all evil forces, acting on them with terrible incendiary and bloody violence. By the third stanza, in typically burlesque fashion, the cross-dressed king is said to exert a sexual appeal on otherwise forbidding female spectators who presumably regret they will not themselves be persecuted by her. Thus, his violence is transformed into a sexually appealing quality. There are three levels at which the cross-dressed king interacts with his public: at the narrative level, the most straightforward, in which he plays a fury pursuing Jupiter; at the level of contradictory commentaries that introduce secondary allegorical senses with both political and sexual motifs; and finally, at the level of physical performance, wherein, it seems, the king's actual presence is called on either to unite these disparate interpretations or to succumb to their competing meanings. Here, the anomaly is less the cross-dressed king per se then the different interpretive claims being made for his energy and presence. To be pursued, as it were, by such competing texts would also be, for the Fury, necessarily to remarshal them in the name of her own violence or unlimited force—which is named as sex, violence, and magic. But s/he is caught up in a wider web that includes all facets of the performance tradition under study: legitimacy, resistance, and seduction (fig. 3.3).

Hermaphroditism, which has been shown to underwrite the ritual significance of royal succession in *Le Ballet de Madame*, underwrites in *Les Noces* the exceeding of power by force, of attraction by magic. Hermaphroditism, initially a balletic icon of royal succession, later a tool of dissident critique, finally became with Louis XIV the balletic sign of unpredictable royal agency. We could refer to it in general terms as seduction. At this juncture, let us note how dance studies induce a return to the issue of agency without discarding ideological critique.

Appropriative Cross-Dressing and Force

When Louis XIV performs a cross-dressed role one can assume the intersection of several appropriations. He references the earlier burlesque style by appropriating it; but he also asserts the "double body" doctrine: he performs his own mortality as the weaker part of a *corporation sole*. In this assertion of mortality, however, the "body politic" is manifested as the invisible presence of a missing (male) sex. It is engendered by the possibility of seduction. Although we know full well that the king performs, we are also confronted with his insistently travestied presence.

Figure 3.3 Louis XIV as a fury in *Les Noces de Pelée et de Thétis*, 1654. Reproduced by permission.

His body as present and coded female presents the king's "body natural"—the "weaker" and therefore "mortal" (feminine) sex of the hermaphrodite. In other words, unlike the wafer, cross-dressing is harder to swallow because it activates no transubstantiation, whether theological or political. It does present, however, his agency, and where it does not, the performance risks becoming anomalous. So, for example, the king's role as Coquette in *Les Festes de Bacchus* (1651) was cut, presumably because it did not activate the proper images of terrifying agency.[33]

How are we to understand this deployment of balletic force in the light of the much elaborated collusion of power and representation in seventeenth-century royal iconography? Is it a cul-de-sac of the balletic form itself? Or does it add a dimension to ideological calculations in their representational effects that actually exceed the logic of representational strategies? Is there a logic of presence as seduction? It might be useful to close this discussion by recalling the ultimate rationale of representation as power.

Every institution in Marin's reading of Pascal is founded on an originary or mythical deployment of force (a fight to the death) in which the stronger triumphs.[34] Institutions become established to obviate reenactments of this founding force. Such institutions—the monarchy, for example—are founded in and through symbols that effectively place their force in reserve and defer any desire to repeat the battle to the death, to reenact violence as an absolute of force. Thus the complicity of representation and power. Representations of power defer the necessity for force to display its absolute. But by the same token, power itself becomes an effect of representation, a force that is reconfigured by means other than its initial violence, by artistic means. Power, in other words, is necessarily flawed, because it exists only as a representation. Thus Marin's definition of power as "force in mourning."[35]

My point is that the cross-dressed king is not powerful in the con-

33. This *entrée* became known to dance historians as the "Entrée supprimé" (suppressed entrée) because it was never performed and was only printed as an appendix to the original libretto. Lacroix declined to reprint it in his republication of ballet libretti for its "lack of nobility and seemliness," even though, as he remarks as well, the king played the role of a thief in the same ballet (*Ballets et mascarades*, 6:304). The libretto for *Le Ballet du roy des Festes de Bacchus*, published by Robert Ballard in 1651, is housed at the Bibliothèque Nationale, In-4o BN Yf Rés. 1210. The Bibliothèque Nationale also holds sixty-nine original watercolor costume and set drawings for this work by Henry de Gissey or his atelier; a facsimile album exists in the Dance Collection of the New York Public Library (*MGZEB 87–264).

34. See Marin, *Portrait du roi*, 11–13, as well as his "La Raison du plus fort est toujours la meilleure," in *Aims and Prospects of Semiotics: Essays in Honor of A. J. Greimas*, ed. H. Parret and H. G. Ruprecht (Amsterdam: John Benjamins, 1985), 726–47; republished in *La parole mangée et autres essais théologico-politiques* (Paris: Meridiens Klincksieck, 1986), 61–88.

35. Marin, *Portrait du roi*, 138.

ventional sense, because s/he is not a representation. In fact, s/he contradicts power's representations: s/he re-presents force. Her performance, oddly lacking as an incarnation of the monarchical institution, replays the force at that institution's origin and thus performs the basis of theatrical doubling itself, the founding violence at the origin of institutions that enable the "inscription of morality as style."[36] Cross-dressing is the inscription of force as style, violence as style, the amorality at the origin of theatrically stylized behavior. Modes of surrogation constituting period style project ideologies not only forward in time (fodder for reconstructions) but also, as it were, backward toward an uncoded energetics, figures of desire, bodies as empty spaces inhabited by an unpredictable and seductive energy.[37] In the area of historical dance reconstruction, such figures that themselves remember in lieu of bestowing memory upon us, who account for their own form as the disruptive necessity to reenact the origin of their own institutionalization, are in need of theatrical construction. They would bring a new and compelling sense of agency to the convention-bound reenactments of history.

The king's body of force, feminized as mortal but present nonetheless as the king—*this* king—does not offer herself up to symbolic consumption but stands instead as a figure of desire, an empty space that his public can fill only with what they fear to be her own agency, her force beyond representation, her sexuality, her body natural. After all, he herself performed these roles, and made them known as extensions of his own physicality, unique moments in her own life in which physical means and performative intention took the center of attention. What I am claiming to have been witnessed in Louis XIV's cross-dressed roles is not court ballet's imaginary, but its real; not its power, but its force: its figuration of agency, neither role as thing-prop nor ideas as presenced effect. Furthermore, the cross-dressed king deconstructs the system of flattery haunting the traditional exaltation and consumption of the royal person. In the irony between her transgressive appearance and his glorious reality, the king risks the stability of his power by presenting her mortal body, but also asserts a terrifying and sexualized agency, by taking it, so to speak, out of its representational mourning and putting it into presence.[38]

36. Joseph R. Roach, "Power's Body: The Inscription of Morality as Style," in *Interpreting the Theatrical Past: Essays in the Historiography of Performance*, ed. Thomas Postlewait and Bruce A. McConachie (Iowa City: University of Iowa Press, 1989), 109.

37. And this is precisely the sense in which Pascal critiqued the Port-Royalist theory of language and revealed that the nonadequation of rationality and power allowed for the return of force in the figure. See Marin, *La Critique du discours*, 273.

38. This conclusion invites further exploration of the relationship between agency, force, and femininity, an exploration that is beyond the immediate scope of this essay.

4

Unruly Passions and Courtly Dances

Technologies of the Body in Baroque Music

SUSAN MCCLARY

Most musicians and classical music connoisseurs today assume they have some acquaintance with French baroque dance: they can identify its principal types (allemande, courante, sarabande, gigue, etc.); they can recognize or even perform several examples of each. Yet the examples of French dance they are most likely to know and hold in highest regard as musical works were composed not at Versailles, but by a German—Johann Sebastian Bach. Without question, the frequency with which Bach composed French dance suites and drew on the characteristic rhythms of its specific types, even in his sacred music, testifies to the international prestige of the genre. But Bach's posthumous status as the cornerstone of the German musical canon has encouraged many to receive his homages to French dance as paradigms of the genre itself. Consequently, we have learned to hear the dances actually produced at Versailles through the filter of Bach's music; we value them as important influences, yet often dismiss them as immature or deficient in comparison to the standard later set by Bach.

We could entertain several reasons for Bach's high esteem relative to his forebears in French dance. To mention only the most obvious, *most* composers pale in direct comparison with Bach. But I would suggest that the contrasts between Bach and his French models do not reflect merely his unparalleled technical skill; rather, they emerge from the very different cultural contexts within which these musicians worked, especially their radically different notions of the relationship between music and the body.

In this essay, I want to examine the place of the body in baroque music. I have two principal reasons for doing so. First, the body has become a topic of tremendous interest in recent years in the humanities and social sciences: the pioneering studies by Michel Foucault have made the history of the body in its relationships to power a matter of unusual urgency;[1] feminist theorists such as Genevieve Lloyd, Susan Bordo, and Judith Butler have likewise focused extensively on the body in their efforts to unravel the tangled cultural associations between gender and mind/body metaphysics;[2] and philosopher Mark Johnson and linguist George Lakoff posit the body as the very basis of all knowledge, thus clearly privileging the body in their resolution of the mind/body opposition.[3] In my own work, I have claimed that music constitutes a cultural medium that involves not only the activities of the mind but also multifaceted aspects of embodied experience. By studying music's engagements with the body at various moments in history, I hope to inject music into those discussions that now flourish in other parts of the academy.[4]

Second, I am raising issues concerned with the body because of their potential for illuminating music itself, especially French baroque music, which was so strongly tied to the dance. To do so, however, means violating some of musicology's fundamental aesthetic tenets. Roman Ingarden, for instance, has written: "We may doubt whether so-called dance music, when employed only as a means of keeping the dancers in step

1. For Foucault, see especially *Discipline and Punish: The Birth of the Prison*, trans. Alan Sheridan (New York: Vintage Books, 1979); and *History of Sexuality*, vol. 1: *An Introduction*, trans. Robert Hurley (New York: Vintage Books, 1980). See also Bryan S. Turner, "Recent Developments in the Theory of the Body," in *The Body: Social Process and Cultural Theory*, ed. Mike Featherstone, Mike Hepworth, and Bryan S. Turner (London: Sage, 1991), 1–35; Randy Martin, *Performance as Political Act: The Embodied Self* (New York: Bergin & Garvey, 1990); and Susan Rubin Suleiman, ed., *The Female Body in Western Culture* (Cambridge, Mass.: Harvard University Press, 1986).

2. See Genevieve Lloyd, *The Man of Reason: "Male" and "Female" in Western Philosophy* (Minneapolis: University of Minnesota Press, 1984); Alison Jaggar and Susan Bordo, eds., *Gender/Body/Knowledge: Feminist Reconstructions of Being and Knowing* (New Brunswick, N.J.: Rutgers University Press, 1989); Judith Butler, *Gender Trouble: Feminism and the Subversion of Identity* (New York: Routledge, 1990); and idem, *Bodies That Matter: On the Discursive Limits of "Sex"* (New York: Routledge, 1993).

3. Mark Johnson, *The Body in the Mind: The Bodily Basis of Meaning, Imagination, and Reason* (Chicago: University of Chicago Press, 1987); and George Lakoff, *Women, Fire, and Dangerous Things: What Categories Reveal About the Mind* (Chicago: University of Chicago Press, 1987). Translation theorist Douglas Robinson similarly identifies the body as the primary site for the production of linguistic meaning; see *The Translator's Turn* (Baltimore: Johns Hopkins University Press, 1991).

4. See my *Feminine Endings: Music, Gender, and Sexuality* (Minneapolis: University of Minnesota Press, 1991); and, coauthored with Robert Walser, "Theorizing the Body in African-American Music," *Black Music Research Journal* 14 (1994): 75–84. See also Richard Leppert, *The Sight of Sound: Music, Representation, and the History of the Body* (Berkeley: University of California Press, 1993).

and arousing in them a specific passion for expression through movement, is music in the strict sense of the word."[5]

Such disavowals of the body have resulted in skewed views of musical culture, which always relates strongly to the human body in some way, even if the relationship sometimes takes the form of denial or attempted transcendence. When we turn to baroque music, especially in France, we cannot avoid the body's centrality without making nonsense of the music—as performers and scholars trained in the Italo-German tradition have demonstrated repeatedly. It is not, therefore, for the sake of following fads that questions about the body need to be brought to music, for the body has always been there. Rather, the current interrogation of the body in the academy finally bestows legitimacy on a topic that ought never to have been banished: the constant interaction between music and bodies.

Let me clarify a few issues before proceeding. By "the body" I do not refer to some strictly biological, transhistorical entity. This is not, in other words, an essentialist project. Quite the contrary: if humans are born with bodies having certain organs, characteristics, and potentials, they are from birth exposed to cultural forces that shape the uses and experiences of those bodies. Thus, matters that seem "natural"—such as kinetic repertories, gendered behaviors, structures of erotic feelings, and what baroque theorists called "the passions"—are in fact heavily mediated by socially based codes, customs, rituals, and discourses. In the title of this essay I use Foucault's expression "technologies of the body" to identify music as one of the means by which people learn about their bodies—how to move, how to feel, how (finally) to *be*.

In pluralistic societies, the power of music to thus affect what is perceived as "natural" often provokes heated debates. This should be self-evident to us in the twentieth century, when so much ink has been spilled decrying the influences of African-American music—the ability of its rhythms to mold those attracted to it, first by introducing an articulate vocabulary to parts of the physique that many white Americans would like to pretend do not exist, and then by suggesting alternative modes of behavior or ways of being. Testifying for the defense, the grand master of funk George Clinton gleefully flaunts his motto: "Free your ass and your mind will follow."

This is, of course, precisely what the other side dreads, and denunci-

5. Roman Ingarden, *The Work of Music and the Problem of Its Identity*, trans. Adam Czerniawski (London: Macmillan, 1986), 46.

ations of music's capacity for corrupting listeners by means of improper appeals to the body recur throughout Western history, from Plato's arguments for policing music in the *Republic* to Augustine's and Calvin's fears that the wrong kinds of music incite sensuality.[6] Such battles resurfaced with particular vehemence in France during the seventeenth and eighteenth centuries. For instance, in his account of the hysteria over music generated during the *guerre des bouffons*, d'Alembert presented the following satirical version of the argument he opposed: "All liberties are interrelated and are equally dangerous. Freedom in music entails freedom to feel, freedom to feel means freedom to act, and freedom to act means the ruin of states. So let us keep French opera as it is if we wish to preserve the kingdom and let us put a brake on singing if we do not want to have liberty in speaking to follow soon afterwards."[7]

D'Alembert here parodies a kind of slippery-slope logic, whereby we slide rapidly from music to feeling to action to collapse of the state, exactly as in Plato, whom this passage deliberately echoes in its apparent horror of liberty. The assumed culprit here is neither the luxury-loving Lydians so despised by Plato nor the purveyors of rhythm and blues condemned by evangelists in the 1950s, but rather the usual demonized Other of the French establishment, namely, Italian music. For d'Alembert writes in the midst of yet one more in a long series of attempts to purge from France the pernicious example of Italian musical license.[8]

We tend to scoff at such debates today, secure in the belief that music is only music. But I would argue that French authorities were absolutely right in trying to suppress Italian music, given their ideological priorities. Indeed, nothing less was at stake than two radically incompatible epistemologies, each grounded in a different concept of the body. If George Clinton celebrates the liberation of mind by way of the ass, Louis XIV most assuredly did not.

Musicologists have long been aware of some of the relationships between the body and the music at Versailles. The scholarly contributions on court

6. See my "Music, the Pythagoreans, and the Body," in *Choreographing History*, ed. Susan Foster (Bloomington: Indiana University Press, 1995), 82–104; and "'Same as It Ever Was': Youth Culture and Music," in *Microphone Fiends Youth Music and Youth Culture*, ed. Andrew Ross and Tricia Rose (New York: Routledge, 1994), 29–40.

7. J. le Rond d'Alembert, *La Liberté de la musique* (1759), in *Oeuvres de d'Alembert*, vol. 1 (Geneva: Slatkine, 1967), 520; my translation.

8. For French documents lauding and condemning Italian music, see the excerpts from François Raguenet's *Parallèle des Italiens et les Français* (1702) and Le Cerf de La Viéville's *Comparaison de la musique italienne et de la musique française* (1705), both in *Source Readings in Music History*, ed. Oliver Strunk (New York: W. W. Norton, 1950), 473–507.

dances by Meredith Little and Wendy Hilton, for instance, emphasize the necessity of knowing something of the steps and choreographic moves assumed by contemporaries when we play, say, a courante at the keyboard.[9] Nor do their guidelines apply only to pieces identified explicitly as dances, for dance so pervaded French culture that it informed most other musical genres as well. In accordance with Louis's priorities, French musicians maintained dance at the center of their activities; even vocal pieces often moved according to the rhythmic impulses of dance-types.

Why should dance have been the central idiom in France at this time? One reason, of course, is that Louis XIV was himself an accomplished dancer who took personal delight in performing in ballets and at balls. Explanations that rely too heavily on pleasure, however, can invite trivializing assessments—such as this one by Paul Henry Lang (notice the language dripping with feminizing tropes): "The music all these [French baroque] composers cultivated was in the sign of the dance, so congenial to the French, with its neat little forms, pregnant rhythms, great surface attraction, and in tone and structure so much in harmony with the spirit of the age. This music, though slight and short-breathed, was elegant and so different from any other that the whole of Europe became enamored of it."[10]

But pleasure was only part of the reason for the French court's interest in dance. As José Maravall and Lorenzo Bianconi have argued, much baroque art was designed to function as propaganda to further the agendas of the state or church in consolidating power. Robert Isherwood's *Music in the Service of the King* traces the extensive networks of political control that governed artistic production specifically at Versailles, and he shows how Louis XIV employed dance and its music to regulate—indeed, to *synchronize*—the bodies and behaviors of his courtiers.[11] Yet this po-

9. See Meredith Little, "Recent Research in European Dance, 1400–1800," *Early Music* 14 (1986): 4–14; and Wendy Hilton, *Dance of Court and Theater: The French Noble Style, 1690–1725* (Princeton: Princeton University Press, 1981); also Patricia Ranum, "Audible Rhetoric and Mute Rhetoric: The Seventeenth-Century French Sarabande," *Early Music* 14, no. 1 (1986): 22–39; and Betty Bang Mather, assisted by Dean M. Karns, *Dance Rhythms of the French Baroque: A Handbook for Performance* (Bloomington: Indiana University Press, 1987).

10. Paul Henry Lang, introduction to *Jean-Baptiste Lully and the Music of the French Baroque: Essays in Honor of James R. Anthony*, ed. John Hajdu Heyer (Cambridge: Cambridge University Press, 1989), 1.

11. See José Antonio Maravall, *Culture of the Baroque: Analysis of a Historical Structure*, trans. Terry Cochran (Minneapolis: University of Minnesota Press, 1986); Lorenzo Bianconi, *Music in the Seventeenth Century*, trans. David Bryant (Cambridge: Cambridge University Press, 1987); and Robert Isherwood, *Music in the Service of the King: France in the Seventeenth Century* (Ithaca: Cornell University Press, 1973). See also Rudolf zur Lippe, *Geometrisierung des Menschen and Repräsentation des Privaten im französichsen Absolutismus* (Frankfurt am Main: Syndikat Reprise, 1979).

litical control rarely revealed itself as raw power; rather, it was cloaked in appeals to *bon goût* or platonic order. Thus the formal balls at which courtiers danced served as moments where the ideals of court society were realized in a literal sense, with participants enacting—as though spontaneously and with supreme grace—a world in which everyone operated of one accord, following a schema seemingly as inevitable as the *harmonia* of the Pythagorean spheres.

Note that within this ideological system the body—far from representing a subversive element—was aligned with mathematics, for Renaissance Neoplatonists held that the properly disciplined body served as a conduit between celestial order and the soul.[12] Drawing on such beliefs, codes of official behavior at Versailles arranged for the body to perform and make visible hegemonic structures of mind and political authority, just as the geometrical grid of trees at Versailles seemed to reveal the platonic law of nature itself. A long tradition of Western transcendentalism contends that the spirit is cruelly confined within the corruptible body. In *Discipline and Punish*, however, Foucault argues that beginning in this period it was the body that was imprisoned by the soul.[13] He views the court of Louis XIV as a transition between a time when punishment was meted out ritually upon the body to one in which authorities employed surveillance and disciplines to colonize interiority, so as to control behavior from the inside.

Nor did the king exempt himself from this regimen of ideological control. His body was glorified as the state-made-flesh, and Louis himself appropriated sacramental imagery and ritual to elevate his corporeal being into the realm of divine mystery.[14] Every aspect of his physical appearance was sculpted and choreographed to maximize the desired effect. And in his ideal society courtiers followed suit—in dance, in deportment, in behavior, and (at least theoretically) in thought.

12. See Gary Tomlinson, *Music in Renaissance Magic: Toward a Historiography of Others* (Chicago: University of Chicago Press), esp. chap. 3. Although bodily affects were viewed as potentially discordant, music of the proper sort could have the effect of aligning the soul with the cosmos, thus bringing together (as the Greeks had not) the categories of *musica mundana* and *musica humana*.

13. Foucault, *Discipline and Punish*, 30: "The soul is the effect and instrument of a political anatomy; the soul is the prison of the body." For an exploration of the more traditional view, see Michael A. Williams, "Divine Image—Prison of Flesh: Perceptions of the Body in Ancient Gnosticism," in *Fragments for a History of the Human Body*, pt. 1, ed. Michel Feher (New York: Urzone, 1989), 128–47.

14. See Louis Marin, *Portrait of the King*, trans. Martha M. Houle (Minneapolis: University of Minnesota Press, 1988); and Peter Burke, *The Fabrication of Louis XIV* (New Haven: Yale University Press, 1992).

If French authorities assumed that the minds of noblemen would adopt the patterns given to them in cultural practices such as dance, this was not necessarily the way things actually worked. Recent historians have questioned the extent to which such ideological structures were in fact internalized by courtiers. Norbert Elias argues that courtiers accommodated themselves to codified rituals not because they were duped, but because the conspicuous consumption demanded by peer pressure made them economically dependent on the king and thus vulnerable to his whims. Moreover, as they watched their power as feudal heirs drain away, they increasingly defined their nobility in opposition to other classes: their affiliations with other aristocrats thus became largely a matter of performance as they participated collectively in a choreography of the ethos that distinguished "good society."[15] Jonathan Dewald, however, reveals that courtiers often bridled under the "gentle" coercion to which they were subjected: in diaries and other personal narratives, the gap between the ideal and the real seethes with resentments, family conflicts, and illicit desires and behaviors.[16] Recall too that many French writers took up the cause of Italian music, in open resistance to official policy.

In other words, the consensus celebrated in official courtly art was but a thin veneer. Not even the most carefully controlled piece of propaganda can rely on surefire results, free from gaps, moments of slippage, and promiscuous chains of signifiers. As Mark Franko, for instance, demonstrates in his book on dance and the ideology of the French baroque body, even the most geometrical dances still had to include motion (the movement of bodies from one pattern to the next), a necessary element that always threatened to undo the mapping of bodies onto mathematics. And in moments of greater license—especially in the period before Louis XIV came to power—court dances gravitated away from the Pythagorean allegories of the sixteenth-century *ballet de cour* and into burlesque performances that foregrounded narrative action, verbal play, and the Bakhtinian grotesque body (Louis himself occasionally performed in drag during his youth).[17] It was in that same relatively open period that Mazarin in-

15. Norbert Elias, *The Court Society*, trans. Edmund Jephcott (New York: Pantheon Books, 1983).

16. Jonathan Dewald, *Aristocratic Experience and the Origins of Modern Culture: France, 1570–1715* (Berkeley: University of California Press, 1993).

17. Mark Franko, *Dance as Text: Ideologies of the Baroque Body* (Cambridge: Cambridge University Press, 1993); see also Franko's essay in this collection. See further Peter Maxwell Cryle, *Geometry in the Boudoir: Configurations of French Erotic Narrative* (Ithaca: Cornell University Press, 1994).

troduced Venetian opera into France and that Louis Couperin developed the unmeasured prelude.[18]

When Louis XIV ascended the throne, he didn't so much put away childish things as he harnessed them to do his bidding. Geometrical dance returned with a vengeance, and courtiers were pressed to submit to its discipline as they performed the ritual of dancing two-by-two before the king. Now, this was no small requirement, for a typical ballroom choreography lasted two to three minutes, with few repeated patterns, and courtiers had to have about twelve of these elaborate arrangements on call at any given time.[19] Saint-Simon recounts how a young noble newly arrived at court destroyed his career when he tried to dance without knowing the proper moves: as he turned continually in wrong directions and pranced out of the designated orbit, he betrayed his status as an outsider and provoked gales of malicious laughter from the assembly. He was driven from court in disgrace, his social and economic future reduced to rubble, so privileged a place did dance occupy within the intricate web of social knowledge that defined court society.[20]

Thus whether or not the official imagery succeeded in disciplining not only the body but also the mind, it is crucial for those concerned with the history of such images to observe how they were engineered to accomplish those purposes. And here we must turn to Jean-Baptiste Lully, an Italian dancer who became Louis's music czar and who worked self-consciously to develop a musical practice that would reinforce the reigning ideology.[21] In pragmatic terms this involved negotiating among various demands, imposed by the drama at hand, the prevailing, carefully measured style of speech declamation, and the bodily patterns of dance.

Let us take as an example a brief air from the prologue to Lully's opera

18. On the introduction of Venetian opera into France, see Neal Zaslaw, "The First Opera in Paris: A Study in the Politics of Art," in Heyer (ed.), *Jean-Baptiste Lully*, 7–23.

19. Hilton, *Dance of Court and Theater*, 11–12.

20. M. le duc de Saint-Simon, *Memoirs of Louis XIV and the Regency*, trans. Bayle St. John (London: George Allen & Unwin, 1926), 19–20; quoted in Hilton, *Dance of Court and Theater*, 15.

21. Lully (1632–87) began his career as a fourteen-year-old dancer in an Italian opera troupe that was visiting Paris. When the troupe returned home, Lulli/Lully remained, insinuated himself into Louis's favor through his abilities in dance, and eventually was granted a monopoly over most musical production at court. It is therefore not surprising that he bent official style so as to spotlight his own talents. Paul Henry Lang writes: "In this ascent to a commanding position he deftly used everyone from the king down. The *lettres patentes* and the *privilèges* he secured from the king were so outrageous that they could not have stood the slightest legal scrutiny, but they could not be scrutinized because they came directly from the king. This adroit manipulator did succeed in becoming the virtual dictator of French musical life" (introduction to Heyer [ed.], *Jean-Baptiste Lully*, 2).

Alceste (1674).[22] As with most of the productions designed for Louis's court, this prologue presents an allegory in praise of the Sun King, commemorating an earlier triumph over Franche-Comté. A figure identified as a "Nymph of the Seine" bemoans the absence of her "hero" and languishes while awaiting his return. Eventually, a fanfare announces the hero's victory, and Louis himself is fêted—honored both as the principal spectator of the drama about to unfold and as the principal spectacle around whose glory all else revolves.

The Nymph's air adopts the rhythmic impulses of the sarabande, which, though rumored to have descended from a New World ritual of unbridled sensuality, had long since been tamed into the most stately of the court dances. Its primary characteristic is a slow triple meter in which the second beat receives unexpected emphasis, associated in dance with a lift onto the toes that is sustained for the remainder of the measure (not an easy feat, given the tendency of ankles to wobble). The resulting contrast between motion and suspended animation marks the sarabande and informs the Nymph's sung discourse. A set of conventions designed for regulating the body pervades the air, from its note-to-note sequences to its periodic phrases that correspond to groups of dance steps. And although Lully sprinkles his tune with graces (indicated by the marks above the staff), these *agrémens* serve as much to reinforce the dance gestures and to brake any inadvertent momentum as to adorn the melody.[23]

The Nymph's air follows the formal plan of a rondeau, in which a refrain returns between slightly contrasting sections (ABACA; ex. 4.1). In this particular rondeau, the refrain itself operates recursively as an ABA structure. The first line, "Le Héros que j'attens ne reviendra-t'il pas?," divides symmetrically, each half contained within two measures, thus setting the pace, the norm against which the rest of the air unfolds. With the next phrase, "Serai-je toujours languissante / Dans une si cruelle attente," the Nymph begins to resist the established rhythm; as she works toward continuous motion she threatens (as much as was allowed within this style) to overflow the bounds of the expected phrasing. But reason saves the

22. Jean-Baptiste Lully, *Alceste;* recording, La Grande Ecurie et le Chambre du Roy, Jean-Claude Malgoire, conductor (Columbia M3 34580); score: *Oeuvres Complètes de J.-P. Lully, Opèras*, vol. 2, ed. Henry Prunières (Paris: Editions de la Revue Musicale, 1932), 13.

23. Note that such music was also analyzed in terms of poetic meters. See, for instance, Bénigne de Bacilly, *A Commentary upon the Art of Proper Singing* (Paris, 1668), trans. Austin Caswell (New York: Institute of Mediaeval Music, 1968). Although airs such as this one were thus multiply constrained, I am concerned here with intersections with the body.

Example 4.1 Lully, *Alceste*, Prologue: The Nymph of the Seine, mm. 1–15

day: her increased animation leads back safely to the opening line, which recontains and seals the refrain with a gesture of closure.

Lully's strategy recalls one of the instances of *bon goût* recorded admiringly by Madame de Sévigné. A young woman of the court had been jilted by the chevalier de Lorraine. When she encountered him one day, she launched into a tirade against him. He—ever mindful of her best interests—deflected attention to the pet she had with her: "That's a pretty little dog you've got there. Where did you get it?" As Madame de Sévigné explains it, the chevalier thereby preserved the lady's dignity, restraining her from a display of passion that would have proved distasteful to the community.[24] This extraordinary disciplining of body and feelings was to be accomplished through the internalization of rules of rational order. As Elias explains,

24. As recounted in Wilfrid Mellors, *François Couperin and the French Classical Tradition* (New York: Dover, 1968), 32.

Why this attitude becomes important to court people is easily seen: affective outbursts are difficult to control and calculate. They reveal the true feelings of the person concerned to a degree that, because not calculated, can be damaging: they hand over trump cards to rivals for favour and prestige. Above all, they are a sign of weakness; and that is the position the court person fears most of all. *In this way the competition of court life enforces a curbing of the affects in favour of calculated and finely shaded behaviour in dealing with people.*[25]

To be sure, the Nymph's air contains conventional signs of sorrow: the minor key, the halting motion, the drooping melodic lines, the yearning appoggiaturas (ornaments that delay expected arrivals but that also enhance by "leaning" into them), and the depressed altered pitch on *cruelle* and in the harmony of m. 3. But these are subordinated to the patterns of dance—which, it turns out, is typical also of French performance treatises: whether the issue is violin bowing, text declamation, or ornament placement, the metrical impulses constitute the deciding factors.[26] Expressivity per se is rarely addressed; formal precision presides.

Modern scholars and performers have tended to ignore seventeenth-century French musical compositions, for these pieces work only if a bodily sense of weight shifts or lifts onto the toes can be perceived in the music; and such gestures depend on minute details of timing—details that cannot truly be captured with the blunt instrument of notation. But our problem is not only the difficulty of reconstituting nuances in the absence of any heard experience of the music. Far more daunting is a conceptual barrier, grounded in the mind/body metaphysics that has dominated thought about music since the nineteenth century: most modern performers actively resist having to factor in the body when studying "purely musical" phenomena. If French music relies on the body, then it would seem to be trivial *as music;* if it works *as music*, then the body ought to be irrelevant—or so the argument goes.

To return to Lully: if standard criteria of expression or formal innovation were brought to the Nymph's air, the piece would count as little more than competent. As we have seen, the affective devices Lully employs are quite minimal: emotional content clearly is not his main concern, nor would we expect it to be, given French taste. Moreover, the air follows restrained harmonic and structural conventions. What it *does* offer,

25. Elias, *Court Society*, 111; emphasis in the original.

26. Kenneth Cooper and Julius Zsako, eds. and trans., "George Muffat's Observations on the Lully Style of Performance," *Musical Quarterly* 53 (1967): 220–45; Bacilly, *Commentary on the Art of Proper Singing;* François Couperin, *L'Art de toucher le clavecin* (Paris, 1716), trans. Mevanwy Roberts (Leipzig: Breitkopf & Härtel, 1933); and Betty Bang Mather, *Interpretation of French Music from 1675–1775* (New York: McGinnis & Marx, 1973).

however, is a subtle series of nuances made up of varying degrees of motion, hesitation, and stability. If we are sensitive to the kinetic impulses of the sarabande, the constant motion that emerges with the words "Dans une si cruelle attente" is exquisitely tense—a detail that strains slightly against the greater regularity of the surrounding context, making the return to the refrain and its lifts all the more gratifying.

The listener's body can experience vicariously those tentative hoverings, the unanticipated sequence of continuous steps, the reestablishment of equilibrium, but only if the performers articulate with the physical precision of French dance the delicate nuances indicated by Lully's ornaments and placement of harmonies. Performed well, the air appears to enact the aural equivalent of a geometric pattern or a theorem in the physics of motion; human expression seems almost trivial in comparison with this embodiment of Pythagorean order.

Like any repertory that influences the body, French baroque music went far beyond facilitating social dance. Through dance and its music, the Sun King could watch the social world move to the tunes he called: dance music at the French court thus filled functions similar to those Plato designated for Dorian music in his republic (indeed, Louis not only praised dance for its ability to enhance military discipline, but he also instituted the custom of having troops parade by him in choreographed review).[27] And this ideological relationship among dance, music, the body, and the state apparently had to be carefully insulated from alternatives—thus the polemical wars that sought to ward off the influence of foreign musics.

The music French critics regarded as the foremost threat to social order was the Italian music that swept through and conquered the rest of Europe precisely because it offered "freedom to feel." At first glance, Italian genres seem far less grounded in the body: dances appear on occasion, but they do not constitute the core of the repertories as they do in France.

27. The patent for dance, for instance, states: "The art of dance has always been recognized as one of the most respectable and necessary to train the body and to give it the first and most natural dispositions to every kind of exercise, to that of arms among others; consequently, it is one of the most advantageous and useful to our nobility and to others who have the honour of approaching us, not just in war times, but even in times of peace in the divertissements of our ballets" (Peter Wollen, "Government by Appearances: The Arts, the Media and the Body Politic," paper delivered at the conference series "Constructing the Body," Los Angeles, 1992–93). A picture of Louis reviewing his troops appears in Foucault's *Discipline and Punish;* see fig. 1, following p. 169, and discussion pp. 188–89. See also Georges Vigarello, "The Upward Training of the Body from the Age of Chivalry to Courtly Civility," in *Fragments for a History of the Body*, pt. 2, ed. Michel Feher (New York: Zone, 1989), 148–99.

Rather than manipulating the body in motion, the Italians sought primarily to invent a musical vocabulary for simulating—and stimulating—the passions.

Yet if they seemed to focus on producing analogues for the interior self, their images were grounded in somatic or bodily experience. Thus sorrow was represented by musical analogues to the body as it suffers grief, with slow, drooping motions; anger was recognized by its angular, aggressive gestures; anguish by its painful dissonances; happiness by rising, ebullient qualities; and so forth.[28] Once this inner landscape (what Stephen Greenblatt calls "inwardness") emerged,[29] culture sought to furnish and arrange it. What Julia Kristeva theorizes in music as the "semiotic" is not the privileged locus of the preoedipal imaginary, but rather the target of choice for cultural work.[30] That we often take these images as reflecting our own souls indicates why they should matter to historians.

By making a distinction between the body's inside and outside, I do not mean to ascribe any transhistorical reality to those categories: quite the opposite. If French music seems to favor moving the physical body at the expense of inwardness and Italian appears to prefer mapping interiority, both discourses remain constructs; each divides up and shapes human bodily experience in its own way. Yet their status as constructs did not prevent them from exercising tremendous influence in the social world. Indeed, French authorities exerted considerable effort to protect their subjects from Italianate musical images. Was this simply the result of monopoly logic or resistance to what Neal Zaslaw argues was Mazarin's attempt to colonize France with Italian culture?[31] Or was there something to fear in the music itself?

It is within the context of the sixteenth-century madrigal that composers

28. See, for instance, Zarlino, *Istitutioni harmoniche*, bk. 4, chap. 32; paraphrased in English by Thomas Morley, *A Plaine and Easie Introduction to Practicall Musicke*, ed. Alec Harmon (New York: W. W. Norton, 1973), 290–91. Subsequent theorists were influenced by Descartes's *The Passions of the Soul*. For an eighteenth-century account of musical affect, see Johann Mattheson, *Der vollkommene Capellmeister* (Hamburg, 1739), trans. Ernest Harriss (Ann Arbor: UMI, 1981). For a philosophical discussion of these issues, see Peter Kivy, *The Corded Shell: Reflections on Musical Expression* (Princeton: Princeton University Press, 1980).

29. Stephen Greenblatt, *Renaissance Self-Fashioning: From More to Shakespeare* (Chicago: University of Chicago Press, 1980), esp. chap. 3.

30. Julia Kristeva, *Desire in Language: A Semiotic Approach to Literature and Art*, ed. Leon S. Rondiez, trans. Thomas Gora, Alice Jardine, and Leon S. Rondiez (New York: Columbia University Press, 1980), 133–47.

31. See Zaslaw, "First Opera in Paris," for an excellent account of what he calls Mazarin's attempted "politico-cultural colonization" of France by Italian art (7). He also explains that the politics were not only aesthetic, but often quite literal: because foreign musicians had opportunities as performers to infiltrate even private chambers, they often operated as spies (8).

first began to develop a musical vocabulary for denoting human feelings. Along with its other constructs, the madrigal produced the earliest explicit musical representations in the West of desire and pleasure, all spelled out in lavish detail. From Arcadelt's simulation of orgasm in "Il bianco e dolce cigno" to the erotic settings of the Song of Songs Schütz wrote during his Venetian sabbatical, Italian music thrived on excess, on transgressing rules of order.[32] If the French *vers mésuré* sought to align poetry with platonic number, madrigalists notoriously ran roughshod over texts that were themselves prone to enjambment, overflowing bounds at every occasion. As the French admirer of Italian music François Raguenet describes it:

> Everything is so brisk, sharp and piercing, so impetuous and affecting, that the imagination, senses, the soul, and the body itself are all betrayed in a common transport; 'tis impossible not to be borne down with the rapidity of these movements. A symphony of furies shakes the soul; it undermines and overthrows it in spite of all its care; the artist himself, whilst he is performing it, is seized with an unavoidable agony; he tortures his violin; he racks his body; he is no longer master of himself, but is agitated like one possessed with an irresistible motion.[33]

To give a relatively obvious example of the kinds of images and qualities of motion I mean (and the kinds that Louis's court demonized), Monteverdi's seventh book of madrigals, inspired by the baroque excesses of Marino's poetry, includes several pieces that explore what Stephen Greenblatt has called "friction to heat." At the time, it was thought that conception could not occur unless the female partner in the sex act were brought to fulfillment—a process of arousal that, according to Greenblatt, Shakespeare's quick, witty exchanges between lovers attempted to simulate.[34] (In our more enlightened time, "friction to heat" is more likely to be called foreplay, and it has been reduced from a status of necessity to one of mere courtesy or even altruism.)

Monteverdi's "O come sei gentile" is a duo, which allows the communicative immediacy of monody and also the complex images exploited by the polyphonic madrigal.[35] Guarini's text compares the state

32. For a discussion of the Arcadelt, see my "Music, the Pythagoreans, and the Body"; Schütz's "Anima mea liquefacta es" will be discussed in my *Power and Desire in Seventeenth-Century Music* (in progress).

33. Raguenet, *Parallèle des Italiens et les Français*, in Strunk (ed.), *Source Readings*, 478–79.

34. Stephen Greenblatt, *Shakespearean Negotiations* (Berkeley: University of California Press, 1988), 66–93.

35. Listen, for instance, to the recording by the Concerto Vocale on the CD titled *Monteverdi, Lamento d'Arianna*, Helga Müller-Molinari and René Jacobs, voices; William Christie, harpsichord (Harmonia Mundi 901129); score: *Settimo Libro de Madrigali* (1619), ed. G. Francesco Malipiero (Vienna: Universal Edition, n.d.), 35–40.

Example 4.2 Monteverdi, "O come sei gentile," mm. 1–9

of a lover with that of a caged bird: both lover and songbird are imprisoned by their mistress and both sing for her; but the bird lives singing, while the lover singing "dies." The duo begins in a state of erotic languor as the first voice traces an extended moan of arousal, only to be choked off in a sudden frisson and release (ex. 4.2). This is an extravagant mapping of the feelings of the body, not as it operates within the social domain of dance, but as it is experienced most intimately. It gives public voice to private erotic feelings, or as Bakhtin says of cultural discourses: "Everything internal gravitates not toward itself but is turned to the outside and dialogized, every internal experience ends up on the outside."[36]

To accomplish this within a milieu that stressed listener response, Monteverdi had to invent analogues that resonated sufficiently with shared experiences to be comprehensible. Of course, the mediated body he constructs here is far from universal: we have only to recall the disgusted responses of the French or to ask undergraduates to accept Monteverdi's languishing images as depictions of masculine subjectivity.[37] Yet such analogues allowed certain representations of sexuality to circulate widely as public currency, and they not only reflected but also helped to shape contemporary experiences of the erotic. In other words, Monteverdi's Marinist imagery also constitutes a technology of the body, albeit one that catered to the hedonistic individualism of Italian patrons, the subjectivist agendas of the Counter-Reformation, and the market economies cultivated for printed madrigals and Venetian commercial opera.[38]

By the end of the duo, the images have shifted considerably, the result of much friction between the two voices (both of which together, however, represent a single speaking subject—at least on one level). With the last line, "vivi cantando ed io cantando moro," the floodgates break and the voices careen forward unrestrained (ex. 4.3). Each seeks a point of closure, yet every would-be point of arrival is but the preparation for cadence by the other voice. The harmonies tumble vertiginously by fifths, occasionally moving obliquely so as to permit yet another downward spiral. The momentum is such that the cadence, when it arrives, cannot absorb the accumulated energies, and the process repeats even more extravagantly. That this too is an image based metaphorically on bodily experiences seems clear enough, though it is an imaginary body within the "virtual reality" of which we can soar, have orgasms that last for five minutes, and overwhelm all boundaries. If, as many of the French apparently did, we associate boundaries with rules of social propriety, it is easy to understand how such unabashed transgression of limits could

36. Mikhail Bakhtin, *Problems of Dostoevsky's Poetics*, ed. and trans. Caryl Emerson (Minneapolis: University of Minnesota Press, 1984), 287.

37. See also musicologist Gary Tomlinson's squeamishness about these pieces, which he sees as evidence of the collapse of Renaissance rhetorical prowess, in *Monteverdi and the End of the Renaissance* (Berkeley: University of California, 1987).

38. See Lauro Martines, *Power and Imagination: City-States in Renaissance Italy* (Baltimore: Johns Hopkins University Press, 1988); Maravall, *Culture of the Baroque;* Stanley Boorman, "What Bibliography Can Do: Music Printing and the Early Madrigal," *Music and Letters* 72, no. 2 (May 1991): 236–58; and Ellen Rosand, *The Rise of a Genre: Seventeenth-Century Opera in Venice* (Berkeley: University of California Press, 1991).

sound like the overthrow of the state, as d'Alembert's antagonists suggested much later.

I want to turn now to one of the musicians who responded to Italianate models in the years after Lully's death, namely, Marin Marais—a composer whose work unexpectedly reached a mass audience in 1992 with the release of the biographical film *Tous les matins du monde*.[39] Most of us shaped by the Italian style (later adopted by the Germans) find even the music from this period of détente alien, and we often characterize it largely in terms of what it *lacks*—namely, the teleological impulses of Italian tonality. To our ears, it may sound stagnant and rudderless, its motions minimal and arbitrary.[40] Yet Marais and his contemporaries can be heard as enacting a delicate cultural fusion. While the greater artistic leniency of Louis's later court permitted fusions of French and Italian procedures, Versailles still was committed to social discipline. Thus the problem facing Marais was how to negotiate between a French aristocratic sense of bodily propriety and the affective power of the Italian style.

Marais's "Tombeau pour M. de Ste-Colombe" is a piece in which the court composer commemorates the death of his teacher.[41] It displays several Italian traits, most obvious among them the descending chromatic tetrachord (theorized by Ellen Rosand as the emblem of the lament as it developed in mid-seventeenth-century Venice)[42] and an unusual number of harsh and sustained dissonances on strong beats. Occasionally, as in m. 11, a melodic *passaggio* will hurl the action forward. Moreover, a Corellian modulatory schema holds the composition together, directing its progress away from and back to the tonic. In other words, many of the elements that had been associated with the emotional exhibitionism of Italian music appear here, along with the devices that produce teleological propulsion.

39. *Tous les matins du monde*, directed by Alain Corneau; soundtrack under the musical direction of viol virtuoso Jordi Savall (Valois V4640, 1991).

40. Even the dean of American French baroque studies often expresses such sentiments. In his *French Baroque Music from Beaujoyeulx to Rameau* (New York: W. W. Norton, 1978), James Anthony damns a whole genre with the faintest of praise as follows: "In summary, French lute music of the seventeenth century is mannered, precious, even decadent; its melodies are surcharged with ornaments, its rhythms fussy, its harmony often aimless, and its texture without unity. Yet at the same time, it is never pretentious, it never demands more from the instrument than the instrument can give. In its own fragile way, it is honest to itself" (243).

41. Marais, *Second Livre de pièces de viole* (Paris, 1701), ed. John Hsu (New York: Broude, 1986), 170–72; on soundtrack for *Tous les matins du monde*.

42. Ellen Rosand, "The Descending Tetrachord: An Emblem of Lament," *Musical Quarterly* 55 (1979): 346–59.

Example 4.3 Monteverdi, "O come sei gentile," m. 78–end

Example 4.3 *(continued)*

Yet it does not sound the same as Italian music, and cannot be made to sound the same. In my years coaching baroque music, I have repeatedly encountered incomprehension and frustration in performers trying to deal with the French repertory, which they often dismiss as incoherent. Marais, however, knew exactly what he was doing in producing this fusion, even though we need to recall his French priorities in order to make sense of his strategies. Most important, the piece is still inscribed on the dancing body: the tombeau is a special category of either the pavane or allemande. Thus, while it is an elegiac genre (in this case, explicitly invoking lament), it is still grounded in the regularized alternations of bodily motion typical of dance.

To be sure, it is heavily stylized as well; yet Marais ensures the latent physicality of his tombeau in a variety of ways. First, he distributes *agrémens* liberally and precisely throughout the piece. These ornaments serve a radically different function from those that flourished in contemporaneous Italian music. Unlike the improvised *passaggi* of Italian performers, French *agrémens* became standardized and virtually obligatory during the reign of Louis XIV: if ornaments represented the moments of greatest personal freedom and potential excess in the Italian style, they were the moments most heavily policed in France. The ornament tables that proliferated in France bear witness to this site of discipline. By contrast, Italians learned to add their extravagant melodic passages by listening, in apprenticeships, or by studying manuals on improvisation. In Italy, ornaments changed ideally with each performance; in France, they were determined by the composer and were to be executed accordingly.[43] If French music exhibited extraordinary grace, this grace was to signify the joy of submitting to authority: ornaments made these moments seem like the voluntary surrender to *bon goût*.

But it was not simply the autocratic desire to control that led French composers to dictate ornamental practice in their music. The sense of bodily motion central to the style relies on carefully choreographed patterns of weight shifts, and this, too, is accomplished in no small part by the *agrémens*, which secure any accumulated tensions to strong beats and release them. Jacques Attali advises us to pay attention to the ways musical styles define and negotiate between order and noise,[44] and in French baroque music the noise is localized, intensified, and dispelled through these frequent clusters of dissonance. Alternations of tension and release occur on a very low level, in keeping with the demands of dance. Recall that Mark Franko points to motion as the destabilizing force in geometrical French dance; motion also is the element most carefully patrolled in French music.[45] Italian music of the time works in almost the opposite fashion, as structural dissonances coalesce into prolonged upbeats that eventually find resolution in distant goals. To affix trills and mordents onto most Italian music is to cripple it, to hamper its flight. Trills occur (as one might expect) in preparation for cadence, where they serve to focus the energy and halt the momentum.

43. See, for instance, the admonishments that the performer obey the composer's indications exactly in the preface of François Couperin's third volume of *Pièces de clavecin*: "Je suis toujours surpris (apres les soins que je me suis donné pour marquer les agrémens qui conviennent à mes Piéces, dont j'ay donné, à part, une explication assés intelligible dans une Méthode particuliere, connüe sous le titre de L'art de toucher le Clavecin) d'entendre des personnes qui les ont aprises sans s'y assujétir. C'est une négligence qui n'est pas pardonnable, d'autant qu'il n'est point arbitraire d'y mettre tels agrémens qu'on veut. Je déclare donc que mes piéces doivent être exécutées comme je les ay marqueés: et qu'elles ne feront jamais une certain impression sur les personnes qui ont le goût vray, tant qu'on n'observera pas à la lettre, tout ce que j'y ay marqué, sans augmentation ni diminution" (François Couperin, *Pièces de clavecin*, ed. József Gát [London: Boosey & Hawkes, 1970], 5).

44. Jacques Attali, *Noise: The Political Economy of Music*, trans. Brian Massumi (Minneapolis: University of Minnesota Press, 1985).

45. Franko, *Dance as Text*, 26: "The ideological impulse behind geometrical dance could only achieve a partial colonization of space by the verbal/figural text. The human action needed to produce the figure could not itself submit to figurality. Thus, the monarch's control of geometrical dance was, of necessity, partial and incomplete."

Significantly, Marais's motion is always under the cautious control of a hand brake. Yet played by Jordi Savall, this tombeau proves profoundly moving, for Savall's subtle shadings, minute inflections, and physical gravity bestow on the music that exquisite blend of sorrow and stoic restraint so prized by French courtiers. Signs of grief abound, especially in the chromatic descent of the lament, but they are held in constant check through rhythmic tactics. The kind of motivic web that commonly grants the illusion of unity to the surface of a contemporaneous Italian piece is avoided, except for fragmentary reiterations of the lament emblem and the dotted rhythmic cell. For motives would pull the ear above the surface, encouraging it to make long-term connections of larger groupings (which would lead, as d'Alembert warns, to the collapse of the state . . .).

Marais produces an affect of bittersweet resignation in this tombeau, in part by focusing on two versions of the sixth scale degree (ex. 4.4). In m. 2, for instance, the viol pushes down to c♯, which seems to convey a ray of hope until the line moves on to c♮, then drops defeatedly to b. The bass takes over the lament figure now and dwells again on that same flickering sixth degree that offers, then withdraws, hope. Meanwhile, the viol seems to try to rise above the gloom, twice (mm. 3 and 5) pushing upward through the springboard of a dotted pattern. In m. 5, the line collapses down by a tritone; the second time it holds out its high note even past the chromatic descent in the bass, then concedes to a cadence on e, executed nonetheless with noble dignity.

A brief episode in G brings a modicum of relief—note especially the achingly prolonged f♮ in m. 9 that initiates the reorientation to the major mode. But the relief is short lived: sharp rhythmic impulses in m. 16 pull toward A minor, and a harsh cluster in m. 19 drives us back to V/e, at which point the lament recommences. Later in the tombeau, moments of too-poignant grief are balanced by brusque *coups d'archet* that prevent a descent into despondency.

In *Tous les matins du monde*, Marais hides under S[te]-Colombe's shed to steal his ornaments—not the signs written in the score, but precisely this science of how to give every note its proper attack, sustain, and weight. Savall keeps the half note perfectly steady in keeping with the dance, yet he plays freely within the half note as a means of infusing the piece with what François Couperin called *âme* (soul). Couperin complained that foreigners played French music badly because they lacked sensitivity to the rhythmic details that allowed this subtle and supple quality of motion. Only if one invests in each half note as if it were a world in itself, yet at the same time keeps the bodily gestures of the dance moving, can the

Example 4.4 Marais, *Tombeau pour M. de Ste-Colombe*, mm. 1–28

tombeau breathe. And although the piece proceeds through its Italianate series of modulations, there are no streams of thwarted desire dammed up in anticipation of long-term resolution. Marais's constant lingering and draining of tensions keeps the attention riveted on the moment.

For the most part, this method of composing was idiosyncratic to France. Although certain aspects of French propriety were imported to the Italian courts, the propulsive drive of Italian musical procedures remained fundamental. Unruly passions may have been domesticated as they were contained within da capo formats, standardized tonality, and affective codes, but the point was to display turbulence successfully channeled by reason. By contrast, the French rarely tolerated ungrounded energy for more than a few seconds at a time. Yet if French style had limited impact on Italy, it was embraced and even institutionalized in parts of Germany and Prussia, where petty courts pumped themselves up in slavish imitation of Versailles. In some courts, the nobility spoke only French, disdaining German as barbaric. Thus, some of our most detailed accounts of French performance practices come to us from German sources, from those who wanted to be able to replicate authentic French models down to the last detail.[46]

Because we no longer have any stake in what rival procedures might have signified, we often trivialize differences as "mere style." But this does not hold true in literary studies. Court poets in Germany at the time had to master French and write within its codes, which guaranteed the qualities that constituted what was known as *civilisation*. When in the mid-eighteenth century a number of poets began writing in their despised native language, they sought to challenge *civilisation* (which restricted its effects to the surface of the body and its behaviors) with what they called *Kultur*: the cultivation and expression of inner resources and feelings that revealed the superiority of the sensitive German bourgeois over the shallow artificiality of Francophile nobles. As Norbert Elias has shown, the rise of *Kultur* produced the beginnings of German nationalist literatures, with *Sturm und Drang* and Romanticism identifiable as successive waves.[47]

J. S. Bach worked within contexts in which he was relatively free to appropriate whatever musical styles came his way. We know that he admired

46. See, for instance, Cooper and Zsako, "Muffat's Observations"; and Johann Joachim Quantz, *On Playing the Flute*, trans. Edward R. Reilly (New York: Schirmer Books, 1966).

47. Norbert Elias, *The Civilizing Process*, vol. 1: *The History of Manners*, trans. Edmund Jephcott (New York: Pantheon Books, 1978), pt. 1.

Example. 4.5 Bach, Partita in D Major, Courante, mm. 1–16

Example 4.5 *(continued)*

the Italian opera performed in Dreşden and that he fell under the spell of Vivaldi's way of channeling musical energies. Beginning in the 1710s, propulsive tonality became his modus operandi, and he continually reread other genres (fugues, chorale preludes, etc.) in terms of his adopted Italianate procedures. The same is true of the dozens of ostensibly French dances he wrote over the course of his career.

In many of his dances, it is possible to overlook the way the French and Italian aspects of his music chafe. In the D Major Partita for harpsichord, however, he enacts a collision between the two that resonates strongly with Elias's subverting of *civilisation* by the forces of *Kultur* (ex. 4.5). Despite the work's Versailles trappings, each movement enacts the disruption of French *bon goût* by means of Italian energy. Thus the opening movement is a French overture, yet the dotted section loses its marchlike quality in a sequence of suspensions that begins parsing the motion out in three-beat units, and the allegro that follows is nothing less than a Vivaldian concerto. Similarly, in the allemande, a serene opening gives way to streams of Italianate figuration, devolving into the tortured pathos of interiority.

It is in the courante, though, that French platonic order most suffers at the hands of surging Italianate desire. Each of the first two measures operates within the patterns long associated with this most complex of the French dance types. A bar in a courante may be grouped into three half notes or divided down the middle into two dotted halves, and in a ballroom situation the dancer would execute different steps depending on the placement of the accents.[48] As in many courantes, Bach's begins ambiguously: the opening gesture would seem to come to rest on beat 4, suggesting division of the bar into two equal halves. Yet the melodic ornament on beat 5 tilts the motion forward, even though equilibrium is reinstated on the following downbeat. The second measure repeats the first, with the materials in the two hands exchanged.

But already in bar 3 this ambiguity begins to seek some kind of continuation other than the dependable resolution on the downbeat—a resolution that would be necessary if the body were actually to dance this composition. Thus the right hand condenses its pattern and arrives a beat earlier than usual, while the bass compensates by moving to g halfway through. The melody divides the bar into three and the harmonic rhythm into halves, and even though consolidation occurs again on the downbeat, the internal jarring within the measures becomes quite uneasy.

After the cadence prepared for measure 5 is displaced by a melodic suspension that refuses to cooperate, Bach drops the pretense that this is a refined, courtly dance. Instead, he unleashes the motives that had been harnessed to the regulated alternation of tension and release, and once unleashed, they start straining forward. A running bass enters to propel the motion toward a possible cadence in m. 9. The action stops momentarily, although the absence of the bass on the downbeat also renders this would-be arrival unbalanced. As though making a bid to reinstate orderly conduct, the melody begins a sequence in bar 9. Yet sequences, even if they spell order within an Italian context, were regarded as suspicious by the French: since it is in the nature of sequences to point forward in time through megagroupings to a delayed, hence all-the-more-desired moment, it takes attention away from the here and now, from the discipline of repeated bodily motions. Not only does Bach's sequence create that kind of long-range yearning, but its accent groupings become irregular with respect to the courante's meter.

Again, we approach cadence—this time, the dominant. But a defiant

48. See Wendy Hilton, "A Dance for Kings: The Seventeenth-Century French Courante," *Early Music* 5 (1977): 161–67.

d in the bass in m. 11 prevents the resolution, and the melody arrives on g disappointed, frustrated. Another sequence ensues, built from the opening motive replicating itself end to end. Here again, while the first two units of the sequence acknowledge the downbeat, both overshoot the goal, pulling ever upward. By m. 14, the meter is sacrificed to the exigencies of climax, and the melody cascades downward, heedless of downbeats. Suddenly Bach rearranges the accents so that an elegant hemiola touches us down at a cadence of m. 16 as though nothing could have been easier. But it requires merely taking the repeat to show how far we have traveled in a mere sixteen bars. The headlong hurtling of that concluding sequence suddenly has to revert to the etiquette of Versailles—something akin to stuffing a rampant genie back into its bottle.[49]

Although Bach obeys the letter of the conventional law by coming to repose on a dominant triad at halftime, he also problematizes that moment: the restless, narrative-impelled exuberance of *Kultur* abruptly backs off, granting us that guarantee of *civilisation*'s propriety. But it is not that Bach escapes social grounding in his courante. If he wreaks havoc on the dance, he does so by means of pitting it against another set of practices, another conception of the body.

This courante arises from the basic incompatibility of these two worlds and Bach's attempt at forging a coherent relationship: four times over the course of the dance he takes us from what he sets up as the static rigidity of the ancien régime to the impulsive desire for self-generation that stood as the ideal of the emergent German intelligentsia, showing step by step how emancipation feels. He implodes the aristocratic conventions so fetishized by the German upper classes, just as German bourgeois poets were to define themselves in opposition to French *civilisation*. In other words, Bach can be heard as participating in the important early stages of German national culture, where identity was enacted by taking the forms of court and infusing them with a new energy that disdained the strictures demanded by civilized manners.

Yet what is enacted in Bach's courante can be (and has been) read as

49. Score: J. S. Bach, *Erster Teil der Klavierübung*, neue Ausgabe sämtlicher Werke, ed. Richard Douglas Jones, ser. 5, vol. 1 (Kassel: Bärenreiter, 1976), 62. Unfortunately, I have not been able to locate a recording that conceives of this courante as I do, for most performers play the piece rather mechanically, according to the meter. In a pinch, try Gustav Leonhardt, *Les Six Partitas*, Klavierübung 1 (Harmonia Mundi 20315/17). When I have given this paper as a talk, I have performed the courante myself. My rationale for my evidently unusual reading of the piece is presented above. The blow-by-blow narrative style of this discussion is, incidentally, deliberate: it is designed to simulate in words what I perceive as the particularities of Italo-German procedures.

the triumph of spirit over body, in the way the kinetic groundedness of the first bars are made to seem fettered by the dance, while the continuation appears as free flight—or, as Ludwig Tieck says of German Romantic music, as "insatiate desire forever hieing forth and turning back into itself."[50] Terry Eagleton shows throughout *The Ideology of the Aesthetic* that German idealist aesthetics sought to transcend the material world, to escape in particular the body and its associations; yet he also argues that the body—by virtue of its centrality to human experience—remains as the foundational Repressed throughout the subsequent history of aesthetics.[51] To the very large extent that many classical musicians were shaped under their presumably universal criteria of idealist aesthetics, the middle-class German poets, philosophers, and composers of the eighteenth and nineteenth centuries succeeded in transmitting their horror of French customs and the body that still persists today, without our necessarily knowing why.

Consequently, those of us who know about courantes or sarabandes primarily through Bach's compositions with those labels know rather less about French dance than we assume. Indeed, our experience with Bach's anti-French dances may render us less receptive to the genuine article than we might be if we had had no contact at all with such dance types, for it can make us impatient with the particular qualities of physical motion and the affective restraint characteristic of cultural forms nurtured at Versailles.

Understanding the very different agendas of French and German composers of dance pieces requires that we give up any claim to the universality not only of music but also of bodies. Nevertheless, by observing carefully the ideological debates surrounding musical practices we can gain invaluable information—information available through no other medium—concerning the historicity of the body. At the same time, an understanding of ideologies surrounding the body can help musicians as we try to reconstitute from stale notation the gestural vitality of a previous era.

50. Ludwig Tieck, quoted in Carl Dahlhaus, *The Idea of Absolute Music*, trans. Roger Lustig (Chicago: University of Chicago Press), 18.

51. Terry Eagleton, *The Ideology of the Aesthetic* (Oxford: Basil Blackwell, 1990), 21 and passim.

5

Body of Law

The Sun King and the Code Noir

JOSEPH ROACH

"Who are my people?"
Ward Connerly

In March of 1685 at Versailles, when Louis XIV affixed beneath his signature the great seal of green wax ornamented with green and red silk ribbon, he enacted into French law the theory and practice of West Indian slavery. The document he authorized with this ceremonial gesture consisted of the sixty articles of the Code Noir, the "Black Code," a body of law "Concerning the Discipline and the Commerce of Negro Slaves of the Islands of French America." The Code Noir inscribed the legal particulars of the Gallic role in the vast Eurocolonial project of the economic exploitation of the Caribbean (and later Louisiana) using African slave labor. It also provided a general structure for the partial incorporation of hundreds of thousands and eventually millions of Africans into the body politic of the ancien régime and its successors. In the visionary imagination of omnipresence and immortality that characterizes such absolutist pronouncements, the Sun King addressed the preamble of the Code Noir "to all present and to come."[1]

1. *Regulations, Edicts, Declarations, and Decrees, Concerning the Commerce, Administration of Justice, and the Policing of the French Colonies of America; with the Black Code and*

His salutation proved prophetic, I believe—not only in the legal and social history of the American state that bears his name, but also, more subtly, in the formation of the national body politic of the United States in the crucible of race. The practice of embodying power in seventeenth- and eighteenth-century France, notwithstanding its particular manifestations as documented elsewhere in this volume, also constitutes a limited but consequential contribution to what Michel Foucault memorably called the "history of the present."[2] Reading the articles of the original Code Noir today, one hundred years after *Plessy v. Ferguson* (1896), the Louisiana civil rights case whereby the Supreme Court of the United States in effect established the doctrine of "separate but equal" as the law of the land until 1954, discloses an unexplored relationship between two legal constructions of race and nation. The first is located in the articles of the Code Noir (adopted in amended form in Louisiana in 1724) and the practices and customs they embodied. The second, in part an unacknowledged descendant of the first, is very much alive today. It animates the claim, now heard ever more bluntly from the bench and from neoconservative opinion makers, that fairness requires the law to ignore race. It also animates the physical bodies of Louisiana creoles past and present, bodies that have been deployed to undo the very concept of race as a meaningful category of difference under the law.

The constitutional address of "We, the People" defers a fundamental question, the one posed on behalf of the individual subject or citizen by the epigraph to this essay: "Who are my people?" This very question was recently asked by Ward Connerly, a Louisianan by birth, now a University of California regent and successful proponent of Proposition 209, a ballot measure that has ended racial preferences in education and government contracts. His question resonates across space and time. It resonates across the century from the Plessy case, which itself represents a catastrophic anglicization of the old Code Noir, to the current crisis of affirmative action and "racial quotas." It resonates even more expansively, in fact—across conventional boundaries of now/then and here/there. Boundaries like that allow us to believe, falsely, that power embodied in seventeenth- and eighteenth-century France pertains only to the dead.

Additions to the Said Code, trans. Olivia Blanchard (Baton Rouge: Survey of Federal Archives in Louisiana, 1940), Black Code of 1685, Preamble. Subsequent citations will be given in the text.

2. Michel Foucault, *Discipline and Punish: The Birth of the Prison*, trans. Alan Sheridan (New York: Vintage Books, 1977), 31.

Such an approach to the "history of the present" is best described by Jonathan Boyarin in *Remapping Memory: The Politics of TimeSpace*, whereby history (as a narrative of more or less linear temporal periods succeeding themselves within fixed national borders) obscures the presence of the very past it seeks to evoke. Boyarin asks:

> Is it possible for us to think otherwise, as cultural actors evidently do, and conceive of "past" events being truly effective in the present—conceive of them, that is, as not really past? To try to imagine the latter possibility, I suggest, requires that we complicate the model of a one-dimensional arrow of time along which we move through or within a separate, three-dimensional "space." *I further suggest that our reified notions of objective and separate space and time are peculiarly linked to the modern identification of a nation with a sharply bounded, continuously occupied space controlled by a single sovereign state, comprising a set of autonomous yet essentially identical individuals.*[3]

Since the consolidation of modern nation-states amid the turbulence of colonial and imperial expansion in the seventeenth century, the legal organization of people into different nationalities has been variously expounded and contested. The word *nation* itself, cognate as it is to *nativity, native*, and *nascent*, once meant a breed, a stock, or a race. Over time the idea of a nation as a political aggregation has tended to supersede this more restrictive racial sense (*OED*), but, as Elizabeth Colwill shows in her essay in this volume, that change of meaning has occurred unevenly and uncertainly. It remains incomplete today.

Louis XIV proclaimed the slave codes in the same year that he announced the Revocation of the Edict of Nantes, which drove hundreds of thousands of Huguenots out of France. Significantly, the Sun King's policies, however failed and misguided, aimed more at assimilation of the Protestant minority, through conversion and intermarriage, than at segregation and exile. No proclamation of national identity before or since resounds more euphoniously than the one current at the time of the Revocation of the Edict of Nantes: *Une foi, un roi, une loi*, or "One God, One King, One Law."[4] To this totalizing trinity, however, the contingencies of African slavery and New World colonization added another and even more problematic term: "One Blood." As its name implies, the

3. Jonathan Boyarin, "Space, Time, and the Politics of Memory," in *Remapping Memory: The Politics of TimeSpace* (Minneapolis: University of Minnesota Press, 1994), 2; emphasis in the original.

4. John B. Wolf, *Louis XIV* (London: Victor Gollancz, 1968), 379–401.

Code Noir directly confronted the problem posed by racial as well as religious difference to the formulation of the French body politic as a matter of law. Despite the undeniable color consciousness of its title, the detailed provisions of the Code Noir of 1685 worked to create a new society in "our islands of America" in which the races would eventually be subsumed into the genius of a single superior "race"—the Gallic one.

This approach to the law and its cultural formation across conventional boundaries of nation and period reflects my interest in the historic transmission of social behaviors and attitudes through performance—the public execution of actions and utterances with revision over time.[5] It also reflects a recent trend within critical legal studies to reexamine a wide range of historical and theoretical issues in light of performance—to think of justice, for instance, not as something that exists merely as abstract principle, but rather as something that must be *done*.[6] "As a cultural system dedicated to the production of certain kinds of behaviors and the regulation or proscription of others," I have written elsewhere, "law functions as a repository of social performances, past and present." As incorporated memory within the law (or as resistant actions outside of it), "performance infuses the artifacts of written law with bodily action, a meaning that obtains when it is said that a party to a contract performs."[7] Performance transmits the meaning and force of the law through the medium of corporeal action. As in the production of a classic play, the efficacy of the transmission resides in the physical embodiment of the textual artifact by living actors.

To approach the law from the perspective of performance is to take the idea of the body politic as literally as Louis XIV did when he addressed the Code Noir to the most distant and even the most abject of his sub-

5. I have recently explored related issues in *Cities of the Dead: Circum-Atlantic Performance* (New York: Columbia University Press, 1996). For a general orientation to the current work in the field of performance studies, see Andrew Parker and Eve Kosofsky Sedgwick, eds., *Performativity and Performance* (New York: Routledge, 1995); Susan Foster, ed., *Choreographing History* (Bloomington: Indiana University Press, 1995); Elin Diamond, ed., *Performance and Cultural Politics* (London: Routledge, 1996); and Peggy Phelan and Jill Lane, eds., *The Ends of Performance* (New York: NYU Press, 1997).

6. Bernard J. Hibbitts, "Coming to Our Senses: Communication and Legal Expression in Performance Cultures," *Emory Law Journal* 41 (1992): 873–960. Hibbitts writes: "The dynamism of performance is arguably reflected in the performative inclination to think of law not as things but as acts, not as rules or agreements but as processes constituting rule or agreement. A performative contract, for instance, is not an object, but a routine of words and gestures. A witness to a contract testifies not to the identity or correctness of a piece of paper, but to phenomena seen and heard. Likewise, members of performance cultures tend to think of justice not as something that simply is, but rather something that is done" (959).

7. Roach, *Cities of the Dead*, 55.

jects: "Although they inhabit countries infinitely far from our land, we are always near them, not only by the extent of our power, but also by the promptness of our will to assist them in their needs" (preamble). Imagining that the state is in some sense a body, in some sense *his* body, the king spoke confidently of the long arm of its law. Invoking the ancient Anglo-Norman doctrine of the "king's two bodies"—the body natural and the body politic—Louis projects himself as being in two places at once. The king's physical person (the body natural) served him as a symbolic iteration—through the spectacular fêtes at Versailles and kindred state performances—of his other body, the one that can project its power over time and distance through the medium of his law-abiding subjects (the body politic). This body physically exists in the performance of itself by an ensemble of actively affiliated bodies—their gestures, actions, utterances, and attitudes—which may be transmitted across vast territories as custom or handed down as tradition. By making the one into many and the many into one, such communications were vital to the expansion of the medieval dynastic state into the modern imperial nation state, which Benedict Anderson has described so influentially as an "imagined community." These communications became all the more urgent, as Anderson shows, in the face of the secessionist energies exerted by the "Creole pioneers" along the intercultural frontiers of the New World,[8] and especially along the Caribbean rim, which includes Louisiana. Unlike the body natural, the body politic cannot die—but it can and will be subject to periodic crises over its efficacy or its legitimacy as it changes through time. An informed answer, therefore, to the question "Who are my people?" more often than not requires an inquiry into what those people *do*, especially what they do as obedient (or resisting) subjects on the inside (or the outside) of the law.

The Code Noir of 1685 required, first, that the people made clear by their actions who they were not. Consistent with the Revocation of the Edict of Nantes, the preliminaries of the code were explicit and dispositive: article 1 banished all Jews from "our islands"; article 3 outlawed the practice of any religion except Catholicism; article 8 forbade the contract of legal marriage to non-Catholics and bastardized the children of such unions. The rest of the code dealt with masters and slaves as legally differentiated from one another in the duties required of them but nonetheless united in the same body politic. The exact nature of their affiliation

8. Benedict Anderson, *Imagined Communities: Reflections on the Origin and Spread of Nationalism*, rev. ed. (London: Verso, 1991), 47–65.

and difference reflected the scope of the Sun King's ambition for the future of the French in the New World. It also showed the influence of the visionary designs of Colbert, even though the code was signed two years after that formidable minister's death.

When Louis XIV declared that "we owe equal care to all the people whom Divine Providence has placed under our authority" (preamble), he made it clear that he expected that the benefits of his paternal concern would be transmitted through the regulation of his slaveholding subjects. In contrast to the Anglo-Saxon common law's predilection for the elaboration of rights, French law, which follows the traditions of the Roman civil code, tends to impose duties. By the terms of the prescriptions of the Code Noir, it was mostly the masters who were required perform. They were specifically obligated, for instance, to carry out various rituals and practices that would incorporate their slaves into the body politic.

These performances were various. Although the fact of slavery deprived slaves of their rights of property in themselves as bodies, the Code Noir recognized their status as autonomous "souls" by requiring their masters to see to their baptism and instruction within the Roman Catholic religion (article 2). Masters were also enjoined from making their slaves work on the Sabbath or on feast days (article 6), from marrying them off against their wills (article 11), from torturing or mutilating them except as provided for by law (article 42), from taking their lives arbitrarily (article 43), from abandoning them when they became old, infirm, or incurably ill (article 27), and from leaving their bodies unburied: baptized slaves were to be buried "in consecrated ground, in the cemetery designated for that purpose," unbaptized "in some field near the place of their demise" by dark of night (article 14). The secular regulation of rites of passage has been described as a characteristic practice of the modernizing nation-state, the goal of which is to mediate between the abstraction of imagined community and the tangible performances of daily life.[9] Mortuary ritual is especially powerful in this regard, and the Code Noir meticulously appropriated the rites of death and burial (as well as baptism and marriage) to this agenda of secular incorporation. As for the physical needs of the living, the code stipulated that masters must provide their slaves with "two linen suits" each year (article 25) and each week victuals equivalent to five pounds of manioc flour, two pounds of salt beef, three pounds of fish, "or something else in proportion" (article 22). Nonperformance by the

9. David I. Kertzer, *Ritual, Politics, and Power* (New Haven: Yale University Press, 1988), 114–19 and chap. 5: "The Ritual Construction of Political Reality," 77–101.

master in any of these articles entitled the slaves to complain to the *procureur*, the king's agent, for redress (article 26).

Feeble as these paper guarantees seem and ineffectual as their enforcement may have been in fact, they may be contrasted revealingly with the general silence of Anglo-American law on the welfare of slaves. Judge Thomas Ruffin of North Carolina epitomized this silence when he concluded that the law could confer but never amend the authority of the master over the slave: "The power of the master must be absolute to render the submission of the slave perfect. . . . We cannot allow the right of the master to be brought into discussion in the courts of justice. The slave, to remain a slave, must be made sensible that there is no appeal from his master; that his power is in no instance usurped; but is conferred by the laws of man at least, if not the law of God" (*State v. Mann*, 1829). Judge Ruffin's opinion is preoccupied with the elaboration of a "right" belonging to privileged persons in the absence of any corresponding obligation under the law. He imagines a community of a very particular kind, one that is ruled by an American version of divine-right absolutism, creating two completely separate classes: those whose rights are absolute and inalienable and those whose rights do not exist. In Anglo-American practice, moreover, the particular conditions of involuntary servitude were explicitly linked to race: in contrast to bonded servitude, into which white folks might fall temporarily, African slavery was constituted as a perpetual and inherited condition. As Thomas Beverley's *History of Virginia* (1705) puts it: "Their servants they distinguished by the Names of Slaves for Life, and Servants for a time. . . . Slaves are the Negroes, and their Posterity, following the Condition of the Mother."[10] On this point at least—of the necessary connection of race and slavery—the community that Louis XIV and Colbert imagined under the Code Noir was more complex.

On the one hand, the condition of slavery in the French territories, as in Virginia, was to follow the status of the mother: the children of a slave father and free mother were born free; those of a free father and slave mother were enslaved (article 13). On the other hand, the code provided for the manumission of slaves (articles 55–58), the emergence of a free black population (article 59), and intermarriage between slaves and slaveholders (article 9). The last-mentioned article, after providing for the confiscation of the children fathered by a free black or slaveholder with a slave

10. Thomas Beverley, *The History and Present State of Virginia*, ed. Louis B. Wright (Chapel Hill: University of North Carolina Press, 1947), 271.

concubine, continues: "However, the man who, not being married to another person during his concubinage with his slave, shall marry the said slave according to the decrees of the church, and they shall be enfranchised thereby, and the children made free and legitimate" (article 9). Such provisions reflect the tendency of the Latin Caribbean plantations to develop three-caste societies, roughly divided into African and Indian slaves, free people of color, and whites. With crisscrossing patterns of intermarriage and less formal arrangements of kinship, however, the lines between the castes functioned more like open frontiers than closely patrolled borders. In view of the tendency of frontier populations to band together in the face of hardship and uncertainty, propinquity alone might be supposed to offer a sufficient rationale to intermingle bloods. The generally different histories of the English-speaking North American colonies in this regard, however, highlight the effects over time of French rule in Canada and French (later Spanish) rule in Louisiana. If no other memory remained, the specialized lexicon of racial mixture itself would disclose its Latin derivation: *métis*, *griffes*, *mulattoes*, *maroons*, *quadroons*, and *octoroons*.

Miscegenation was, in fact, a geopolitical strategy of Louis XIV's France. When Colbert assumed responsibility for the administration of Canada in 1663, he formulated a policy, already implemented ad hoc by the *coureurs-de-bois*, of populating its vastness with Frenchmen by assimilating Native American peoples through enculturation and intermarriage. At his direction, a state-financed dowry was offered to any woman, French or Indian, who would marry a man of the other race, "in order that, having one law and one master, they may form only one people and one blood."[11] In other words, there was nothing inherent in the body natural (the "blood") that prevented its complete absorption into the body politic under the paternal aegis of one God, one king, and one law. Although the assimilationist strategy was contested and unevenly successful—skeptics in the colonial administration expressed fear about the proliferation of half-breeds and complained that Frenchmen were being turned into Indians instead of the other way around—it is important to remember that Louisiana was founded and developed in its early years by French Canadians, many of whom brought with them a willingness to sponsor the performances that would, in the fullness of time, turn "one law" into "one blood." In the West Indies and Louisiana, of course, the assimila-

11. Cited in Jerah Johnson, "Colonial New Orleans: A Fragment of the Eighteenth-Century French Ethos," in *Creole New Orleans: Race and Americanization*, ed. Arnold R. Hirsch and Joseph Logsdon (Baton Rouge: Louisiana State University Press, 1992), 23.

tionist project was complicated by the growing presence of Africans and their commingling with Native Americans. On that subject, perhaps the most remarkable article of the Code Noir of 1685 provided for the full enfranchisement of freed slaves: "We give to the enfranchised the same rights, privileges, and immunities enjoyed by free-born persons, so that the merit of an acquired freedom might produce in them, for their persons as well as for their possessions, the same benefits that the happiness of natural freedom gives to our other subjects" (article 59).

The intent of this clause seems to anticipate by nearly two hundred years the Fourteenth Amendment to the Constitution of the United States, guaranteeing equal protection under the law to all regardless of former condition of servitude. Of course, one of the "benefits of freedom" bestowed on the enfranchised by the Code Noir was the right to own not only property in oneself, but property generally, including slaves—which *gens de couleur libre* of Louisiana did in growing numbers throughout the colonial and antebellum periods. Although article 59 and other liberal provisions were struck from the revised version of the Code Noir in 1724 and miscegenation was outlawed at that time, the imagined community of "one blood" had already rooted itself in certain popular behaviors and practices that were further reinforced under Spanish rule. What those cultural performances embodied for many, particularly for the newly enfranchised, was the vision of an emergent society in which race, if it continued to exist as a concept at all, might remain beneath the notice of the law.

Such a vision is enabled by a habit of mind that allows a people to think beyond the body natural in order to imagine an expanded body politic. Frenchmen in the age of Louis XIV could do that, but not without deep ambivalence. Rather than thinking of "our islands" in the Caribbean as a place where a new world had been discovered, they sought to act on them as a place where a new world could still be invented, notwithstanding the unprecedented cultural disruptions and the staggering human costs involved. The Code Noir is not the only evidence of this perplexed vision. These dangerous utopias were in a sense rehearsed, I believe, in the great court entertainments performed by and for Louis at Versailles in the 1660s. In these festive rituals of state, on the cusp of feudal tournament and modern national spectacle, the actors and scenes rendered visible the anxieties provoked by the salient material fact of the practice of one blood, its culturally revolutionary hybridity.

In an essay on these fêtes, Orest Ranum rightly notes the importance of fantastic islands in their boldly synoptical scenography, which enfolded the chivalric games and courtly mythology of dynastic tradition within the technological wonders wrought by the innovations of the imperial machinists and designers. Ranum argues that the resulting performances drew on sources deep in European cultural memory, to which I would add that they simultaneously appealed to aspirations directed toward far distant shores and scarcely imaginable futures:

> The Ptolemaic theory of the four elements that make up the world—earth, air, fire, and water—implied that islands, and particularly volcanic southern islands, were the natural locations of mutation, or at least of copulation between species occupying different positions in the hierarchy of species that ranged from angels to devils. . . . Acts of sexual frenzy were considered more likely to occur on the tropical islands that were the encounter zones between inhabitants of Olympus, man, and the sea. Southern islands were shown as inhabited by fishy creatures that were a bit human: a fin was not all that different from a wing. An island resident might possess the passions of a human housed in a scaly hulk.[12]

The ambivalence of this imagery, reminiscent of the oscillation between nostalgia and nausea in Shakespeare's *Tempest*, derives, I believe, from both the reassuring representation of a mythic world of the Mediterranean past and the anxious creation of an unprecedented one in the Caribbean future.

The most significant of the fêtes, *Les Plaisirs de l'île enchantée* (The pleasures of the enchanted island, 1664), took place in the same year that Colbert initiated his plans for the crash development of a sugar-refining industry in France, with the mercantilist aim of monopolizing the final production and distribution of the most profitable commodity of the New World; during the next year the finance minister, who also had overall charge of the fêtes, imposed prohibitive tariffs on sugar imported from any other country. The scope of these designs may be measured by some statistics: French trading ships in Caribbean waters, which numbered 4 in 1662, amounted to 205 by 1683, the year of Colbert's death. By that year there were also twenty-nine sugar-refining factories prospering in metropolitan France, consuming approximately eighteen million pounds of semiprocessed West Indian sugar annually. Sugar plantations were the most labor intensive of all, requiring one slave for every two acres, compared with one slave for every ten acres of cotton or thirty acres of corn.

12. Orest Ranum, "Islands and the Self in a Ludovician Fête," in *Sun King: The Ascendancy of French Culture During the Reign of Louis XIV*, ed. David Lee Rubin (Washington, D.C.: Folger Shakespeare Library, 1992), 17.

From 1680 French slave importation into Haiti alone averaged 8,240 slaves per year, making a total of 800,000 slaves by 1776.[13] This number excludes those who disembarked at Martinique, Guadeloupe, and St. Christophe; it also excludes those who perished during the Middle Passage (from disease, neglect, abuse, murder, and suicide), a wastage that averaged approximately one-third of those who embarked in African ports and one-fifth of the ships' crews.[14]

Enchanted islands, beckoning in the distance where horizon becomes mirage, must have been on the minds of many at court in 1664, but *The Pleasures of the Enchanted Island*, a complex pageant with a number of subsidiary entertainments that took several days to perform, was created by the combined talents of Lully, Quinault, Molière, Le Notre, and Torelli out of materials drawn from Ariosto's *Orlando Furioso*. As spectacles of abundance, the entries enacted the natural distribution of commodities to the far corners of the world and their providential return to a centripetal locus of accumulation at Versailles. This bounty, not for the eyes alone, included the lavishly sugared *patisseries du roi*.[15] In the opening dramatic scenes, Louis himself enacted the leading role of Roger. In the climactic action of the Third Day, however, the hero, now played by a stand-in or stunt double for the king, breaks the spell of the enchantress Alcina, who has entertained and bewitched him with a ballet that featured giants, dwarfs, sea monsters, and eight Moors carrying torches. It is Alcina's power to summon these Caliban-like creatures to perform for her delight that defines her magic. Upon the successful conclusion of a siege and the occupation of her island, Roger destroys Alcina's palace with fireworks. Replacing the enchantress, Roger acquires her magic, which is now in a larger sense the magic of the state, legitimated physically by the royal presence under a canopy at the symbolic center of the realm.[16]

In the most frequently reproduced image of *The Pleasures of the Enchanted Island*, Louis (always locatable by the size of the plume in his hat) is shown as he witnesses the rout of Alcina, who is riding on a sea monster, one of three afloat on Le Notre's ingeniously managed waters (fig. 5.1). Between the king and the enchanted island lies an empty plane

13. Eric Williams, *From Columbus to Castro: The History of the Caribbean* (New York: Random House, 1984), 145, 161–63.

14. C.L.R. James, *The Black Jacobins: Toussaint L'Overture and the San Domingo Revolution* (1938; New York: Vintage Books, 1989), 6–9.

15. Jean-Marie Apostolidès, *Le Roi-machine: Spectacle et politique au temps du Louis XIV* (Paris: Editions de Minuit, 1981), 93–113.

16. Molière, *Oeuvres complètes*, ed. Maurice Rat (Paris: Gallimard, 1956), 1:675.

Figure 5.1 *Les Plaisirs de l'île enchantée*, Third Day, 1664. By permission of the Bibliothèque Nationale.

populated only by two armed guards. He watches as his stand-in (or "body double," in Hollywood parlance) lays down the law at a considerable distance across the water, underscoring through bodily performance the political theory of colonial rule that "although they inhabit countries infinitely far from our land, we are always near them" (Code Noir, preamble).

The symbolic economy of the Code Noir, like that of *The Pleasures of the Enchanted Island*, requires belief in the efficacy of corporeal action at a distance. For the modern state to work its magic, the symbolic and the physical dimensions of the body politic must be unified so that the king's immortal body may reconstitute itself into a body of laws. But these laws must be repeatable as specific performances at distant sites. They must serve as a *constitution* as that word has enlarged in meaning from an individual physique to an instrument for governing diverse and even refractory interests in a commonwealth. The constitutional imperative of bodily performance attains its greatest clarity in the Code Noir's provisions for the punishment of runaways. The slave absent without leave for one month "will have his ears cut off and [will be] branded on one shoulder with the fleur-de-lys; if he is guilty of a second offense . . . , he shall be hamstrung and also branded with the fleur-de-lys on the other shoulder, and a third time he will be put to death" (article 38). Branding with the Lily of France, the time-honored emblem of her monarchical continuity and national identity, subjects the slave who rejects the king's legal incorporation to a most rigorous reminder of the long arm of his law.

By providing for the marking of the rejectionist's body by maiming amputations and identifying brands, the Code Noir insisted on the existence of the slave as a legally distinct but nonetheless integral constituent of France. This is demonstrated by article 57: "We declare that enfranchisements acquired in our islands will be held in lieu of their being born on the islands, and enfranchised slaves [have] no need of our letters of naturalization in order to enjoy the advantages of native subjects of the Kingdom, lands, and countries under our authority, although they were born in a foreign country." Prior to enfranchisement, however, although slaves may be fully French, they cannot be fully French subjects. Contradicting its prior recognition of the "souls" of Africans, the code thrice defined slaves as chattel: "appurtenances" (article 44), "movable objects" (article 45), and "movable goods" (article 46). By the legal logic based on this definition, flight is theft—stealing oneself from one's master. But the brand that is then applied punitively to the flesh of the thief is not the mark of the private owner. It is rather the historic and sacred emblem of the body politic itself.

Like any legal code, the Code Noir was also subject to the dictates of a higher law—that of unintended consequences. As the checkered history of its enforcement in Louisiana makes clear, Africans who represented the majority of the population it was designed to incorporate came to America from the French concessions of Senegambia, bringing powerful laws and customs of their own. As Gwendolyn Midlo Hall has shown, conditions therefore favored "the emergence of a particularly coherent, functional, well integrated, autonomous, and self-confident slave community."[17] This African community operated within and around the one that Europeans believed they alone had imagined. In fearful recognition of the power of public performance to consolidate imagined communities, the Code Noir prohibited slave assembly: "We also forbid slaves belonging to different masters to gather together, day or night, under pretext of weddings or otherwise, whether on the premises of the masters or elsewhere, and especially along the highways or remote places, under penalty of corporeal punishment which must not be less than the lash or fleur-de-lys; and in the case of frequent repetition and other aggravating conditions, they may be punished by death" (article 26).

In actual practice, the records of the festive and ritual life of the French plantations show plentiful evidence of a flourishing tradition of public performance. Some of these the code required or implicitly condoned, contradicting article 26—at funerals, on feast days (especially Mardi Gras), and on Sunday afternoons. In "Congo Square," an unofficial New Orleans marketplace, the slaves danced bamboulas, calindas, and carabines accompanied by African instruments.[18] On the island of Martinique during Mardi Gras season 1808, Pierre Laussat, Napoleon's deputy, came upon a festive assembly of slaves who danced both the bamboula and European-style contredanses on Ash Wednesday, saying their "farewells to Carnival."[19] Although he had reinstated the Code Noir of 1724 when he briefly served as Louisiana's last French governor in 1803, Laussat's laissez-faire account recalls an apocryphal story, part of the folk tradition of New Orleans Mardi Gras, that Louis XIV issued a special decree exempting carnival activities in Louisiana from the rigor of the law.[20] This story prob-

17. Gwendolyn Midlo Hall, *Africans in Colonial Louisiana: The Development of Afro-Creole Culture in the Eighteenth Century* (Baton Rouge: Louisiana State University Press, 1992), 159.

18. Jerah Johnson, "New Orlean's Congo Square: An Urban Setting for Early Afro-American Culture Formation," *Louisiana History* 32 (1991): 117–57.

19. Pierre Laussat, *Mémoires sur ma vie, à mon fils* (Pau: E. Vignancour, 1831), 137.

20. Hodding Carter, ed., *The Past as Prelude: New Orleans, 1718–1968* (New Orleans: Pelican Publishing, 1968), 342.

ably had its origin in article 6 of the code, which forbade work on Sundays and feast days, a considerable loophole through which the great performance traditions of West Africa, evolving in their own way in proximity to European festivities, could pass. They inaugurated a genealogy of related forms that today include Second Line parades, Mardi Gras Indian processions, and jazz funerals. Although the musical life of the Sun King's court is justly celebrated in the genius of Lully and others, the cornucopia of popular forms associated with New Orleans might be considered a more consequential, though distant and indirect, contribution of his policies.

More certainly, the enfranchisement of the *gens de couleur libre* and the development of a three-caste society under French and Spanish sovereignty in Louisiana profoundly complicated the issue of race for the Anglo-Americans after 1803. The first American governor, William C. C. Claiborne, was alarmed by the sight of armed colored militia drilling in the main square and under their own officers.[21] In 1812–15, however, their numbers increased by immigration from Haiti, *gens de couleur* were freely recruited by the Americans, who were happy to have their military services. Addressing himself "to the free coloured inhabitants of Louisiana," Andrew Jackson appealed to them as fellow Americans: "As sons of freedom, you are now called upon to defend our most inestimable blessing." He hastened to assure them that if they enlisted, "due regard will be paid to the feelings of freemen and soldiers. You will not, by being associated with white men in the same corps, be exposed to improper comparisons or unjust sarcasm."[22] For the next hundred years after the victory at the Battle of New Orleans, however, the position of free people of color deteriorated as white Americans attempted with increasing vehemence to impose a binary system of racial classification and to disenfranchise anyone with a trace of "negro blood." As recounted by Rodolphe Desdunes in *Nos Hommes et notre histoire* (1911), the losing battle for full citizenship—once guaranteed under the old regime—was fought in the law courts and in the court of public opinion.[23] Organized into the Comité des Citoyens

21. Roland C. McConnell, "Louisiana's Black Military History, 1729–1865," in *Louisiana's Black Heritage*, ed. Robert R. MacDonald, John R. Kemp, and Edward F. Hass (New Orleans: Louisiana State Museum, 1979), 39.

22. "Proclamation. Head-quarters, 7th military district, Mobile, September 21, 1814," Louisiana State Museum.

23. Rodolphe Desdunes, *Our People and Our History*, trans. Sister Dorotea Olga McCants (Baton Rouge: Louisiana State University Press, 1973). See Caryn Cossé Bell, *Revolution, Romanticism, and the Afro-Creole Protest Tradition in Louisiana* (Baton Rouge: Louisiana State University Press, 1997).

and inspired by the memory of the Revolution of 1848, which ended slavery in the French West Indies and enfranchised all the former slaves, francophone creoles of color maintained a position rooted in their past but focused on their American future: race could not be a factor in the determination of legal rights. In this regard, the body natural is legally superseded by another body, an invisible one that enjoys equal protection of the law, an inalienable one that is constituted as a civic soul.

Homer Adolph Plessy, born in 1862 to Rosalie Debergue and Adolphe Plessy, French-speaking Catholics of New Orleans, was described as "an octoroon," a person of one-eighth "African blood." Legally black, he could pass as white. In the Anglo-American zeal to establish a defensible color line in the ethnic gumbo that was creole Louisiana, many definitions of race were tried, including the test of one thirty-second "negro blood." All failed.[24] On behalf of the Citizens Committee, a successor to the Comité des Citoyens, Homer Plessy volunteered his body natural, the blackness of which was invisible, to assert his right to equal protection of the law on behalf of his body politic.

The aim of Plessy and the Citizens Committee was to explode the idea of race in American law. In June 1892 the octoroon entered a "whites only" railway car in violation of the Louisiana Separate Car Law of 1890, which provided for "equal but separate" accommodations for people of the "white" and "colored" races. Plessy was arrested and charged as planned. Testing the law's definition of race, the Citizens Committee performed the juridical memory of "one blood," which existed not only in the dusty archives of the Cabildo—the old colonial building where the Louisiana Supreme Court heard the case—but also in the crowded, polyglot New Orleans streets outside. In a letter to Albion Tourgée, Plessy's attorney, Louis Martinet of the Citizens Committee described the historic effects of French law and custom as they manifested themselves in an increasingly segregationist American urbanscape of 1891: "There are the strangest white people you ever saw here. Walking up & down our principal thoroughfare—Canal Street—you would [be] surprised to have persons pointed out to you, some as white & others as colored, and if you were not informed you would be sure to pick out the white for colored & the colored for white."[25]

24. Virginia Dominguez, *White by Definition: Social Classification in Creole Louisiana* (New Brunswick, N.J.: Rutgers University Press, 1986), 56–89.

25. Cited in Otto H. Olsen, ed., *The Thin Disguise: Turning Point in Negro History. Plessy v. Ferguson—A Documentary Presentation, 1864–1896* (New York: Humanities Press, 1967), 56–57.

Although he did not cite article 59 of the Code Noir, Tourgée's brief developed a similar argument against racial segregation by recourse to the equal protection clause of the Fourteenth Amendment of the United States Constitution. He further attacked the Separate Car Law because it failed to define (because it could not) what it meant when it said "white" and "colored" races. Tourgée's brief asks: "Is not the question of race, scientifically considered, very often impossible of determination? Is not the question of race, legally considered, one impossible to be determined, in the absence of statutory definition?"[26] Moreover, because it could not define what race meant, the law in effect deputized the railroad conductors of Louisiana, while punching tickets, to make their own judgments about what the legislators might possibly have been thinking of when they specified "white" and "colored" races. Despite the logic of Plessy's plea and the material fact of his body natural, the Supreme Court of the United States decided that there is a clear and important distinction between "white and colored races—a distinction which is founded in the color of the two races, and which must always exist as long as white men are distinguished from the other race by color."[27] The court thereby legalized race relations for the United States in the twentieth century that were, as the old saying goes, somewhere to the right of Louis XIV.

The question of the status of race under the law continues to circulate within the larger conundrum of the body politic. Many of the issues that surfaced in *Plessy* a century ago have turned up again in current debates over affirmative action, race-based admissions to colleges and universities, and minority set-asides. I have argued here that their particular genealogy extends further back in time. They are the consequence of a particular history, one that cannot be adequately represented solely by the documents left behind because it also exists in the physical bodies, practices, and attitudes that it continues to produce.

As a regent of the University of California and chairman of the ballot initiative to end racial preferences under affirmative action, Ward Connerly recently explained his personal perspective on race and the law to the press. Although he is described as "a black man pushing to end the very policies meant to help black people," his story is in fact more complicated—and, I hope, by now more familiar. Growing up poor in Louisiana under Jim Crow, the orphaned Connerly was raised by his Choctaw Indian grandmother. His other grandmother was white. One

26. Cited in ibid., 81.
27. *Plessy v. Ferguson*, 163 U.S. 537.

grandfather was a white man of French descent, the other was black. The grandmother who raised him taught him to believe that "race just didn't matter"—a fair summary of Plessy's argument if she may be understood to have meant that race *ought* not to matter. It is not coincidental that on these two occasions—that of *Plessy v. Ferguson* and that of California Proposition 209—a national challenge to race as a legal category emerged among the descendants of a community first imagined under a law that gave to freed slaves and their descendants "the same rights, privileges, and immunities enjoyed by free-born persons" (Code Noir, article 59) and for a time permitted (and thereafter never wholly or effectively prevented) their intermarriage. Connerly itemizes his kinship ties with the clear intent of demonstrating that in the face of their unifying consanguinity—multiple, complex, ambiguous—the concept of separate races is unworkable under the law: "Who are my people? . . . I can identify with blackness, I can identify with white, I can identify with Indian."[28] Across three centuries, his body thus performs as bidden—one blood under one law.

28. Donna St. George, "Black University Regent Fights Affirmative Action," *New Orleans Times-Picayune*, April 7, 1996, A-18.

6

Louis *le Bien-Aimé* and the Rhetoric of the Royal Body

THOMAS E. KAISER

It is fortunate for our monarch that he became the well-loved; if not, he would have been the well-dethroned.

Marquis d'Argenson

When at his death Louis XV's eulogists recalled and celebrated the most memorable events of his long and not always glorious reign, they almost invariably came to fix upon that moment in August 1744 when, following his successful debut as a field commander, Louis had fallen ill in the city of Metz—gravely so, it had seemed—miraculously recovered, and soon after "received" the title of *bien-aimé* (well-loved) from his adoring and grateful people. "Oh Metz!" intoned the abbé Coger, "you were . . . the theater of the most touching scene that has ever been offered to humanity! All hearts, in unanimous concert, proclaimed him Louis *le Bien-Aimé;* superb monuments announce this title to posterity."[1] During the last two centuries, Louis's biographers have surely presented a far more critical view of his reign than did his eulogists; yet they have

I should like to thank the following for their cogent comments on and criticisms of this article: Sarah Hanley, Sarah Maza, Robert Morrisey, Jan Goldstein, Katie Crawford, and Jo Margadant.

1. François Marie Coger, *Oraison funèbre de . . . Louis XV . . . prononcée le 3 octobre 1774 au Collège Mazarin* (Paris, 1774), 12.

continued to reconstruct the restoration of the royal body at Metz in much the same way as did many of his contemporaries—namely, as a major boon to the monarchy that, as one recent biographer has put it, left "no doubt that the French loved their monarch passionately."[2] Together with the victory of Fontenoy less than a year later, the events of Metz have been commonly considered to be the high point of the reign, after which diplomatic disappointments, military reversals, and Jansenist controversy eroded the great popularity Louis had allegedly enjoyed in happier, earlier years.[3]

But did Metz really constitute such an undiluted triumph? In this essay I reconsider the events of Metz in order to place them within a larger perspective of royal self-representation and contemporary judgment of Louis XV. To be sure, Louis's recovery may in fact have given his subjects temporary hopes for the rejuvenation of the French state, a reflection of the belief, explicated in the contributions to this volume of Jeffrey Merrick and Abby Zanger, that the king's two bodies—his mortal *corps* and his immortal office—had come to intersect within the ideology of dynastic absolutism. Yet the generation of these hopes, I argue, occurred at a time of increasing despair regarding the health of the king and the direction of the monarchy. Louis's subsequent acclamation as the *bien-aimé*, hardly so spontaneous an affair as has been traditionally believed, was in fact most notable for reinforcing a vision of kingship that Louis XV—already suspected of abdicating his royal responsibilities in the pursuit of pleasure—could not sustain. Crucial in this regard was Louis's return to sexual promiscuity, which not only raised traditional fears of female usurpation of royal power but also appeared to violate an implicit "love" contract between Louis and his people that royal propaganda efforts—seemingly crowned with success by the events of Metz—had underscored for decades as the informal basis of royal authority. In the end, I will demonstrate how the monarchy, by seizing on the events at Metz as its most important moment of self-definition, wound up advancing a strategy that placed it in an untenable rhetorical position with regard to its critics and thereby placed in jeopardy the very authority it had sought to strengthen.

The title of *bien-aimé* bestowed on Louis XV—the first French king since Charles VI to bear it—had roots deep in the traditions of the medieval

2. Olivier Bernier, *Louis the Beloved: The Life of Louis XV* (Garden City, N.Y.: Doubleday, 1984), 130.

3. See, for example, Michel Antoine, who has written of a "volte-face" in public opinion around 1748 that gave rise to "aversions unknown until then." Michel Antoine, *Louis XV* (Paris: Fayard, 1989), 603.

French monarchy. That French kings and their subjects were tied together by a special, divine love was a commonplace of medieval French political theology, a correlate of the deeply embedded idea that collectively the French nation constituted a divinely blessed *corpus mysticum* to which all members owed a supreme obligation as part of their Christian duty.[4]

Paternalistic models of kingship could be easily accommodated within the conception of the *corpus mysticum* as a society held together by love. As head of the family/nation, a father / king might on occasion appear as a punishing patriarch, but he was much more frequently associated with the "softer" bonds of mutual affection and indulgence that supposedly joined together king and subjects. In Claude de Seyssel's estimation, a king bound to his subjects by "paternal love, justice, and fair treatment" stood in bold contrast to "princes and monarchs who wish to dominate and command their subjects beyond reason and who try to hold them in servile fear by ambitious and tyrannical domination."[5]

Demonstrated through acts of justice and reason, royal paternal love was also manifested through the establishment of peace and harmony that promised in their wake times of material abundance. The propaganda halo painted around Henri IV continually reinforced the notion that this monarch, whose "benevolence toward his people aroused a reciprocal love," was responsible for restoring pastoral tranquillity after the conflict of the religious wars and thereby represented through his very presence a "horn of abundance." Mythologically represented as the Gallic Hercules, Henri IV was hailed as restorer of a Saturnine age, the bringer of arts to humanity and thereby the instigator of peace, fertility, and plenty.[6]

4. As Jacques Krynen has recently pointed out, there is as yet no study of love as a political virtue; see his *L'Empire du roi: Idées et croyances politiques en France, XIIIe–XVe siècles* (Paris: Gallimard, 1993), 458. But cf. Ernst H. Kantorowicz, *The King's Two Bodies: A Study in Medieval Political Theology* (Princeton: Princeton University Press, 1957), 232–72; Gaines Post, *Studies in Medieval Legal Thought: Public Law and the State, 1100–1322* (Princeton: Princeton University Press, 1964), chap. 10; and Colette Beaune, *Naissance de la nation France* (Paris: Gallimard, 1985), 334–35.

5. Claude de Seyssel, *Proem . . . to the Translation of the History by Appian of Alexandria Entitled "The Deeds of the Romans,"* in *The Monarchy of France*, trans. J. H. Hexter (New Haven: Yale University Press, 1981), 180. On the king as father, see Pierre Ronzeaud, *Peuple et représentations sous le règne de Louis XIV: Les Répresentations du peuple dans la littérature politique en France sous le règne de Louis XIV* (Aix-en-Provence: Presses de l'Université de Provence, 1988), chap. 9.

6. Quoted in Jacques Hennequin, *Henri IV dans ses oraisons funèbres, ou la naissance d'une légende* (Paris: Klincksieck, 1977), 127, 125. See also Corrado Vivanti, "Henry IV, the Gallic Hercules," *Journal of the Warburg and Courtauld Institutes* 30 (1967): 176–97; and Frances A. Yates, *Astraea: The Imperial Theme in the Sixteenth Century* (London: Routledge & Kegan Paul, 1975), conclusion.

The pastoral image of monarchy based on love, harmony, and peace was far too useful for the French monarchy ever to be abandoned during the Old Regime, and it would continue to be invoked routinely upon the resolution of troubling domestic and foreign conflicts. At the same time, it constituted only part of the monarchy's arsenal of political mythology, having to compete—when it could not be effectively integrated—with other myths, especially those associated with the powerful cult of heroic kingship that found its main theme in the pursuit of glory, particularly military glory. According to one close study, allusions to Henri IV as a pacific monarch were outnumbered by allusions to him as a conquering hero, the reincarnation of Jupiter, Mars, Alexander, and Caesar; according to another study, Louis XIV's reign was similarly characterized by a hegemonic discourse whose "webs of myths and facts . . . bound the prince to the pursuit of *gloire*."[7] Clearly, the best strategy from the standpoint of royal image-makers was to maintain images of the king as both conqueror and *père du peuple*. Court librettists under the Sun King tried earnestly to reconcile these images of Louis XIV with such phrases as "he has served himself with Victory in order to enable Peace to triumph," while other masters of royal rhetoric sought the same end by routinely drawing sharp lines between the fear the king inspired in his enemies and the love he inspired in his people.[8]

Notwithstanding such efforts, the space between these two mythologies was never completely sealed. As Robert Isherwood has shown, alternations between peace and war policies forced Louis XIV's court musicians to shift abruptly and sometimes awkwardly between tropes of love and glory; as one contemporary complained politely, "The muses find in him so many different qualities that they do not know how to blend the ones suitable for praising a conqueror with the sweet and amorous tones which are suitable to his pacific virtues."[9] Similarly, the distinction made between fear among enemies and love among subjects did not always persuade; as one academician later put it, "It is difficult for a great King to

7. François Bardon, *Le Portrait mythologique à la cour de France sous Henri IV et Louis XIII: Mythologie et politique* (Paris: A. & J. Picard, 1974), 243; Orest Ranum, *Artisans of Glory: Writers and Historical Thought in Seventeenth-Century France* (Chapel Hill: University of North Carolina Press, 1980), 337. On the war image in general, see Joel Cornette, *Le Roi de guerre: Essai sur la souveraineté dans la France du Grand Siècle* (Paris: Payot, 1993).

8. Robert M. Isherwood, *Music in the Service of the King: France in the Seventeenth Century* (Ithaca: Cornell University Press, 1973); Jean de La Bruyère, "Discours prononcé dans l'Académie Française le lundi quinzième juin 1693," in *Les Caractères de Théophraste traduits du grec avec Les Caractères ou les moeurs de ce siècle* (Paris: Garnier Frères, 1962), 511.

9. Isherwood, *Music*, 287.

make his neighbors tremble without making his Subjects groan."[10] On balance it is hard to avoid the conclusion that Louis XIV's image as conqueror tended to obscure his image as *père du peuple* and that this result was intentional; informed seventeenth-century opinion followed Machiavelli in supposing that fear provided a more reliable bond between sovereign and subject than did love.[11] And whatever the other avenues available, it was in war, as one academician put it, that great princes "principally arrive at glory, because the most renowned have arrived there through valor, victory, and conquests."[12]

With the rise of foreign and domestic sentiment against Louis's wars and repressive religious policies in the late years of the reign, an ever-growing chorus of royal critics came to impugn Louis's apparent lust for conquest, invoking the *père du peuple* image as a means for showing just how far Louis had fallen short of his royal responsibilities.[13] Most prominent among these critics was the exiled ex-courtier and archbishop Fénelon, author of the widely read roman à clef *Les Aventures de Télémaque* and advocate of what one historian has termed "Christian agrarianism."[14] Calling Louis to account for his material extravagance, his reckless pursuit of military conquest, and his indifference to the sufferings of his subjects, Fénelon employed a language of the pastoral and "pure love," drawing inspiration from traditional notions of the king as *père du peuple*, provider of justice, peace, and abundance. This language was notable for the way it tended to subvert, rather than blend, with the cult of military glory.[15]

10. *Recueil des harangues prononcées par messieurs de l'Académie Françoise* (Paris, 1735), 4:425.

11. Gabriel Naudé, for example, believed that only "the rigor of punishments" and the "fear of the gods and their thunder" could maintain people in their duty; see his *Considérations politiques sur les coups d'état* (Paris: Editions de Paris, 1989), 141. On the Machiavellian outlook in general, see the useful E. Thuau, *Raison d'état et pensée politique à l'époque de Richelieu* (Paris: A. Colin, 1966).

12. *Recueil des harangues*, 1:382.

13. Ronzeaud, *Peuple et représentations*, 334–38. For eighteenth-century appropriation of the patriarchal image by royal critics, see the excellent article by Jeffrey Merrick, "Patriarchalism and Constitutionalism in Eighteenth-Century Parlementary Discourse," *Studies in Eighteenth-Century Culture* 20 (1991): 317–30.

14. The phrase is taken from Lionel Rothkrug, *Opposition to Louis XIV: The Political and Social Origins of the French Enlightenment* (Princeton: Princeton University Press, 1965), chap. 5. On the pervasive influence of Fénelon, see Albert Cherel, *Fénelon au XVIIIe siècle en France (1715–1820), son prestige, son influence* (Geneva: Slatkine, 1970). According to Cherel, the *Télémaque*, originally published in 1699, appeared in sixteen editions by the end of the reign and was widely imitated.

15. On Fénelonian "pure love," see Nannerl O. Keohane, *Philosophy and the State in France: The Renaissance to the Enlightenment* (Princeton: Princeton University Press, 1980), 338–43. As Keohane makes clear, Fénelonian "pure love" differed from Jansenist notions of

Confronted by such growing criticism, royal propagandists responded in kind, demonstrating far more resourcefulness and flexibility in their packaging of monarchy than most historians, content with reducing all Old Regime royalist ideology to a monolithic "absolutism," have attributed to them. Just as the creatures of Foreign Minister Colbert de Torcy answered the widely circulated attacks on French foreign policy in much the same juridically and historically based idiom in which these attacks were expressed,[16] court poets, who had often been obliged to seek their own glory in praising the military achievements of their king, gradually shifted their emphasis to praise of the king's promotion of domestic tranquillity. As the cardinal Polignac observed before the Académie Française in 1713, the Muses had always preferred times of peace and tranquillity: "If sometimes they sing of combat to celebrate the virtues of heroes, soon after they deplore the tumult of arms, which causes the fine arts to languish; but when Peace returns on earth . . . it is then that they reach the height of their desires."[17] Very gently the notion of glory itself was detached from conquest. As the abbé Mignon explained, to locate Louis's virtues it would be necessary to look "beyond his victories," for his virtue is "stronger than that of his armies" and the "grandeur" of all true heroes "resides in their souls and not in the arms of their soldiers."[18]

Elaborated at length by the academician Louis de Sacy in his *Traité de la gloire* of 1715, this notion of glory was used to project a notion of kingship distinct from that associated with Alexander and Caesar. A hero was not just a "valiant man" but a "valiant, good, just, human, wise, modest man, who does not rush into danger, and who does not spill blood like ferocious beasts out of love of carnage or hope of booty." Service to his people alone had to be the sole concern of the king/hero, for only through such service could he win their abiding love. "The only taste they [kings] seek to satisfy is to reconcile themselves to the love of their sub-

---

love, which were built on the idea that pursuing enlightened self-interest promoted social utility. In proclaiming that a prince should "gratify all wishes," crafters of the image of Louis as the *bien-aimé* borrowed more from the latter than the former; love for the prince was hardly selfless. See Houdar de La Motte, *Fables nouvelles dediées au roy* (Paris, 1719), 138. On Fénelon and the image of the *père du peuple*, see Ronzeaud, *Peuples et répresentations*, 329–31.

16. See Joseph Klaits, *Printed Propaganda Under Louis XIV: Absolute Monarchy and Public Opinion* (Princeton: Princeton University Press, 1976); also Thomas E. Kaiser, "The Abbé Dubos and the Historical Defense of Monarchy in Early Eighteenth-Century France," *Studies on Voltaire and the Eighteenth Century*, no. 267 (1989): 77–102.

17. *Recueil des harangues*, 3:525–26.

18. Ibid., 409–10.

jects; the sole interest that dominates them is to make their subjects happy."[19]

Two points regarding this utilitarian notion of monarchy based on love between king and subjects deserve emphasis here. First, it was notable for its narrowing of the social and political distance between subject and sovereign that had appeared so enormous in the propaganda of Louis XIV's early and middle reign, propaganda in which Louis had been made to appear a colossus, a godlike figure well beyond the status of ordinary mortals.[20] Taking a cue from the anti-French propagandists who had sought to diminish Louis's stature by stressing his personal failings, Sacy acknowledged that kings were fallible, that they were subject "to all weaknesses, exposed to all the misfortunes of humanity."[21] Second, Sacy sought to invest the ultimate judgment of royal glory in the public at large, in what he called "public opinion." Although he conceded that the public—which he never defined very precisely—might make temporary errors, Sacy, like other contemporaries who sought to rehabilitate the validity of "public opinion" and the political judgments made by it, believed that in the long run the public—"always equitable, and sole legitimate dispenser of great reputations"—would make fair and responsible decisions regarding their kings when guided by men of letters, and that these decisions could "not be too much respected" if only because such attributions of glory originated in the hearts of the king's own subjects.[22]

Already articulated before his accession to the throne, these notions underpinned the entire presentation of monarchy during Louis XV's early reign. Fully aware of the opprobrium heaped on Louis XIV and critically aware of the desperate need for peace felt by a country weakened by protracted warfare and a government facing bankruptcy,[23] the Regency, established in September 1715, took no time representing itself in images of pastoral monarchy. The last words supposedly said by the dying king to

19. Louis de Sacy, *Traité de la gloire* (Paris, 1715), 184–87, 190, 195.

20. Nicole Ferrier-Caverivière, *L'Image de Louis XIV dans la littérature française de 1660–1715* (Paris: Presses Universitaires de France, 1981), 181: "Grandiose and immovable, grandiose because immovable, thus appears the monarch."

21. Sacy, *Traité*, 194.

22. Ibid., 54, 59, 241. On the rehabilitation of "public opinion" in this period from various perspectives, see my articles "The Abbé de Saint-Pierre, Public Opinion, and the Reconstitution of the French Monarchy," *Journal of Modern History* 55 (1983): 618–43; "Rhetoric in the Service of the King: The Abbé Dubos and the Concept of Public Judgment," *Eighteenth-Century Studies* 23 (1989–90): 182–99; and "Money, Despotism, and Public Opinion: John Law and the Debate on Royal Credit," *Journal of Modern History* 63 (1991): 1–28.

23. The best general treatment remains Henri Leclercq, *Histoire de la Régence pendant la minorité de Louis XV*, 3 vols. (Paris: E. Champion, 1921–22).

his successor—in which the Sun King warned his great-grandson against imitating his war policies and urged him to succor his subjects—were soon published by the government and frequently recalled thereafter in royal discourse.[24] In his appearance before the Paris Parlement on the eve of his confirmation as regent, the duc d'Orléans—who, according to Saint-Simon, believed himself to resemble the fondly remembered Henri IV and affected his mannerisms—invoked Fénelonian rhetoric from the *Télémaque*, which had granted the king as *père du peuple* "an absolute power to do good" and "tied his hands once he wishes to do evil."[25] Fénelonian references continued to appear over the course of Louis XV's early reign, during which Louis was hailed as the "new Telemachus," and his tutor, the maréchal Villeroy, as his "Mentor."[26] Much the same point was made through persistent references to Louis XV as the new Solomon, whose virtues as the peace king were discreetly, but nevertheless firmly, distinguished from those of his predecessor, the reincarnation of the more warlike David. "The pacific Solomon has succeeded the bellicose David," pronounced an academician in 1721. "He will triumph over our domestic problems through abundance, just as Louis XIV triumphed over our enemies through the terror of his arms."[27]

At the heart of this revived image of a pastoral, paternal monarch lay the celebration of the young king as both the giver and recipient of his subjects' love. Louis XV's childhood copybooks reveal a vigorous effort on the part of his preceptor, the future cardinal Fleury, to teach the young monarch that love, not fear, should bind him to his people. They are filled

24. Louis XIV, *Derniers paroles du roy Louis XIV au Louis XV, son arrière petit-fils* (n.p., [1715]), published by the Imprimerie du Cabinet du Roy, gives one version of these words. They were recalled, for example, by the court poet Antoine Danchet in his "Discours dans l'Assemblée publique tenue au Louvre le jour de Saint Louis, 25 août 1732," in which Louis XV was said to be "bound by the last instructions of his August great-grandfather" and was hailed not as "a Conqueror who burns to extend his domination" but as a "father who seeks to make his children happy" (*Oeuvres mêlées de M. Danchet* [Paris, 1751], 4:206).

25. Louis de Rouvroy, duc de Saint-Simon, *Mémoires*, ed. A. de Boislisle, 41 vols. (Paris: Hachette, 1879–1928), 26:268; François de Salignac de la Motte Fénelon, *Les Aventures de Télémaque*, ed. A. Cahen (Paris: Hachette, 1927), 1:191; François Isambert et al., *Recueil général des anciennes lois françaises* (Paris: Belin-Leprieur, 1821–33), 21:20. The similarity between the texts has been noted in George Havens, *The Age of Ideas* (New York: H. Holt, 1955), 62.

26. Carolet, *Bouquet présenté au roy le jour de Saint Louis de l'année mil sept cent vingt un* (n.p., [1721]). Another example is the reference made in the speech of Louis de Sacy before the Académie Française in 1718: "Cast your eyes on those who nurture this precious see of the common happiness, and never stop promising yourselves a Telemachus, because there are still Mentors" (*Recueil des harangues*, 4:128).

27. *Recueil des harangues*, 4:229.

with fables preaching messages such as "a king who is the terror of his subjects instead of being their defender and father is more unfortunate than the vilest of all animals"; with precepts such as "to call the King father and pastor of the people is not so much to recite a panegyric as to call him by his proper name and define what it is to be a King"; and with promises to his subjects such as "I will act so that I am loved by my subjects, because it is much better for a king to be loved than to be feared; he who is loved is protected from all snares, he who is feared fears as well and he who fears cannot be happy."[28] Impressed upon the young sovereign himself, such messages were broadcast publicly throughout the early reign with monotonous regularity. Upon his recovery from what appeared to be a serious illness in 1721, Louis was regaled by the court poet Danchet with the words "It is not the magnificence, / Nor the glory of great deeds, / It is the mutual love of peoples and kings / Which from a brilliant throne establishes power / . . . We love him, our love desires / That he govern his subjects, / Less as King than as Father." Similarly, on the occasion of his marriage, Louis was complimented at Fontainebleau for preferring "the sweet pleasure of making himself loved to the most legitimate right of making himself feared by his Subjects."[29]

Although Louis remained without an official sobriquet until the late summer of 1744, anticipations of the *bien-aimé* title are not hard to find much earlier. On Louis's return trip from his coronation in 1722, he was hailed in a celebration by the court poet Houdar de La Motte as "the most lovable King" and "the most loved King" (*le Roi le plus aimable, le Roi le plus aimé*), and upon his recovery from an illness in 1729 he was acknowledged as "the most cherished of Kings" (*le plus chéri des Rois*).[30] It would thus not require much of a linguistic stretch when, upon recovery from another apparently life-threatening illness, Louis was recognized as the *bien-aimé* for the first time on the Day of St. Louis 1744.[31]

If such were the messages regarding Louis XV imparted by the monarchy, how were they received? The standard notion that Louis XV enjoyed

28. Bibliothèque Nationale [henceforth cited as BN], ms. fr. 2325, fol. 73; ms. fr. 2324, fol. 8; ms. fr. 2322, fol. 216.

29. Danchet, *Oeuvres*, 4:9; Louis Pierre Daudet, *Journal historique du voyage de S.A.S. Mademoiselle de Clermont* (Chaalons, 1725), 302.

30. Louis Pierre Daudet, *Journal historique du premier voyage du Roi Louis XV dans la ville de Compiègne* (Paris, 1729), 277.

31. The first attribution I have been able to document is that of the abbé Josset, *Compliment fait à la Reine . . . lorsqu'il a prononcé devant sa Majesté le Panégyrique de Saint Louis dans l'église des R.R. P.P. Jésuites de Metz, le 25 août 1744* (n.p., n.d.), 4. Josset later claimed to

a relatively high reputation among his subjects until the late 1740s has recently been undermined by Arlette Farge through her research into the most complete extant record of early-eighteenth-century French political sentiment—namely, the reports of Parisian police spies (*mouches* or *mouchards*), who infiltrated Parisian courts of law, cafés, public walkways, and private houses.[32] These reports must be used critically and do not constitute scientific opinion polls; gathered from a nonrandom segment of the population, they no doubt reflect biases of their compilers. Yet, particularly when corroborated by other sources, these reports offer an invaluable window on public political sentiment, providing at the very least a useful sampling of different kinds of contemporary political discourse and one indication of the frequency of such discourse. Moreover, since the monarchy—including the king, who often read them—relied on these reports as indices of public sentiment, they are evidence for what public authorities took to be "public opinion" regarding major figures within the monarchy and its political initiatives.[33]

---

have been the first to use the title with regard to Louis XV; see Charles Philippe d'Albert, duc de Luynes, *Mémoires du duc de Luynes sur la cour de Louis XV, 1735–1758* (Paris, 1860–65), 9:117. A query into the use of the term *bien-aimé* in texts for the period 1550–1789 in the database of the American and French Research on the Treasury of the French Language (ARTFL) at the University of Chicago reveals that it was commonly used as a term of endearment between lovers and among family members in secular literature and frequently used in reference to biblical figures, especially Jesus, in religious literature. I should like to thank Robert Morrisey for facilitating my use of this excellent research resource.

32. Arlette Farge, *Dire et mal dire: L'Opinion publique au XVIIIe siècle* (Paris: Seuil, 1992). These reports are partially to be found in the Bibliothèque de l'Arsenal [henceforth cited as BA], AB MSS. 10155–10170, which cover the period 1724–41. For the period 27 July 1742 through 18 August 1743, see Edmond-Jean-François Barbier, *Chronique de la Régence et du règne de Louis XV (1718–1763), ou Journal de Barbier* (Paris, 1857–66), 8:129–348. Another series, which Farge has apparently not consulted, can be found in the Bibliothèque Historique de la Ville de Paris [henceforth cited as BHVP], MSS. 616–26; it extends from 1737 through the critical year of 1744. Although I agree with Farge's general conclusions regarding negative opinion of Louis XV, I do not accept all her contentions regarding the nature of the public surveyed, nor her view that this opinion was unresponsive to the more elitist controversies between the monarchy and the parlements. See also Frantz Funck-Brentano, *Figaro et ses devanciers* (Paris: Hachette, 1909), 175ff.; and Arlette Farge and Jacques Revel, *Logiques de la foule: L'Affaire des enlèvements d'enfants Paris 1750* (Paris: Hachette, 1988).

33. That Louis was informed of these reports is indicated by various sources, including the reliable Charles Philippe d'Albert in his *Mémoires*, 4:280; and a letter of 29 January 1743 from Maurepas to Marville published in A. de Boislisle, ed., *Lettres de M. Marville, lieutenant-général de police au ministre Maurepas, 1742–1747* (Paris: H. Champion, 1896–1903), 1:104. Lest one assume that pressure from above inclined police spies to underreport or soften comments critical of the government, consider the police report of 17 June 1743, which, after recording unflattering public discussion of royal "dissipation," recalled—undoubtedly for purposes of self-protection—the issuance of "definite orders that have been received to produce a faithful account of all that is said even with respect to the king" (Barbier, *Chronique*, 8:301).

Judging from contemporary journals and *mémoires* that recorded public opinion before the police reports begin in 1724, it appears that Louis, a beautiful, if often sickly, orphan, who had barely managed to survive the wave of death that had swept over the royal house in the last years of the previous reign, enjoyed a period of public infatuation that lasted until his adolescence. To be sure, any assessment of public perceptions of the king throughout the early decades of the reign must take into account the public's knowledge that, had Louis died, France, already nearly financially prostrate from Louis XIV's last war, would almost certainly have been drawn into yet another disastrous international conflict. In the event of Louis's death, Philip V, king of Spain and, according to French dynastic law, Louis's heir to the French throne until the birth of the dauphin in 1729, would in all likelihood have reasserted the right to succeed that he earlier had been obligated to renounce, thereby unraveling the entire peace settlement reached at Utrecht in 1713.[34] This knowledge notwithstanding, it is hard not to credit royal image-makers with some measure of success, given that accounts of Louis are saturated with the same sentiments of love and affection that the monarchy itself wished to project. Upon Louis's recovery from his illness in 1721, recorded Charles Duclos, Paris exploded with a "transports of joy," the hearts of its people "feeling the tenderest love" for their prince. To Mathieu Marais, the king at his coronation in 1722 "resembled Love" itself; his status as the "new Solomon" was confirmed when, still a child, he "wisely" settled a rather silly dispute over which ballet was to be performed at a court function.[35]

Such nearly universal adulation began to dissipate as the king entered adolescence. Jansenist dissent may well have played a role here, but it is hard to deny that the king, too, by virtue of his own shyness, his craving for privacy, and his apparent indifference in the face of his subjects' suffering, contributed to malaise across the wider population.[36] Already in No-

34. For one standard account of the renunciation and its diplomatic aftermath, see Alfred Baudrillart, *Philippe V et la cour de France*, 5 vols. (Paris: Firmin-Didot, 1890–91). I have dealt with some of the legal and ideological considerations in "Abbé Dubos and the Historical Defense of Monarchy." Philip had been anxious to reassert his claim many times, as during the Cellamare conspiracy.

35. Charles Duclos, *Mémoires secrets sur les règnes de Louis XIV et de Louis XV*, in *Nouvelle Collection des mémoires pour servir à la France* (Paris, 1839) 10:578; Mathieu Marais, *Journal et mémoires de Mathieu Marais . . . sur la régence et le règne de Louis XV* (Paris, 1863–64) 2:364, 47–48.

36. On Jansenism, see Dale K. Van Kley, *The Damiens Affair and the Unraveling of the "Ancien Régime," 1750–1770* (Princeton: Princeton University Press, 1984); and Jeffrey W. Merrick, *The Desacrilization of the French Monarchy in the Eighteenth Century* (Baton Rouge: Louisiana State University Press, 1990). As for Louis himself, a number of biographers have

vember 1722, Marais recorded that at age twelve Louis "no longer wishes to study" and was openly mocking his tutors. Two years later, according to policy spy reports, it was said that Louis's pursuit of pleasures "promises nothing good." "He is, people say, very proud, very absolute, and pleases himself by doing everything according to whim." In 1725, rumor had it that the king "thinks of nothing but his pleasures, that he likes nothing that might divert him from them." In the following year, it was said that the king had become "addicted to hunting." Hunting was by no means considered an inappropriate activity for a king, but Louis's immoderate passion for it led observers to conclude that he "does not want to open his eyes to the state of the Kingdom." One wisecrack of 1728, which revealed some of the problems inherent in the projection of Louis as the pastoral king, had it that Louis could only be spoken of as "a do-nothing king, of whom history will not say that he had defeated all the Nations of Europe as had his great-grandfather, but that he made war only on deer."[37]

Beginning in 1736, public dismay at Louis's addiction to hunting was joined by worries over his reported heavy drinking. Reports that Louis's personality was being altered "by the excessive quantity of wine [he] drinks at parties with the lords of his court" began to raise public fears that the king was ruining his health. By 1737 rumor had it that because of the "excess of wine" consumed daily, the king had aged, lost weight, and was seriously ill, and that his physicians had given him only six months to live if he did not restrict his drinking. It was soon reported that wine was no longer strong enough for the king, that he was now mixing different liquors which he and his "companions in debauchery" consumed until they collapsed on the floor and "lost their reason." Additional "evidence" for the corruption of the royal body came from reports in 1738 that the king had promenaded drunk along the roof of Versailles, causing some to fear that "the mind of this prince is dissipating, and that he was falling into madness." It would not be long before it was said that the king was spitting blood.[38]

---

tried to rescue him from the charge of laziness and indifference, but acknowledge that Louis's retiring personality did not help matters; see especially Antoine, *Louis XV*. On Louis's withdrawal from the public sphere, see J. de Viguerie, "Le Roi et le public: L'Exemple de Louis XV," *Revue historique*, no. 563 (1987): 23–34.

37. Marais, *Journal*, 2:421; BA, AB MS. 10155, fols. 17, 145, 153; AB MS. 101558, fol. 164. A similar rhetorical strategy was used in a song circulating in 1732 that satirized the government's handling of the Jansenist stronghold of St. Médard: "Without powder and without canon / He [Louis] closed St. Médard in his name / These are his war exploits" (BN, ms. fr. 15133, fol. 113).

38. BA, AB MS. 10165, fol. 501; AB MS. 10166, fols. 139, 159, 165, 216, 248, 524. The duc de Luynes (*Mémoires*, 1:287–88) corroborates the claim that Louis walked on the roof of Versailles with his companions in this period, though he does not indicate that Louis was intoxicated at the time.

While public concern for the king's health and sanity was reported to be genuine, police spy reports suggested that this concern was less a result of genuine affection for the king than of the political effects his death might have. Fears persisted of a possible Spanish intervention in French dynastic affairs. To be sure, in 1729 a dauphin was born, and he was for three years joined by a brother who died in 1733. But given the dauphin's young age and reportedly uncertain health, "many people" were said to think that Louis's death would still be "the worst disaster that could happen to the state," that it would create division within the kingdom and allow a pro-Spanish party to form and seek the succession of a Spanish Bourbon should the dauphin die in turn.[39] As for Louis's rapport with his people, the king was time and again reported to be a figure both remote and uncaring. One report had it that he had failed to punish a royal Swiss guard who had raped and killed a girl of nine. Another indicated that Louis had given the fishwives of Paris such a cold reception when they arrived at Versailles to offer their compliments on one of Louis's many recoveries from illness—a much colder reception, they said, than those they had received on similar occasions under Louis XIV—that they promised never to come again. Speculating on an appropriate sobriquet for an effigy of the king, one wag reportedly suggested that none was more appropriate than "Louis the Taciturn."[40] But much more was at issue here than callousness and diffidence: during the food shortage of 1740, persistent rumor directly implicated the king in a plot to profit from grain speculation at the expense of his own people, as it would ten years later in a plot to abduct children.[41]

Louis's reported behavior understandably led some observers to impugn his innate moral character and intelligence; in their eyes, Louis appeared "stupid" and an "imbecile."[42] But the more common and more charitable interpretation of his behavior was in its way more politically explosive. Louis, according to one endlessly repeated line of argument, was inclined toward selfishness and self-indulgence and avoided serious involvement in state affairs because he had been purposely miseducated

39. BA, AB MS. 10166, fol. 485; AB MS. 10167, fol. 115.

40. BA AB MS. 10158, fols. 120, 317; AB MS. 10165, fol. 44.

41. On the king's involvement in the "famine plot," see BA, AB MS. 10167, fol. 133; and for a general analysis, Steven Kaplan, *The Famine Plot Persuasion in Eighteenth-Century France*, Transactions of the American Philosophical Society, n.s., 72, pt. 3 (Philadelphia: American Philosophical Society, 1982), 44–45. On the king's imputed role in child abduction, see Farge and Revel, *Logiques de la foule*, 121ff.

42. BA, AB MS. 10161, fols. 181, 207. As one political song put it, "Is he a Tyrant, (no) / He is a fool" (AB MS. 10161, fol. 403).

by the cardinal Fleury, who had sought to concentrate power in his own hands by endlessly diverting the king from his duties. "He is not naturally bad, and if something happens in his Kingdom detrimental to his Subjects, it is not his doing, but that of his Ministers." Lacking not so much a will to do good as any controlling political will at all, the king became discursively represented as a slave of his own appetites and the puppet of a ministerial clique, while the body politic incorporated within his own rotting person became depicted as vulnerable to the influence of nefarious forces, not the least of which was the Jesuits. "Those who frequent the court say the king in no way knows what is happening in his kingdom, that His Majesty leaves everything to M. Cardinal Fleury, . . . in short, that M. Cardinal Fleury is the King of the King."[43]

Serious as matters seemed, the public persistently nursed the hope that the king would retake control of his body and his state—the connection between the two is clear—and it reacted positively to whatever sporadic evidence it had that such was taking place. A report of 9 May 1737 noting how the public was "thrilled to learn the King is taking precautions to manage his health according to the salutary advice given to His Majesty" contained as well the news that the public thought Louis was finally getting interested in affairs of state, "for which people hope the most and expect to result in a great good."[44] Although this apparent invigoration of the royal will passed quickly, the death of cardinal Fleury in January 1743 once again raised hopes that Louis would finally settle down to the business of governing himself, now that this former preceptor, first minister, and reputed royal alter ego was gone from the scene. Even if skeptics remained, the diarist Barbier reported that the public in general regarded "the king with admiration" for having declared to his ministers that he would be ready to hear pressing concerns of state at any time. "He is accessible, he speaks wonderfully, he renders justice, and he works with knowledge of affairs," Barbier observed, a sentiment reflected as well in a police report recording that the public had begun to perceive in the king a trace of Louis XIV's dedication because of his new promise that he would not allow his trips and pleasures to interrupt his work.[45]

As it turned out, Louis's apparent inability to maintain interest in public affairs reasserted itself, causing a particularly serious letdown in many

43. BA, AB MS. 10159, fol. 270; AB MS. 10160, fols. 129, 145, 193; AB MS. 10162, fols. 263, 320; AB MS. 10168, fol. 279; AB MS. 10161, fol. 218.

44. BHVP, MS. 616, fol. 142.

45. Edmond-Jean-François Barbier, *Journal historique et anecdotique du règne de Louis XV* (Paris, 1847–56), 2:350; BHVP, MS. 623, fol. 126.

observers of the monarchy both inside and outside the government and instilling a terrifying sense of political drift. Ministers were being chosen or rejected on temperamental whims, noted the marquis d'Argenson in early April 1743, and what, he asked himself, did the king have to show after two months for his new supposed leadership?[46] Louis's apparently irremediable inability to act decisively, wrote the cardinal de Tencin of the Royal Council to the duc de Richelieu in October, was allowing individual ministers to run their departments virtually without direction from the king.[47] The maréchal de Noailles—the king's confidant and influential adviser, a seasoned government official and a top military commander—summed up the situation in a letter to Louis of 8 July: an escalating crisis of state had now developed, he warned, "a sort of enervation, indolence, and numbness in all the parts of the administration of the government to which the fastest remedy must be applied, without which, Sire, your kingdom will be menaced by the greatest disasters." If paralysis at the top was causing chaos in the state, he contended in a subsequent *mémoire*, the result was not only poor administration, but a crippling blow to the domestic and foreign prestige of the monarchy. "The public and foreigners assert that the government has no fixed plan; it is easy to imagine the bad effects that such an opinion must be producing and the general discredit that must be the result."[48]

In his correspondence with the king, Noailles proceeded to call for a new, general plan intended to reinvigorate and coordinate the various activities of state and "to raise opinion as much at home as abroad," but he frankly warned Louis that the plan would have to bear the king's personal mark; "It must be the work of Your Majesty. . . . It must be [Your Majesty] who speaks, decides, and orders as master."[49] Seizing on an already circulating notion that Louis would now make his debut as field commander of his armies,[50] Noailles on 16 August recognized such a personal intervention of the king as the sine qua non of his entire plan to

46. René de Voyer de Palmy, marquis d'Argenson, *Journal et mémoires du marquis d'Argenson*, 9 vols. (Paris: Mme Veuve Jules Renouard, 1859–67), 4:60–61.

47. Bibliothèque Victor Cousin, MS. 64, fol. 158.

48. Camille Roussel, ed., *Correspondance de Louis XV et du maréchal de Noailles* (Paris: P. Dupont, 1865), 1:147–48, 2:61. According to Antoine, *Louis XV*, Noailles had the greatest influence over the king during this period. See also BA, AB MS. 10029 (Journal de Mouchy), fol. 146, which notes the king's "blind confidence" in Noailles.

49. Roussel (ed.), *Correspondance*, 2:69.

50. Antoine, *Louis XV*, 363–64, cites a letter of April 1743 to the duc de Broglie in which Louis expressed a strong desire to go to the front, not in order to gain personal glory, but to share the pains of his soldiers.

rescue the king and the state, being "indispensable in every respect," "the only means to save your State which is in danger, as one should not hide from you," and the best means to ensure "the personal honor of Your Majesty." What was particularly striking in Noailles's argument was his insistence that royal firmness and recourse to military action not be allowed to inspire fresh visions and imputations of French wars of conquest, which had in the past "revolted all Europe against the ambition of France" and given rise to "all odious reproaches that had called for total sacrifice against its aggrandizement." Declaring war against "the spirit of conquest," Noailles urged the king to work for peace, to act openly, and to commit himself to the rigid rule of law: "A king of France, in governing himself invariably by maxims, is necessarily a great King," wrote Noailles, and "his credit and influence will always be proportionate to the opinion one has of his justice, his fidelity, and his firmness."[51]

Over the next nine months, Noailles, supported by the king's mistress, Madame de la Tournelle (later the duchesse de Châteauroux), planned with Louis his arrival at the front, selecting the optimal time for the king's military debut—"the most likely to cover in glory and to reestablish the prosperity of his affairs"—with a studied calculation worthy of the best public relations agent. To be sure, diplomatic and military factors also came into play in this calculation, but clearly more than field position was at issue when, for example, Noailles pointed out to Louis in a letter of 11 September how a defeat soon after the king's arrival "would be one of the most unhappy events."[52] News of the king's intentions began to leak out such that over the early months of 1744 his impending departure for Flanders became a common topic of conversation in such places as the Café Procope.[53] On 3 May 1744, Louis left Versailles for the front in Flanders.

The attempt to rescue the king's glory by way of his personal appearance at the front led a few months later to the critical moment at Metz, but its

51. Roussel (ed.), *Correspondance*, 1:181; 2:90, 121, 123. On the image France tried to cultivate abroad in the mid–eighteenth century, see Albert Babeau, "L'Appel à l'opinion publique de l'Europe au milieu du XVIIIe siècle," *Séances et travaux de l'Académie des sciences morales et politiques*, n.s., 162 (1904): 161–78.

52. Roussel (ed.), *Correspondance*, 2:13. Antoine, *Louis XV*, 364, points out that had the king himself fought at the front in this period, he would have had to do so under the command of the Elector of Bavaria and later Holy Roman Emperor, which would have constituted an unacceptable affront to the royal dignity. The involvement of the duchesse de Châteauroux is indicated in Marie-Anne de Nesle, duchesse de Châteauroux, *Correspondance de Mme. de Châteauroux*, in *Mémoires de la duchesse de Brancas*, ed. Eugène Asse (Paris: Librairie des Bibliophiles, 1890), 106ff.

53. BHVP, MS. 624, fol. 6; BA, AB MS. 10029 (Journal de Mouchy), fol. 131.

political significance can be grasped only if it is placed within the long tradition of early modern political misogyny and sexual slander. For no sooner had Louis arrived in Flanders than two of his mistresses, the duchesse de Châteauroux and Madame de Lauraguais—sisters not only to one another but also to two earlier mistresses of the king—arrived as well, thereby setting in motion a complex of responses that had their roots deep in the political culture of the Old Regime.

Although the history of political misogyny and sexual slander remains to be written, recent research has made abundantly clear the highly gendered nature of Old Regime institutions and the deep fears regarding rule by women that infused them.[54] What motivated such fears was not simply belief in the innate incapacity of women for sovereign rule, developed at length by Jean Bodin,[55] but also suspicions regarding the ease with which women could undermine the entire mission of the state by corrupting the king's natural goodness: "The public danger does not lie at all in that a women is called Queen, or wears a crown," wrote one polemicist, "but in that most often she governs everything through the cravings of immoderate passions."[56] As Bishop Bossuet put it to the court in the next century, nothing puts us further from the path God has chosen for us than the pursuit of sensual pleasure, for it overwhelms and disorients reason, making it unable to "respond to itself" and, in leading us to seek ever-changing ends, distracts us from the one true good.[57]

To be sure, it was generally conceded that the king was entitled to enjoy many pleasures, including sexual gratification outside marriage. Indeed, royal entertainments celebrated the king's pursuit of such pleasures as an agreeable aspect of his humanity, and, as in the case of Louis XIV, even clergymen like Bossuet were forced to accommodate themselves to

54. For a theoretical perspective, see Carole Pateman, *The Sexual Contract* (Stanford: Stanford University Press, 1988); and for institutions, see the now classic article of Sarah Hanley, "Engendering the State: Family Formation and State Building in Early Modern France," *French Historical Studies* 16 (1989): 4–27. On specific cases, see Jeffrey Merrick, "Sexual Politics and Public Order in Late-Eighteenth-Century France: The *Mémoires Secrets* and the *Correspondance Secrète*," *Journal of the History of Sexuality* 1 (1990): 68–84; Thomas E. Kaiser, "Madame de Pompadour and the Theaters of Power," *French Historical Studies* 19 (1996): 1025–44; and the literature, too vast to indicate here, on Marie Antoinette. On the common use of sexual slurs against women in the eighteenth century, see David Garrioch, "Verbal Insults in Eighteenth-Century Paris," in *The Social History of Language*, ed. Peter Burke and Roy Porter (Cambridge: Cambridge University Press, 1987), chap. 5.

55. Jean Bodin, *Les Six Livres de la république* (n.p.: Fayard, 1986), vol. 6, bk. 6, chap. 5.

56. *Discours merveilleux de la vie, actions et déportemens de la reyne Cathérine de Médicis, Roine Mère* (n.p., 1578), lxxxi.

57. Jacques-Bénigne Bossuet, "Troisième Dimanche de Carême . . . prêché à la Cour, en 1662," *Oeuvres complètes de Bossuet* (Paris, 1862), 2:278.

their sovereign's many adulterous relationships.[58] Yet there was a persistent concern underlying the celebration of *les menus plaisirs* that the king might be overindulging himself to the detriment of the public good and that, in particular, royal mistresses—whose proximity to the royal person could give them a special influence over the royal will—had subverted that will through seduction for purposes of retaining their position or, worse, interfering directly in the affairs of state. Hence, the monarchy repeatedly tried to reassure the public that the king was not abandoning his royal duties and that the pleasures he sought humanized him but did not turn his head. "Louis is always wise, he regulates his desires," ran the text of one Benserade royal ballet, "and rises above his pleasures." "The shepherd [i.e., Louis] is never without something to do," went another, " . . . business goes before pleasure." And again: "Even though he is at an age when we feel a strong desire for pleasure, do not believe his pleasure wins out, he always returns to his sheep."[59] In his behavior at court, noted Ezéchiel Spanheim, Louis affected "to have no favorites or mistresses except to refresh his spirit or to satisfy his passion, giving them no more control of his will or of government."[60]

Scattered evidence from court journals indicates that Louis XIV was thought to have successfully insulated his pursuit of women from royal governance during the early part of his personal reign. Louise de La Vallière, who was later held up frequently as a model royal mistress, was considered either to have had too "little mind" (Madame de La Fayette) or been too "tender and virtuous" (Madame de Caylus) to have had political ambitions; as Madame de La Fayette put it, "She dreamed only of being loved by the king and of loving him."[61] As the reign proceeded, how-

58. Jean-Marie Apostilidès, *Le Roi-machine: Spectacle et politique au temps de Louis XIV* (Paris: Editions de Minuit, 1981), 99, points out that royal gazetteers reassured the public after each royal fête that such diversions helped the king do his job better. On royal mistresses and the Church, see Guy Chaussinand-Nogaret, *La Vie quotidienne des femmes du roi d'Agnès Sorel à Marie-Antoinette* (n.p.: Hachette, 1990), chap. 4; and Georges Couton, *La Chair et l'âme: Louis XIV entre ses maîtresses et Bossuet* (Grenoble: Presses Universitaires de Grenoble, 1995).

59. Isaac de Benserade, *Les Oeuvres de Monsieur Benserade* (Paris, 1697), 2:367, 360, 285.

60. Ezéchiel Spanheim, *Relation de la cour de France en 1690* (Paris: H. Loones, 1882), 3. Louis advised the duc d'Anjou to take time to amuse himself, but never to abandon business for pleasure; see his *Mémoires pour les années 1661 et 1666, suivis des réflexions sur le métier de roi, des instructions au duc d'Anjou et d'un projet de harangue* (Paris: Editions Bossard, 1923), 229.

61. Mme de LaFayette, *Histoire de Madame d'Henriette d'Angleterre*, and Mme. de Caylus, *Souvenirs de Mme de Caylus*, in *Nouvelle Collection des mémoires pour servir à la France* (Paris, 1839), 8:189, 480–81, respectively. The abbé Choisy attributed to La Vallière "no ambition, no views" (quoted in Georges Mongrédien, *La Vie privée de Louis XIV* [Paris: Hachette, 1938], 74).

ever, perceptions of the king's mistresses began to change. Madame de Montespan, more "ambitious" for herself and a far more imposing presence at court, was a fairly controversial figure.[62] Yet of all Louis's mistresses, it was Madame de Maintenon, later Louis's morganatic wife, who generated the most vicious and greatest quantity of criticism. Although Maintenon had her defenders, who doted on her piety, her somewhat mysterious relationship with the king—she spent time alone with him almost daily—ignited the worst fears at court and beyond regarding the usurpation of royal authority. "Success, complete confidence, rare dependence, total power, universal public adoration of ministers, generals of armies, the most intimate royal family," wrote Saint-Simon, "all, in a word, at her feet; everything considered acceptable with her, everything objectionable without her, men, business, things, decisions, justice, favors, religion, everything without exception in her hand, the King and the State her victims." "People no longer doubt the refined politics of Mme. de Maintenon, who gives her protection in turn to each minister to engage them in her interests and who balances their authority," noted the marquis de Sourches in 1686.[63] Within and outside the court there circulated songs advancing similar themes.[64] "It is said that one prince today / Controls everything himself; / This is but a slander. / A women in penance, / Widow of a little turd, / Holds the tiller of France; / That is the pure truth." Or: "A King by his victory / Once crowned / Loses the luster of his glory / By a fool governed; / Everywhere one hears it said / Unhappy day! / Cursed is the rule of his love."[65]

In such lyrics and other literature, many of the tropes used earlier in reference to presumed power-hungry women were repeated, just as they

62. For conflicting comment, see Mme de Caylus, *Souvenirs*, 482; Saint-Simon, *Mémoires*, 28:179; and Mme de Sévigné, *Lettres de Madame de Sévigné, de sa famille, et de ses amis* (Paris: Hachette, 1862–66), 5:421. Louis's relatively brief relationship with Mlle de Fontanges appeared more like Louis's relationship with La Vallière; according to Mme de Caylus (*Souvenirs*, 480), the king was attracted only to her face and was ashamed of her speech and "stupidity," while the ascerbic Liselotte thought her "beautiful as an angel . . . but . . . a stupid little fool." See also Elisabeth-Charlotte de Bavière, quoted in John Wolf, *Louis XIV* (New York: W. W. Norton, 1968), 321.

63. Saint-Simon, *Mémoires*, 28:214; Louis-François de Bouchet, marquis de Sourches, *Mémoires du marquis de Sourches sur le règne de Louis XIV* (Paris, 1882–93), 1:379.

64. Like the authorship of this material, the audience for the literature discussed below is hard to determine, but police records suggest that political songs did circulate beyond the capital. BN, ms. fr. N.A. 1891, fol. 75, shows that in 1706 a number of individuals were arrested for having composed "insolent songs against the King and Mme. de Maintenon" and for having "spread them in Paris and in the Kingdom."

65. P. G. Brunet, *Le Nouveau Siècle de Louis XIV, ou choix de chansons historiques et satiriques presque toute inédites de 1674 à 1712* (Paris, 1857), 193, 310.

would be reiterated with regard to Madame de Pompadour and Marie Antoinette: the king has lost control of his reason—"it is Maintenon / who guides the king's reason"; "Gods, what horrible disorder / Louis, your reason sleeps"; the woman is a demon—"I have seen under the cloak of a women / A demon lay down the law"; "this shrew of Hell / Who imposes on us her rule of iron;" "Detestable creole witch / Fatal Maintenon"; the woman is a prostitute—"See this holy whore / How she controls this empire;" the king must reassert control over his own sexuality to reestablish the people as the proper object of his love—"Reign over yourself, it is time / You will make fewer malcontents, / Choose sincere Ministers / And be the Father of your People."[66]

Demonic possession aside, it was by no means immediately obvious to contemporaries precisely how Madame de Maintenon, a woman three years older than Louis and no longer the beauty she had once been, maintained her hold over the king. This was a mystery to which a generation of contemporary prose writers, claiming to base their accounts on "veritable" sources and often concealing their true publishers under fictitious names, devoted ever more fantastic accounts.[67] Two explanations gained currency in this connection. The first, which impugned Maintenon's piety as a mere cover for her supposed nefarious dealings, contended that she had been seduced by the king's allegedly lubricious Jesuit confessor, Père La Chaise, and that La Chaise had used his spiritual influence over Louis XIV to reinforce her position of power while conspiring with her to lead Louis into wars of "universal monarchy" against Protestant powers.[68] A second, more widely circulated explanation—one sufficiently credible for the usually sober marquis d'Argenson to take seriously—centered on Madame de Maintenon's school for aristocratic young women, Saint-Cyr, which, according to such accounts, provided a never-ending source of nubile young females for Louis's pleasure. Having lost her own sexual allure, Madame de Maintenon could maintain her position of power in-

66. BN, ms. fr. 12694, fols. 524, 179; ms. fr. 12695, fols. 675, 654; ms. fr. 12694, fol. 443; Brunet, *Nouveau Siècle*, 237; BN, ms. fr. 12695, fol. 656.

67. Some of this literature is examined in H. Gillot, *Le Règne de Louis XIV et l'opinion publique en Allemagne* (Paris: E. Champion, 1914), 21–27; and P.J.W. Malssen, *Louis XIV d'après les pamphlets répandus en Hollande* (Amsterdam: H. J. Paris, 1936). For the use of one prominent publisher's pseudonym, see Léonce Janmart de Brouillant, *La Liberté de la presse en France au XVIIe et XVIIIe siècles: Histoire de Pierre du Marteau, imprimeur à Cologne* (Geneva: Slatkine, 1971). A useful bibliography to such literature is provided in Ralph Coplestone Williams, *Bibliography of the Seventeenth-Century Novel in France* (New York: Century, 1931), 218ff.

68. Anon., *La Cassette ouverte de l'illustre créole, ou les amours de madame de Maintenon* (Villefranche, 1691); Anon., *Histoire du père La Chaise* (Cologne, 1693, 1695).

definitely by serving as madam of this royal "seraglio" on the periphery of Versailles. "As soon as the King has cast his eyes on some Nymph, . . . Mme de Maintenon takes great care to catechize her and to instruct her in the manner in which she should receive the honor that the King pays her."[69]

The ultimate impact of Madame de Maintenon's usurpation of royal prerogative was represented as the emasculation of the king. The king's oversexuality, his "too much love," was explicitly linked to royal impotence —excess, in other words, giving rise to insufficiency.[70] Much the same symbolic neutering of the royal body was effected mythologically by drawing on an ancient Roman variant of the Hercules corpus, a corpus that had previously often been used to enhance monarchical glory. Directing this variant against the monarchy, satirists now recast Madame de Maintenon in the role of Omphale, a Lydian queen with whom Hercules—the epitome of Louis XIV—had become so infatuated that he had exchanged his lion's skin for her clothes and performed at her feet the traditionally female gender-linked task of spinning yarn. "He wants to follow the path of Hercules," went one political song of 1710, "And for the queen Omphale / Spin until death." Referring explicitly to the same myth, another text remarked upon the "weakness, which effeminates the courage of a hero, and makes him lose all the luster of his most sublime qualities."[71]

Louis XV's accession to the crown in 1715 at the age of five would suspend the leveling of this sort of sexual slander at the reigning king himself, but this did not mean that those who had been or were closely associated with the monarchy would now be spared. For one thing, works directed against Louis XIV and his mistresses and first published during

69. Anon., *Suite de la France galante, ou les derniers dérèglements de la cour*, in Roger de Rabutin, comte de Bussy, *Histoire amoureuses des Gaules, suivie des romans historico-satiriques du XVIIe siècle*, ed. Paul Boiteau and C. L. Livet (Paris, 1856–76), 3:151. See also Anon., *L'Esprit familier de Trianon, ou l'apparition de la duchesse de Fontange* (Paris, 1695); Anon., *Le Tombeau des amours de Louis le Grand, & ses dernières galanteries* (Cologne, 1695); Anon., *Scarron apparu à madame de Maintenon et les reproches qu'il lui fait sur ses amours avec Louis le Grand* (Cologne, 1694). Gillot, *Règne*, 26, discusses variants of this account, including one in which Louis gains his title of *père du peuple* as a result of his seduction of nine-year-olds, and one in which young victims of royal debauch were housed in a convent near Paris. On d'Argenson's discussion of Saint-Cyr as a royal bordello, see his *Journal*, 1:20–21.

70. Anon., *Les Nouvelles Amours de Louis XIV* (1691), in DeBois-Jourdain, *Mélanges historiques, satiriques et anecdotiques* (Paris, 1807), 1:138.

71. BN, ms. fr. 12694, fol. 533; Anon., *Scarron*, 22. On the classical sources of the Hercules/Omphale myth, see *Dictionnaire des antiquités grecques et romaines* (Paris: Hachette, 1900), 3:100.

the previous reign continued to circulate, as indicated by police records that chronicle frequent arrests of individuals accused of distributing such materials through the 1730s.[72] For another, the Regency—infamous for such works as Voltaire's "Puer Regnante" and Lagrange-Chancel's *Les Philippes*, which accused the regent of incest, sodomy, and the attempted murder of Louis XV—provided an ample target for fresh sexual slander, as did, to a lesser extent, the administration of the duc de Bourbon and succeeding ministries.[73] The point to be emphasized here is that at the time Louis XV began his active pursuit of women, the long tradition of sexual slander reflecting deep suspicions of women and of their political influence was surely still alive and available for deployment against any public figure, not excepting the king himself.

Begun sometime in the mid-1730s, the king's extramarital liaisons became matters of public knowledge by 1737, at which time they do not appear to have aroused much negative comment.[74] Indeed, there were those who approved of them, such as the diarist Barbier, who suggested in January 1739 that such dalliance might at least distract Louis from his inordinate passion for hunting and help "improve his mind and sentiments."[75] In these early years, some observers even doubted that the king had much interest in sex, that because he was "susceptible to no passion for women" his liaison with Madame de Mailly would be "without consequence" and that because the king "does not like women and has a fickle mind" no long-term relationship would be possible. Some remarked upon the "modest" sums Louis was said to be granting Madame de Mailly (a mere 10,000 livres a month), suggesting that they were so small it seemed as

72. BN, ms. fr. N.A. 1891, fols. 105ff. As noted above, Mme de Maintenon did not leave behind a uniformly bad reputation. According to La Beaumelle, she was "regarded at Saint-Cyr as a saint, at the court as a hypocrite, in Paris as a person of intellect, and in all the rest of Europe as a women without morals [*moeurs*]." Whatever the precise situation, La Beaumelle, in trying to restore her reputation in his 1756 edition of her works, noted that she had been "outraged in a thousand *libelles*," whose authors—"discontented *officiers*, over-credulous foreigners, impassioned Huguenots"—had impugned her with the "crimes of Agrippina and Brunehault." See Laurent Angliviel de La Beaumelle, *Mémoires pour servir à l'histoire de madame de Maintenon* (Amsterdam, 1756), 1:viii.

73. Joseph de Lagrange-Chancel, *Les Philippiques, odes* (Paris, 1875); François-Marie Arouet de Voltaire, *Oeuvres complètes*, ed. Louis Moland (Paris, 1877–85), 1:296. BN, ms. fr. N.A. 1891, fol. 157, for example, records the arrest of a M. Mahudel in 1725 for distributing *libelles* against the government with illustrations that were "licentious and against good mores." A compilation of the supposed misdeeds of female French rulers over the ages was published anonymously during the French Revolution under the title *Les Crimes des reines de France depuis le commencement de la monarchie jusqu'à Marie-Antoinette* (Paris, 1791).

74. BA, AB MS. 10166, records intermittent comment beginning in the spring of 1737.

75. Barbier, *Journal historique*, 2:212.

though she could not possibly be his mistress, or, if she was, that she must be motivated by true love. If Louis's early liaisons were criticized, it was because of the coldhearted, ungallant way in which he was thought to be hurting the queen by parading his mistresses through Versailles, something that, it was said, Louis XIV had never done out of consideration for Marie-Thérèse. Such actions, according to one report, clearly indicated that "Louis the Fourteenth had feelings, but that Louis the Fifteenth has none of any sort."[76]

Although there remained those who did not begrudge the king the sort of extramarital affairs common among members of the court, commentary began to grow more hostile around 1740. The king's refusal to touch for scrofula—hitherto practiced four times a year—and his nonobservance of Easter in 1739, which, according to Barbier, caused great scandal in Versailles and Paris, were linked directly to his liaison with Madame de Mailly.[77] Although some still thought the two were incompatible—"Bacchus and love do not get along"—the "debauchery" previously associated with the king's heavy drinking now began to become associated with the king's supposedly more active sexual life. "It continues to be said that the court is a land of debauchery and voluptuousness," ran one police spy report of February 1740, "that the ladies there are most lascivious and work at nothing but to corrupt the court with the luxury that surrounds them. . . . There is no lady of the court who does not aspire to become to the King what . . . Mailly is to his Majesty." By April, rumors circulated that the king intended to "wallow" in adultery, that the king's licentious behavior was setting an example that all courtiers had begun to imitate, that all ladies of the court were concubines of the king. In September it was reported that the tower at the royal château of Choisy had been garnished with placards reading "Royal Bordello." In January 1741, drawings of secret parties of the king with Madame de Mailly and other courtiers were reported circulating through Paris, and in March it was reported that the duc de Tremouille had died from smallpox contracted at these "parties of pleasure." By 1742 the king had become sufficiently associated with the pursuit of sexual pleasure to trigger the ancient worries over female usurpation of power. Songs passed through the court and capital attributing to Madame de Mailly "all the hardships we feel."[78]

It is hardly a surprise, then, that when the project to send the king to

76. BA, AB MS. 10166, fols. 355, 365, 217.

77. Pierre Narbonne, *Journal des règnes de Louis XIV et Louis XV de l'année 1702 à l'année 1744* (Paris, 1866), 616; Barbier, *Journal historique*, 2:223–24.

78. BA, AB MS. 10167, fols. 73, 45, 88, 144, 46, 243; BHVP, MS. 626, fol. 251; MS. 623, fol. 123.

the front in Flanders arose, the duc de Noailles—though not the coterie around the duc de Richelieu, who sought to use the duchesse de Châteauroux as a means for exerting influence on the king—opposed her proposals to join Louis at the front. It was not easy, however, to dissuade either the duchesse or Louis—who, police reports suggest, was unaccountably unaware of how the many graces he had granted his new mistress had opened "the door to satire and impertinence." Although a police report of 25 April 1744 indicated that "we have finally made the King understand how it suits his glory that he not allow a mistress to follow him," the duchesse de Châteauroux and her sister joined him in June.[79]

The immediate impact of Louis's taking charge at the front was as great as Noailles had hoped. Reports received by the police praised the actions of the king, noting particularly his affability, goodness, and, perhaps most important, his ability "to make himself adored." Made public shortly after his departure, a letter to the dauphin, in which Louis wrote of his devotion to his people, had a wonderfully tonic effect on his subjects, according to the police, since it helped dispel the belief that Louis cared nothing for them. "The King has advanced a great deal in winning the hearts of his subjects," observed one police report; " . . . times have changed a great deal." When Louis won military encounters at Menin, Courtrai, and Ypres, the gap between the royal image and public opinion appeared to be closing. Although the public seemed proud of the king's military prowess, they emphasized not his lust for conquest, but—taking a leaf from the royal scriptwriters—his desire for peace. "He does not yield to the inhuman ardor / Which has only blood for its object / . . . It is peace that Louis wants to bring to the earth."[80]

Yet the prospect of a visit to Flanders by the king's mistresses haunted the public; while some, like the marquis d'Argenson, saw no real harm in Louis's dalliance at the front, others warned of "the most unhappy consequences for the king's glory."[81] To be sure, Louis XIV had visited the front with his mistresses, but only in the company of the queen, whose presence, as Primi Visconti noted, was necessary for the king to entertain his mistresses "without scandal."[82] But now there seemed no possibility that Marie Leszczynska would join the royal party. At the front, the "superstitious" Flemish reacted badly to the arrival of the duchesse de Château-

79. Roussel (ed.), *Correspondance*, 2:18; BA, AB MS. 10029, fol. 142.
80. BA, AB MS. 10029, fols. 150, 151, 159.; BHVP, MS. 625, fol. 4.
81. D'Argenson, *Journal*, 4:103–4; BA, AB MS. 10029, fol. 161.
82. Primi Visconti, *Mémoires . . . sur la cour de Louis XIV* (Paris: Perrin, 1988), 15.

roux and her sister in Lille, attributing a fire to celestial disapproval of their coming and serenading them charivari-style beneath their windows with the lyrics "Beautiful Châteauroux / I will become mad / If I do not make love to you."[83]

Matters came to a head in August, after eastern France was invaded and looted by the Austrians—and in response to which Louis left Flanders for Alsace. But on 8 August Louis fell ill, thereby setting in motion the celebrated scenes at Metz. Apparently on the verge of death, Louis was forced by the bishop of Soissons to confess and publicly repudiate his sexual promiscuity and to banish the royal mistresses; otherwise the bishop, himself involved in a political cabal against the Richelieu coterie, threatened to withhold last rites. Word of Louis's illness had already spread, causing great and, given the wartime conditions, understandable alarm. Whatever genuine feelings for Louis there may have been, these feelings were hedged with concerns that the Austrians might try to capitalize militarily on his illness, and the prospect of the succession of a dauphin not quite fifteen no doubt aroused fears as well.[84] Given these sentiments and the general hostility to the mistresses—who were widely blamed for Louis's illness and nearly murdered by angry crowds following their humiliating exile from Metz—it is understandable that the combination of Louis's repudiation of these two courtesans and his recovery later in August reportedly sent his subjects into paroxysms of joy, the likes of which France had not seen for decades. In ridding himself of disease and its apparent cause, the king, through the good offices of the bishop of Soissons, appeared, at least for the moment, to have purged the body politic of female-induced corruption and so resacralized it. "If God brings back this Charming King / [God's] Grace has made a Penitent / His Sins will then be Finished / Hallelujah."[85] From the standpoint of monarchical propaganda, what was crucial was the fact that after fifty years of insistence that the king and his people were bound by mutual love, there had now emerged apparently incontrovertible evidence that such truly was the case; the gap between image and reality finally seemed to have been closed.[86]

So critical a moment did this appear that the state's ideological apparatus lost no time in scripting the text for the months of celebrations to

83. D'Argenson, *Journal*, 4:104.

84. BHVP, MS. 625, fol. 90.

85. BN, ms. fr. 15134, fol. 912.

86. Boislisle, *Lettres*, 1:187, contains a letter from Maurepas to Marville that acknowledges "how [Louis] is dear to his subjects."

follow, and none other than Louis himself led this effort, indirectly overseeing the great festival held in Paris on 10 September and even personally selecting the medal struck to commemorate his recovery that bore the inscription "God the Conservator."[87] But it was an abbé Josset, canon of the cathedral in Metz, who on 25 August managed to compress into one sobriquet the most successful of all the laudations offered Louis:

> The Good King! The Great King! From the Other End of the Kingdom he came to our help, he came to defend these Frontiers from the ravages of the Enemy; his love for us made him disregard all the dangers of war. . . . No, no Prince was ever more . . . lamented, more bitterly mourned, more ardently desired; and if History one day gives him some title, what title more merited, more justly acquired, and more Honorable for a King than that of LOUIS LE BIEN-AIMÉ.[88]

It was of course precisely this title that history did grant him—with some considerable connivance of the crown. On 7 September, the police of Paris posted orders, which were also proclaimed orally by town criers, that instigated and regulated the celebration of the king's recovery and in particular commanded citizens to decorate and illuminate their houses. According to official reports, on the evening of 10 September all the shops of Paris, large and small alike, were bedecked with the inscription etched in lights "Long live Louis the *bien-aimé*."[89] On 17 September, Pannard's *Les Fêtes sincères*, hailing Louis as the *bien-aimé*, opened at the Comédie des Italiens, where it played for more than two months to audiences totaling nearly four thousand.[90] At least in one case the monarchy did almost literally put the words it wanted to hear in the mouths of its subjects: Jacques Bailly, general guardian of the king's paintings, composed a vaudeville, including the words "Louis my dear / Long live Louis the *Bien-Aimé*," that was recited by the fishwives of Les Halles on 10 September.[91] Needless to say, official news outlets of the crown covered such stories at length and in great detail, especially the *Mercure de France*, which

87. Archives Nationales, K. 1007, no. 146, contains many details on the organization of various celebrations, including the one on 10 September. On the medal, see Boislisle, *Lettres*, 1:189, 195.

88. Josset, *Compliment*, 4.

89. *Ordonnance de police qui enjoint aux Habitans de la Ville & des Faubourgs de Paris d'illuminer leur Fenestres le jeudy du présent mois, en rejouissance de l'heureux rétablissement de la Santé du Roy, 7 séptembre 1744; Gazette de France* 39 (19 September 1744), 453.

90. Clarence D. Brenner, *The Théâtre Italien: Its Repertory, 1716–1793* (Berkeley: University of California Press, 1961), 141–42.

91. *Mercure de France* 47 (1744): 2315–18.

devoted over a hundred pages to the many celebrations of the king's recovery and to public praise of the king's virtues.

So critical was the acquisition of the *bien-aimé* title to the ideological fortunes of the crown that the monarchy not only never abandoned it, but also turned the events surrounding conferral of the title into one of the reign's essential political myths. Two themes, from the very outset, would be stressed: first, the spontaneous, genuine nature of public grieving for the king in his illness and of public joy at his recovery, and second, the broad social base of such sentiment—comprising peasant, bourgeois, and aristocrat alike. There could be no mistaking the sincerity of the people's response to the king's actions, one journal put it, for it was easy to distinguish between "exterior demonstrations, which are merely the forced tribute of duty or convention, from the natural ecstasy that gives rise to sentiment." Journal coverage of celebrations in Paris by the *Gazette de France* caused at least one reader to remark on "the manner in which the title *Bien-Aimé* was given to the King, not by courtesans, but by the people." "One would say that joy has given place to no other sentiment," the *Gazette* observed, "that all Parisians composed but one single family, united by ties of tenderness as much as by those of blood, and that they were brothers concerned only with rejoicing at what their father has bestowed upon them."[92] It seemed as if the mystical body of the realm had been reconstituted and rejuvenated, held together by love under the paternal care of the king.

How well did the myth of the *bien-aimé* serve the long-range interests of the monarchy? There is no straightforward way to measure its benefits, but the evidence suggests that it ultimately proved highly problematic. At the core of the difficulties lay the contradiction of an absolutist regime deriving its informal—that is, nonjuridical—political authority from the love of its people. As pointed out above, the recasting of the king as the people's love object implicitly, and sometimes even explicitly, narrowed the distance between ruler and ruled, thereby serving to dispel the mystique of monarchy. When censors would grant permission, as they did to

92. *Suite de la clef, ou Journal historique sur les matières du tems* 56 (1744): 312; Président de Levy, *Journal historique, ou fastes du règne de Louis XV, surnommé le Bien Aimé* (Paris, 1766), 2:423n; *Gazette de France* 39 (1744): 454. To be sure, under Louis's later reign there was—understandably, considering the frequent warfare—a return to more militaristic representations of the king, but these representations continued to portray Louis as lover of peace, father, and so on. For an excellent discussion, see Jeffrey Merrick, "Politics on Pedestals: Royal Monuments in Eighteenth-Century France," *French History* 5 (1991): 234–64.

one anonymous poet, to write on the occasion of Louis's return to Paris from Metz, "Ah! to serve what one loves, is that obedience? / Be a citizen King, all citizens are King," obedience may have been made to seem sweeter and hence more acceptable, but at the same time sovereignty in the case of a "citizen King" became perilously close to being represented as popular rule.[93] Indeed, the emphasis on the sincerity and universality of Louis's acclamation after Metz made the king's mandate, albeit originally from God, seem almost elective. No one, Voltaire pointed out, knew whether the people loved the king better than the people themselves; if so, then investment of authority through love could not be a matter of obligation or customary law so much as choice.[94] "What Law solicits us to do," ran one poetic tribute, "Is never as valuable as a Voluntary Act; / . . . He is no longer King except by my free choice, / Such as he has done [is] such as I would choose / . . . If the Scepter is given for merit, / He should be elected, if he is not my born King."[95]

Such discourse would put later critics of royal policy in a strong rhetorical position to put pressure on the king when his policies, as they so often did, failed to attract wide support; for critics could now credibly threaten the king with loss of his authority should he continue to support the unpopular initiatives his administration had undertaken. Opponents of Maupeou would use Louis's sobriquet in such a manner to push Louis into dismissing the hated minister: "If the name of *Bien-Aimé* cannot naturally be taken from a good Prince, the luster of his glory would be obscured, however, by the hardness and tyranny of a Minister, if [the Prince] suffered his violence any longer. . . . Ah! Sire, prisons filled with your faithful subjects: Vincennes, the Bastille . . . *lettres de cachet* without number, hard exiles, espionage that holds us in fear: is that the reign of Louis the *Bien-Aimé*?"[96] Even more hostile critics, like a poet outraged by Louis's arrest of Charles Edward, the Pretender's son, pointed out the irony of the king's title, calling it "specious": "Examine the error of the title that was given to you / Louis the *Bien-Aymé* is Louis without a crown."[97] "Incestuous tyrant, inhuman traitorous forger," wrote another, "How dare

93. Anon., *Au Roy entrant à Paris à son retour de Metz* (Paris, 1744), 4 (censor's approval on 22 October 1744).

94. Voltaire, *Oeuvres*, 23:268.

95. Anon., *La Quatre-jovialinaire* (The Hague, 1745), 79–81.

96. Anon., *Maupeou tyran sous le règne de Louis le Bien-Aimé* (n.p., 1773), 92–93.

97. BHVP, MS. 649, fols. 56, 50. On this affair, see Thomas E. Kaiser, "The Drama of Charles Edward Stuart, Jacobite Propaganda, and French Political Protest, 1745–1750," *Eighteenth-Century Studies* 30 (1997): 365–81.

you arrogate to yourself the name of *Bien-Aymé?*"[98] If it was the people who had the authority to confer this title, it was now "your people" who "declare you unworthy."[99] By making popular acclaim such an important pillar of royal authority, the monarchy had opened itself up to moral blackmail and put the king under a continual obligation to satisfy public demands.

And the plain fact was that, apparently never truly popular during his early reign, Louis was even less so later, as higher taxes, Jansenist controversy, disappointing military outcomes, and other developments took their toll such that even the royalist Jacob-Nicolas Moreau had to admit at Louis's death, "Never was a prince less missed than the poor Louis XV."[100] The bookseller Hardy observed just how problems of the reign had undermined Louis's acquired title: "The decay of finance and the disorder that had been introduced for a number of years in all parts of the administration by a conduct as odious as it was reprehensible of different ministers . . . unhappily had caused Louis XV surnamed the *Bien-Aimé* to lose this glorious title that the people had awarded him in 1744 in the just ecstasy of their love."[101]

Especially important to the erosion of the *bien-aimé* title was Louis's return to promiscuity. For although Louis did banish his mistresses at Metz, he reinstated them three months later, causing much the same sort of letdown among his subjects that had occurred following earlier disappointments of reform hopes. In 1745 his liaison with Madame de Pompadour became a matter of instant public knowledge; and although this relationship did not at first meet with a universally hostile reaction, some almost immediately perceived in it a replay of Louis XIV's relationship with Madame de Maintenon (the Parc-aux-Cerfs under Pompadour would be imagined to serve the same purpose as Saint-Cyr under Maintenon) and yet another threat to the autonomy of the royal will. Inspired in part by the *parti dévot* centered on the queen and dauphin, a new wave of scurrilous attacks on the king's sexual life and on Pompadour passed through the public; devastating verbal assaults in the form of satirical songs and thinly veiled allegorical novels were accompanied by threats of assassination upon the latest object of the king's lust.[102] In the end, Pom-

98. Emile Raunié, ed., *Chansonnier historique du XVIIIe siècle* (Paris, 1879–84), 7:222.

99. Ibid.

100. Jacob-Nicolas Moreau, *Mes Souvenirs*, ed. Camille Hermelin (Paris, 1898–1901) 1:379.

101. BN, ms. fr. 6681 ("Mes loisirs"), fol. 335.

102. BHVP, MS. 580, fol. 244; MS. 649, fols. 55–56. On *dévot* discourse, see Van Kley, *Damiens*, 234–42. The novel literature includes Marie-Magdeleine de Bonafons, *Tanastés,*

padour would be charged with causing "anarchy, disorder, and all the woes of France," indeed, with having brought France to verge of "despotism."[103]

What needs emphasis here is that much as a royal liaison with an "ambitious" mistress might well have triggered anxiety over the custody of the state under any reign, Louis XV's relationships with his mistresses proved particularly problematic in a regime that relied so heavily for its authority on bonds of mutual love between the king and his subjects. For even if it was true, as one bishop thought, that the only thing necessary for a French king to make himself loved by his subjects was for him to love them,[104] Louis's promiscuity indicated that he lacked this minimal but essential prerequisite, since he appeared all too ready to sacrifice the good of his people to placate his ever-demanding mistresses. Already in the case of Madame de Mailly it was said that any natural love felt by Louis for his people had been lost out of "passion" for her, such that "he forgot with her all the rest of the world."[105] In much the same way later on, it would be written that Louis, "in letting the reins of his empire fall in the hands of [Pompadour]," had "seemed to renounce . . . the love of his peoples."[106] As one political song sadly put it, "the King regards Madame de Pompadour tenderly/ . . . and the People indifferently."[107] The crux of Louis's problem lay in the monarchy's inability, despite efforts to prove Louis a king with his subjects' best interests at heart, to overcome his image as a ruler "sensual, indelicate, and lazy," for whom "pleasure was the only object" and the satisfaction of his lusts preferable to winning "the love of all the French."[108] In the end, the king's two bodies appeared to be separating, as the mortal royal person sought pleasure and escape from

---

conte allégorique (The Hague, 1745); François-Vincent Toussaint, *Mémoires secrets pour servir à l'histoire de Perse* (Amsterdam, 1745); and [Laurent Angliviel de La Beaumelle], *Les Amours de Zéokinizal* (Amsterdam, 1748). The police were most concerned about *Tanastés* and incarcerated its author for nearly twelve years; see BA, AB MS. 11582, on her case. At her interrogation Bonafons said "her imagination had been helped by the discourse she had heard in public." According to the police, the work had acquired a wide reputation; see Boislisle, *Lettres*, 3:98–100.

103. [Bouffonidor], *Les Fastes de Louis XV, de ses ministres, généraux, et autres personnages de son règne* (Villefranche, 1782), 2:477; on Pompadour, the separation of the king's two bodies, and "despotism," see Kaiser, "Madame de Pompadour."

104. Jean-Louis Buisson de Beauteville, *Mandement . . . qui ordonne . . . des prières pour le repos de l'âme du feu roi* (Paris, 1774), 11.

105. [La Beaumelle], *Les Amours*, 53.

106. [Mouffle d'Angerville], *Vie privée*, 2:301.

107. BN, ms. fr. 13659, fol. 208*bis*.

108. Raunié, *Chansonnier*, 8:314–15.

responsibility in the boudoirs of the royal mistresses while the immortal royal *dignitas* was effectively abandoned.

In his account of the origins of the French Revolution, William Doyle contends that the French monarchy was "not overthrown by the opposition to its policies, much less by revolutionaries dedicated to its destruction," but fell, rather, "because of its own contradictions."[109] I have sought in this essay to demonstrate how the monarchy helped generate such contradictions with regard to royalist ideology by promoting an image of the king it could not sustain. Just as the monarchy's attempts to answer its critics in their own language of law and history ultimately prompted even more crushing critiques of royal policies and institutions, so did the crown's effort to construct Louis as the *bien-aimé* backfire, allowing opposition parties to exploit the gap between image and perceived reality. Thus, while the *parti dévot* hammered away at Louis's personal failings, the Jansenists and parlementaires struck at the juridical foundations of absolute monarchy. Indeed, the critiques of the king's person could only bolster the monarchy's institutional critics; for once the king's body and will were presumed to be corrupted, the French nation had every reason to seeks restraints and limits on the royal prerogative through constitutional means. The notion of the *bien-aimé*, a rhetorical trap of the monarchy's own design, provided one mechanism whereby the monarchy unwittingly helped to effect its own eventual demise.

109. William Doyle, *Origins of the French Revolution*, 2d ed. (Oxford: Oxford University Press, 1988), 115.

7

Dancing the Body Politic

Manner and Mimesis in Eighteenth-Century Ballet

SUSAN LEIGH FOSTER

Poised in her statuelike pose on the pedestal, choreographer and dancer Marie Sallé may well have glimpsed the swooning melancholy of her partner as he danced the role of the sculptor Pygmalion. Out of the corner of her eye, she may have followed his mimetic gestures as he prayed to Venus to bring her, a stone that he had carved and now the object of his desire, to life. She certainly heard the chordal changes indicating Venus's favorable response and announcing that she, as Galathea, was about to stir to life and participate in her own choreographic rendition of Ovid's story of Pygmalion. Did she realize, however, that the steps she was about to execute would create a scandal of international proportions, that a letter published in the *Mercure de France* describing her production would be reprinted in newspapers across Europe,[1] and that her choreography would inspire numerous plagiarized productions such as the one presented at the Comédie Italienne in Paris two months later?[2] Could she have foreseen that her approach to choreographic experimentation would eventually result in the separation of ballet from opera and the establishment of dance as an independent and autonomous art form?

According to the anonymous author of the *Mercure de France* letter,

1. M***, *Mercure de France*, April 1734, 770–772.

2. Renée Viollier's study of the composer Mouret, *Mouret, le musicien des grâces* (Geneva: Minkoff, 1976), provides a detailed account of the Paris performance whose scenario by Panard and l'Affichart was danced by Mlle Roland and Sr. Riccoboni to music by Mouret, who, according to Viollier, may also have composed the music for Sallé's *Pygmalion* (145).

Sallé's *Pygmalion* merited special acclaim for two kinds of radically innovative choreographic decisions: first, she chose to appear uncorseted and without wig or mask, and second, she interpolated movements from the vocabulary of pantomime to enable the dancing to tell a story without the aid of spoken or sung lyrics. What everyone who read the letter would also have known is that to implement her new choreographic concept she risked her reputation as *première danseuse* at the Paris Opéra and jeopardized her status as an employee of the king representing the most prestigious institutionalization of the arts of music and dance in all Europe.[3] They would also have noted that she presented her choreographic experimentation in a prestigious public, not private, venue, fusing in an unprecedented way the elite values of ballet with the populist medium of pantomime.[4] Pantomime, a familiar staple at fair theaters and street productions, was a medium that subverted, satirized, or circumvented narrative, but it had seldom been invoked as the principal means for sustaining a coherent and sentiment-filled exchange of thoughts and feelings among all those onstage, especially the sanctioned stage of the king.[5] Subsequent productions at the Paris Opéra for which Sallé served as choreographer incorporated pantomime, experimented with costume, and extended the danced dialogue among characters so as to create danced narratives. These pantomime ballets, occurring as single acts within the five-act opera-ballets *Les Indes galantes* (1735), *L'Europe galante* (1736), and *Les Fêtes d'Hébé* (1739), received enormous acclaim and were cited by subsequent generations of aestheticians and dance historians as pivotal works that prefigured in danced form the arguments for choreographic reform made by Denis Diderot and Jean Georges Noverre in the 1750s and 1760s.[6]

3. As an employee at the Opéra, Sallé's career was strictly controlled. Her *Pygmalion* was presented in London during one of the leaves granted her from the Opéra. She was never allowed to perform it at the Paris Opéra, nor was she permitted to dance on other Parisian stages. For details of her life and career, see Émile Dacier, *Une Danseuse de l'Opéra sous Louis XV: Mlle Sallé, 1707–1756* (Paris: Plon-Nourrit, 1909).

4. As early as 1715, the duchesse du Maine organized a highly publicized experiment with pantomime dance at her summer home, but this genre of entertainment had not yet reached patented house stages in France. In London, where pantomime played a more prominent role in many kinds of productions, ballet had never been cultivated to the extent it had in France. Sallé's appearances there exemplified the most refined dancing in all Europe.

5. Robert Isherwood, in *Farce and Fantasy: Popular Entertainment in Eighteenth-Century Paris* (New York: Oxford University Press, 1986), describes the fair theater performances in great detail and sets them in the context of other types of entertainment available to citizens of Paris during the period.

6. See, for example, Jean Georges Noverre's *Lettres sur la danse et les ballets* (Stuttgart and Lyon, 1760), published in English as *Letters on Dancing and Ballets,* trans. Cyril W. Beaumont

Audiences found in Sallé's dances a more compelling expressivity and a clearer and more lively interaction among characters. Yet these dances did not simply evidence a new generation's tastes and sensibilities coming to embodiment. Rather, they gestured toward an aesthetic rupture of enormous proportions. Sallé's choreography for Galathea, the work of art that comes to life, embraced two distinct aesthetic traditions—the baroque opera-ballet and the parodic pantomime—and from them bodied forth a third, the action or story ballet (*ballet d'action*). In so doing, Sallé forecast the dissolution of the opera-ballet and with it the demise of courtly codes of comportment that had informed aristocratic conduct and identity for generations. In its place, newly composed bodies, autonomous, self-propelling, and self-narrating, would take center stage, providing palpable justification for Enlightenment theories of the subject and of citizenship.

This essay examines the overhaul of choreographic conventions that Sallé helped to initiate, finding in them a theorization of the relationship between the individual and the state as eloquent as any articulated by the philosophes. The ballet performed in tandem with the vast array of cultural endeavors that accomplished the sweeping political changes of the eighteenth century. More vividly than most of these endeavors, however, the ballet exemplifies the changing conceptions of body and self on which the reformulation of the body politic would depend. Focus on the ballet and its development, particularly during the period of Sallé's career, yields new perspectives on Enlightenment thought and on the centrality of the body as a primary concern for those who aspired to reimagine the state. The example of the ballet also encourages a new acknowledgment of the persuasive political content of aesthetic form.

By the time of Sallé's productions, the evocative impact of the baroque opera-ballet, with its alternation between characters who sang the story and dancers who displayed the pomp, gaiety, or somberness of the situation, had begun to play itself out.[7] The haunting quality of these elegant danc-

---

(New York: Dance Horizons, 1966); and Denis Diderot's *Entretiens sur "Le Fils naturel"* and his *Discours sur la poésie dramatique*, both conveniently collected in the volume *Diderot's Writings on the Theatre*, ed. F. C. Green (Cambridge: Cambridge University Press, 1936). See also Diderot's "Lettre sur les sourds et muets" (1751), in *Oeuvres Complètes de Diderot*, ed. J. Assézat (Paris: Garnier Frères, 1875).

7. Rousseau's famous critique against the ballet's nonrealistic and antinarrative function can be found in *Julie, ou La Nouvelle Héloïse: Lettres de deux amants habitants d'une petite ville au pied des Alpes*, pt. 2, letter 23, pp. 265–66. But disenchantment with the opera

ing figures by now seemed vacant rather than suggestive. The symmetrical use of the dancers in their placement onstage, the floor patterns wherein two dancers mirrored each other throughout a duet, the just and regulated exchange of bodies in space—all were found boring rather than ennobling. The meaning of the lines they traced in space—a clear reference to noble conduct in former times—was no longer intelligible. An increasingly secularized and bourgeois viewer, searching for relevance in the dancers' abstract allusions, found only stifling references to an obscure gallantry.

The paintings of Antoine Watteau, especially as analyzed by Norman Bryson, provide an elegant account of what was in the process of becoming indecipherable.[8] Bryson argues that Watteau's emphasis on the eyes of his characters lent a passionate quality to the face, whereas the body was always depicted in a more stately and formal posture. The conflicting messages encouraged viewers to engage in endless reverie about the characters' state of being. Conversely, in those paintings by Watteau where figures were pictured at a far distance, the face remained ambiguous and the body became more eloquent. Bryson explains:

> Watteau's strategy is to release enough discourse for the viewer to begin to verbalize the image, but not enough in quantity or in specificity for the image to be exhausted. . . . With Watteau, discourse provides a way of triggering a powerful subjective reaction in the viewer—he hears unplayed music . . . describes the absence of explicit meaning as "melancholy" and "depth," and tries to fill the semantic vacuum set up by the painting with an inrush of verbal reverie.[9]

Through the insufficiency of discursive messages or through the collision of distinct messaging systems, therefore, the figures in Watteau's paintings contoured a plenitude which they always stopped short of filling.

---

ballets can be found much earlier in the writings of Toussaint de Rénard de Saint-Mard, *Réflexions sur l'opéra* (The Hague: Jean Neaulme, 1741); Francesco Algarotti, *Essai sur l'opéra* (1755), trans. into French by [F. J. de Chastellux] (Paris: Chez Rualt, 1773); Gaspare Angiolini, *Dissertation sur les ballets pantomimes des anciens, pour servir de programme de "Semiramis"* (Vienna, 1765); Louis de Cahusac in his article "Danse" for the *Encyclopédie* and also in *La Danse ancienne et moderne, ou traité historique de la danse*, 3 vols. (The Hague, 1754); and Diderot in his *Entretiens sur "Le Fils naturel."*

8. In *Word and Image: French Painting of the Ancien Régime* (Cambridge: Cambridge University Press, 1981), Norman Bryson contrasts the figural nonspecificity of meaning in Watteau's work with the discursive clarity of LeBrun, his predecessor, and Greuze, who followed a generation after. I find significant correspondences between Bryson's analysis of painting and the development of eighteenth-century ballet, as the following argument suggests. For his summary of Watteau's work, see 70–91.

9. Bryson, *Word and Image*, 74.

Choreography for the baroque opera-ballets operated in similar ways. In their relation to narrative, in the spatial configurations and dispositions of dancers in space, in the costuming, these ballets developed a nondiscursive space that allowed viewers the kind of sensuous reverie summoned up in Watteau's work. In baroque operas, characters who engaged in sung dialogues established identities and motivations and created the narrative action. Danced interludes, situated at key moments in the plot's development, suspended narrative action in order to expand on individual and group feelings. Whether joyful, mournful, nostalgic, or troubled, characters' states of being were elaborated through collections of dances whose movements resembled those feelings. Light, quick movements; measured, somber steps; meandering or buoyant phrases—each connected to the characters' identity at that moment in the story. The articulation of physicality presented in these dances never aspired to demonstrate the development through time of the characters' attitudes or feelings, nor was it necessary for dance to function in a narrational capacity. Instead, the dances proliferated the possible resonances of feelings in all their variation and nuance.

Take, for example, the choreographic rendition of an emotion such as melancholy. To elaborate on a character's melancholic reverie, dancers might well perform a slow sarabande in which the poignant suspensions and the stately, slow pacing of steps imparted a sense of restraint from full-blown physical exertion. Dancers seemed to hold back from any invigorating athleticism, and they also indulged in a weighty and languorous phrasing of steps.[10] The following description of a solo sarabande performance, although performed at court rather than onstage, gives a sense of the hesitations and shifts in mood through which melancholy would be constructed:

> Sometimes he would cast languid and passionate glances throughout a slow and languid rhythmic unit [cadence]; and then, as though weary of being obliging, he would avert his eyes, as if he wished to hide his passion; and, with a more precipitous motion, would snatch away the gift he had tendered.
>
> Now and then he would express anger and spite with an impetuous and turbulent rhythmic unit; and then, evoking a sweeter passion by more moderated motions, he would sigh, swoon, let his eyes wander languidly; and certain sinuous movements of the arms and body, nonchalant, disjointed, and passionate, made him appear so admirable and so charming that throughout this enchanting dance he won as many hearts as he attracted spectators.[11]

10. I am grateful to Linda Tomko whose historical and analytical understanding of the sarabande informed this section of the essay.

11. This description of a sarabande performance, translated by Patricia M. Ranum, appears in Father François Pomey's *Dictionnaire royal augmenté* (Lyon, 1671), 22 (copy now

The sudden changes in tempo and the quick retraction of the eyes and body from any fulsome enactment of sadness evoked melancholy through its allusions to the state of melancholia. The dancer did not look like a melancholic person so much as exemplify melancholy's languid, restless, and swooning qualities.

Whether dancing melancholy or joy, the choreography elaborated qualities shared with those feelings and also the requisite spatial harmony between and among all dancing bodies. Floor paths used to organize dancers' movements through space—symmetrical crossings side to side and upstage to downstage, woven circles, pinwheels, and diagonals—enmeshed dancers in harmonious patterns of spatial inscription. These patterns celebrated the justness of groups of dancers in symmetrical opposition to one another, the magnificent variety of geometrical pathways though space, and the felicitous resolution of asymmetrical configurations into balanced groupings. These dispositions for dancers emphasized the connections among bodies and the participation of each body in the ensemble over any individual body's momentum or gestural repertoire. Viewers might focus momentarily on a given dancer, but the choreography consistently reabsorbed the dancer into the overall patterning. This perpetual loss of contact, deliciously arresting, fueled the viewer's desire for further sightings, for more knowledge. Just as the delicate measuring of steps to music evoked innumerable affective associations, so the sweep of all bodies through space drew viewers continually into the affective world of the dance.

Costuming enhanced this inrush of affect, especially when the mask was used. The face, normally the vehicle for a mute form of discursive exchange both among dancers and between dancers and audience, was stilled by the mask. The masked face stared back at the audience, rebuffing spectators' search for familiar forms, transforming the known into the exotic. The absence of such highly specific information as the face would convey imparted a greater articulateness to the gestures of the limbs, the swaying of the torso, and the tiniest inclinations of the head. While the body's movement acquired greater expressivity through the neutrality of the face, the exact nature of the characters' thoughts or feelings remained ambiguous. As a result the character, like Watteau's figures, became a wistful apparition signaling poignantly toward the expressivity of feeling as well as toward feeling itself.

---

in Biblioteque Municipale Rodez). The passage is quoted in full in Meredith Little and Natalie Jenne's book *Dance and the Music of J. S. Bach* (Bloomington: University of Indiana Press, 1991), 93–94.

Choreography for the opera-ballets thus constructed for the viewer a desire to supplement the affective space of the performance. The positioning of dance itself within early-eighteenth-century aristocratic society further reinforced the ballet's powerfully evocative impact. Defined as a kind of metadiscipline that prepared one for all activities, dancing referenced values necessary to the proper performance of all physical endeavors. Its mastery assured the aristocrat the ability to achieve a calm, moderated easefulness—neither too erect nor too floppy, always agile, always cool—in fencing, tennis, and all the martial arts. It equally ensured a defectless body—agreeably proportioned, with each part exercising a relaxed, cordial aplomb. Noble identity depended not only on one's knowledge and proper execution of the correct actions, but also on the body's image in a given position. Undesirable attributes with which anyone might be born, such as knock-knees, a thrusting chin, or sunken chest, impeded the realization of a successful aristocratic identity. As dancing master Pierre Rameau observed, no better remedy than dancing existed for enhancing one's bodily position and consequently one's social position: "Dancing adds grace to the gifts which nature has bestowed upon us, by regulating the movements of the body and setting it in its proper positions. And if it does not completely eradicate the defects with which we are born, it mitigates or conceals them."[12]

Louis XIV had reinforced the body's role in conveying social status from the earliest years of his reign. He pursued a defectless body through his own dancing, and he consolidated rubrics of etiquette and comportment as part of his strategic plan to enhance royal authority. All nobility necessarily danced, and in day-to-day life they comported themselves in the gracefully moderate manner cultivated in dancing. Louis XIV had commemorated this metadisciplinary role for dance in his founding charter for the Académie de la Danse in 1762.[13] The original twelve members of

12. Pierre Rameau, *The Dancing Master* (1725), trans. Cyril W. Beaumont. (New York: Dance Horizons Press, 1970), 2.

13. The charter begins by asserting the centrality of dance's role in providing a base for all other physical activities including the bearing of arms: " . . . the Art of Dance has always been recognized as the most honest and most necessary at forming the body, at providing the most basic and natural foundation for all sorts of exercises, among others the bearing of arms, and consequently, one of the most advantageous and useful to our nobility, and to others who have the honor of approaching us, not only in times of war in our armies, but also in times of peace in the entertainment of our ballets" (. . . l'Art de la Danse ait toujours été reconnu l'un des plus honnêtes & plus nécessaires à former le corps, & lui donner les premières & plus naturelles dispositions à toutes sortes d'Exercices, & entr'autres à ceux des armes, & par conséquent l'un des plus avantageux & plus utiles à notre Noblesse, & autres qui ont l'honneur de Nous approcher, non-seulement en tems de Guerre dans nos Armées, mais même

the academy, and those who replaced or were initiated into the institution by them, were responsible for maintaining standards of excellence in dancing and in choreography, but they were also required to pursue dance as a system of knowledge that would provide its practitioners with an underlying foundation of bodily training useful in all situations.

The professional dancers trained at the academy who appeared onstage throughout the late seventeenth and early eighteenth centuries exemplified the values of a defectless physical appearance and a mannerly social comportment, and drew extensively from the vocabularies of social dance, their syntactic phrasing, and their rapport with musical structure. Even though the theatrical repertoire included many steps of greater intricacy, with each step fashioned for presentation by a dancer onstage to an audience seated in front and often below, the basis for theatrical invention resided in the social dance repertoire, which in turn referenced correct and gracious aristocratic comportment. Whether they danced the roles of gods and goddesses or shepherds and shepherdesses, dancers were concerned less with an illustration of the proper execution of specific actions than with the manner in which any action might signal propriety. Their nested references to generalized physical articulation celebrated the infrastructure that connected all members of French society, a structure whose origins could be found in the monarchic order of things.

In its references to other realms of physical endeavor, dancing gestured a manner of physical being to which all the king's subjects should and could aspire. Its cultivation of a "nonchalant, disjointed, and passionate physicality" established the guidelines for a moderate and moderated behavior through which social affairs should be conducted. Dancers' deliciously ambiguous desirability, their nuanced negotiations of space, glorified what opportunities were available within the highly scripted codes of social protocol. Their command of emotionality and corporeality ennobled the systems of control under which all the king's subjects necessarily operated.

Choreography for the opera-ballets thus elaborated an idealized version of the absolutist body politic. Through their gracefully calibrated distances from one another and the perpetual restraint maintained by all bodies from any expression too fulsome, dancers celebrated the reticulated

en tems de Paix dans le divertissement de nos Ballets) (*Lettres patentes du roi pour l'établissement de l'Académie royale de danse en la ville de Paris*, in *Danseurs et Ballet de l'Opéra de Paris depuis 1671* [Paris: Archives Nationales et Bibliothèque Nationale, 1988], 27).

social space within which the king and his subjects were variously positioned. Identity within that space, established as much by how one moved as by what one said, never existed apart from the patterns of all bodies in regulated motion together. Each body, held carefully in its place and carefully holding its place, depended on the moderated movements of all bodies for its identity and significance. Desire traveled among these bodies, fueled by their restraint and by the ingenious variations on standardized positions and steps they performed. Yet the static quality of the danced interludes belied the choreography of power that authorized all dancing bodies.

By the 1730s and 1740s, the persuasive eloquence of this system of evocation had begun to erode, and choreographers and aestheticians aspired to replace what they construed as the ornamental silliness of the opera-ballet's spectacle with more realistic, moving images of human nature. Following Sallé, dancers, unmasked and clothed in accurate historical costume, would depict actual human beings embroiled in the issues and conflicts of social life. They would enact the dramas inherent in all human relationships, causing viewers to both see and feel the characters' experiences. As in Sallé's production of *Pygmalion*, they would forsake the trappings of aristocratic entitlement in search of authentic human conditions.

To accomplish this choreographic agenda, those who followed Sallé's experiments began to utilize facial expressions within and as a part of the choreographic sequences.[14] They likewise replaced the bell-shaped skirts and stiff tunics (*tonnelets*) that segmented the body into articulate periphery and composed central body with a more supple dress that emphasized the connection of limbs to torso. Characters' identities were thereby established, not through the location of telling emblems on a generically shaped costume, but through imitative resemblance to the real or imagined life fashion of those characters.

Perhaps most significant, their new ballets relied on few if any lyrics to convey the plot. Instead pantomimed dialogues, woven into the syntax of steps, elucidated the action. Laminated to the meter, intensity, and phrasing of the music, these distilled depictions of the emotions desig-

14. Choreographers working within the conventions of the new genre include Jean Baptiste François De Hesse, the choreographer for Mme de Pompadour's private theater; Antoine Buonaventure Pitrot, who presented several works at the Comédie Italienne; Jean Lany, who created danced interludes for the Comédie Française; Jean Georges Noverre, who presented ballets at the Opéra Comique before traveling to Stuttgart and Vienna; and principal dancers at the Opéra Jean Dauberval and Marie Allard.

nated exaggerated and stereotypic versions of human interaction. The face engaged in these stereotypic depictions both as a part of the total bodily response and as the final arbiter of the movement's meaning. It presented the most condensed version of the passion—whether pain, anger, shock, adoration, interest, confusion, flirtation, or amazement—being represented in the drama.

Out of these sequences of postural and gestural mimetic movement, choreographers built new kinds of group interactions that moved the plots forward. Where the opera-ballets had offered pleasant exercises in tracing bodies' progress along geometrical pathways, the new action ballets (*ballets d'action*) engaged bodies in danced dialogues that created dynamic and asymmetrical configurations. The vocabulary's elaboration of several heights for the body—degrees of *plié* and *relevé*—and equally subtle but precise facings for the dancer faded in significance when compared with this vivid use of pantomime. Likewise, the precise location of each body within vertical and horizontal grids mattered far less than the causal logic of each body's response to the unfolding drama onstage. Danced characters began to move in tensile ensembles or froze into *tableaux vivants* in which each character registered a unique participation.

If the painterly analogue to the opera-ballets could be found in Watteau's work, the approach corresponding to the new action ballets existed in paintings by Jean-Baptiste Greuze. Whereas Watteau's images perpetually solicited further clarification, Greuze's tableaux specified everything. Each character's motivation and situation were fully explicated in the careful display of facial expression, calculated postures, and specified distances among figures. The crucial dramatic moment with all its attendant complexities was fleshed out clearly. Like the tableaux onstage, these paintings constructed organic wholes from the individualized participation of each character.

As in Greuze's paintings, the new action ballets staged a feeling like melancholy very differently from the opera-ballets. Along with anger, joy, fear, angst, or intrigue, melancholy assumed a role as one of the lexical units through which characters portrayed their interactions and the narrative sustained its development. A character manifested melancholy in response to new information or a change in events and eventually evolved out of melancholy—again, as motivated by internal or external changes to the situation. To represent this trope, the performer learned to theatricalize schematized elements from the visual appearance of the melancholy person: a drooping of the head to front or side, the slow concave collapse of the torso, or perhaps the back of the hand pressed lightly against the forehead.

This rubric for representation pried both dance and the dancing body loose from their interstitial situatedness among the discourses of health, comportment, athleticism, sociability, and theatricality. It required a stable and solid physical entity to portray accurately the habits and reactions of other bodies and to house the causally related sequences of feelings that characters would enact. To produce such a body, dance pedagogy slowly shifted from the study of dances to the study of exercises that prepared the body for dancing. It incorporated insights from the developing science of anatomy to enhance the effectiveness of routines that addressed the body's strength and flexibility as well as any individual deficiencies.[15] Through these training regimens and the anatomical language they employed, the body acquired a kind of objecthood. Its central function, rather than to participate in the conduct of social, political, and theatrical affairs, was to carry around and communicate the desires of the individual subject.

Thus the action ballets embodied a new conception of individuality as discrete and bounded by each individuated body. No longer enmeshed within webs of spatial-social protocol, the danced character generated his or her own sequence of feelings or else responded uniquely to the initiatives of others. No longer defined in relation to the flux within those webs of signification, the dancing body now maintained an autonomous identity, moving responsively to enact the character it played. This responsiveness caused the body to lose its capacity to engage directly the sensuous fascination of viewers. The character, rather than the body, became the source of erotic and emotional attraction.

Opera-ballet had presented physicality as simultaneously disciplined and articulate, sensuous and lively. Action ballet redistributed these qualities, leaching them from the cultivated body and investing them in the constructed character. The dancing body shifted from the central subject to a prop by which the subject could be displayed. Its facility in assisting the character, rather than its gracefulness in presenting itself, was what demanded evaluation. Gracefulness continued as an evaluative category during the displays of technical prowess, the celebratory scenes of vigorous virtuoso dancing, that choreographers interjected into the ballets. In

15. Published writings on dance pedagogy and choreography from the period reflect an extensive understanding of and focus on anatomy. See, for example, Gennaro Magri's *Theoretical and Practical Treatise on Dancing* (Naples, 1779), trans. Mary Skeaping, Anna Ivanova, and Irmgard E. Betty (London: Dance Books, 1988); Giovanni-Andrea Battista Gallini's *Treatise on the Art of Dancing* (London: printed for the Author and sold by R. & J. Dodsley, T. Becket, & W. Nicholl, 1762); and Noverre's *Letters on Dancing and Ballets*.

these scenes, the body performed on its own. However, its detachment from the signifying capacity to reference other realms of physical action left its breathtaking dexterity without the resonances to emotion and to eros that it once enjoyed.

Nevertheless, the choreography for the action ballets placed all bodies on the same footing. It extended to all human beings regardless of class or profession the same capacities to feel and to empathize with another's feelings. No longer suspended within a web of gestures hierarchized by the perfect perspective of the stage as universe and the single, most favorable viewing location of the monarch, these mimetic bodies opened up the spectacle to a wider range of viewing positions from which their discursive messagings could be apprehended. Their group configurations and their evolving sequences of passions could be seen best—but not most perfectly—from the center of the auditorium. The new mimetic bodies, responding logically to events around them, danced out an independence never before available to them. Freed from the relational protocols they had previously been required to perform, they could now initiate and respond all on their own. Well in advance of the seizure of power by the "people" of France, the action ballets provided palpable images of just how the French citizen's body should behave.

Where the vocabulary for the opera-ballets had referenced courtly codes of protocol, the mimetic sequences utilized by these self-sustaining bodies derived from a seemingly universal language of gesture. Choreographers and aestheticians claimed a primal and innate origin for gesture in the responsiveness of each individual to his or her own feelings.[16] The

16. Librettist, dance historian, and author of several entries for Diderot's *Encyclopédie*, Louis de Cahusac, in *La Danse ancienne et moderne, ou traité historique de la danse* (The Hague, 1754), 1:13, proposed this origin for dance, in a statement highly typical of the period:

> Man experienced sensations from the first moment that he breathed; and the sounds of the voice, the play of features across his face, the movements of his body, were simply expressions of what he felt.
>
> There are naturally in the voice sounds of pleasure and of sorrow, of anger and of tenderness, of distress and of joy. There are similarly in the movements of the face and of the body gestures of all these traits; the ones were the primitive sources of song, and the others of dance.
>
> This was the universal language understood by all nations and even by animals, because it is anterior to all conventions and natural to all the creatures that breathe on the earth.

> L'Homme a eu des sensations au premier moment qu'il a respiré, et les sons de la voix, le jeu des traits du visage, les mouvemens du corps ont été seuls les expressions de ce qu'il a senti.
>
> Il y a naturellement dans la voix des sons de plaisir et de douleur, de colere et de tendresse, d'affliction et de joie. Il y a de même dans les mouvemens du visage et du corps,

motivation and facility for communication thereby originated within each body and not in a socially constructed and politically imposed codification of conduct. Nature and not culture served as inspiration for the new ballet, as Noverre observed in his definition of the genre:

A well-composed ballet is a living picture of the passions, manners, customs, ceremonies and customs of all nations of the globe, consequently, it must be expressive in all its details and speak to the soul through the eyes; if it be devoid of expression, of striking pictures, of strong situations, it becomes a cold and dreary spectacle. This form of art will not admit of mediocrity; like the art of painting, it exacts a perfection the more difficult to acquire in that it is dependent on the faithful imitation of nature.[17]

The universal language of gesture, plainly evident to any who would study nature carefully, provided the means for uniting and communicating with all nations of the globe.

By locating dance's origins in a naturalized, ahistorical time and place, and by representing more realistic characters and events onstage, choreographers removed themselves from their role as direct emissaries of the king's taste. Yet their new choreographic approach contained a tacit ideological argument of its own. Because dancing developed from human and not godly predispositions, it operated with absolute validity outside the purview of the church. Because, moreover, its prehistorical originators dwelled in a classless community, dancing could be seen as an endeavor of a diverse urban society rather than the project of a hierarchically organized court. These Enlightenment goals of decentering church and monarchy were complemented by a third line of argumentation, imperialist in its objectives, that used the presumption of movement as a universal language to rationalize the continuation of expansionist foreign policies. Because dance productions claimed universal accessibility to and significance for the portraits of life they presented onstage, they helped to justify the exportation of French culture just as they provided reassurance that Paris, sited at the center of the world, spoke to and represented all the rest of the earth.

Sallé, poised at the brink of this transformation in representation, may well have chosen the myth of the sculptor whose creation is brought to

des gestes de tous ces caractères; les uns ont été les sources primitives du Chant, et les autres de la Danse.

C'est-là ce langage universel entendu par toutes les Nations et par les animaux même; parce qu'il est antérieur à toutes les conventions, et naturel à tous les etres qui respirent sur la terre.

17. Noverre, *Letters on Dancing and Ballets*, 16.

life to reflect on the impending changes in choreographic conventions. The reflexive ingenuity of her choice resulted, I argue, from her awareness of the aesthetic possibilities of yet a third choreographic approach. Neither mannerly nor mimetic, but rather deeply ironic, this approach to the representation of human feeling was already circulating in the unofficial London and Paris theater productions of the early eighteenth century.[18] It developed a use of pantomime radically distinct from that used in the action ballets.

In both cities, but in Paris especially, an intense and prolonged rivalry sprang up at the beginning of the eighteenth century between the fair theaters and the three authorized theatrical establishments: the Opéra, the Comédie Française, and the Comédie Italienne. As the popularity of the scandalous, irreverent fair productions began to affect audience size and consequently profits at the official theaters, administrative staff at the main houses marshaled government support to harass their cultural and legal inferiors. Based on charters received from Louis XIV that defined their exclusive rights to perform opera, drama, and musical comedy respectively, the three houses began to extract royalty fees from the fair theaters and also to prohibit them from presenting works in any of their genres. Censors, suddenly empowered with new responsibilities, exercised unpredictable, despotic control over texts submitted for their approval. New regulations not only enjoined the fair theaters from presenting comedies, tragedies, or entire operas, but also restricted their use of dialogue and even sung lyrics. Between 1745 and 1751, for example, spoken or sung dialogue was banned entirely.[19]

Capitalizing on an inconsistent and slow-moving bureaucracy, the fair theaters responded with a riotous profusion of strategies for altering presentational formats.[20] Dialogues might be presented with one actor at a time onstage; players appeared speaking nonsense syllables in perfect alexandrines while pantomiming the action; an offstage actor would deliver lines as an onstage actor mouthed them; child actors were used in place of adults; actors might carry their lines on signs around their necks; or verse would be displayed on huge placards that the audience would

18. Artur Michel emphasizes the influence that the English mime tradition had on the French fair theaters by citing the number of English mimes who were imported to perform in Paris, especially between the years 1720 and 1729; see "The Ballet d'Action Before Noverre," *Dance Index* 6, no. 3 (1947): 55.

19. Ibid., 67.

20. For a detailed discussion of these subversive conventions, see Thomas Crow, *Painters and Public Life in Eighteenth Century Paris* (New Haven: Yale University Press, 1985), 49–67.

then sing to popular tunes while the actors mimed the action. Because prohibitions usually denied producers the right to present extended sequences of spoken or sung dialogue, gesture was frequently substituted to convey part or all of the drama.

The demand placed on bodily movement to carry the narrative along inspired substantial changes in the vocabulary inherited from the bawdy, acrobatic, interventionist style of the commedia dell'arte tradition. Players took an increasing interest in the representation of the passions through facial and bodily gestures that indexed a full range of emotional experience, fashioning sequences of such gestures that delineated the narrative structure implied in the music. They adapted the intricate spatial relations developed in acrobatic routines to illustrate relationships among different types of characters. And they began to extend the length and scope of coherent narrative that could be rendered by movement and music alone.

Although the pressure on the fair theaters to avoid classical theatrical genres forced an exploration of pantomime as a medium capable of telling a story, the thrust of the performances remained resolutely antinarrative. Fair theater thrived on the parodic, iconoclastic, and spectacular display rather than the coherent, sentimental tale, using pantomime to mimic in such a way as to deflate power. Many of the productions relied on the audience's familiarity with a classic plot. As they mercilessly satirized, for example, Lully's famous operas and Corneille's dramas, the unorthodox sequences or juxtapositions of events in different mediums unraveled any sense of narrative logic.

Under these conditions, the representation of emotional life acquired a very different modality of presentation. Mimetic renditions of emotional states, for example, would be interrupted by parodic and satirizing gestures that undercut their sincerity. These gestures shifted any empathic connection away from the character and toward the playfully bitter irony on which the entire performance was based. Feelings still coalesced and communicated themselves. Characters evoked pity, erotic fascination, or a sense of outraged injustice, but the parodic gestures intruded on the action so as to force a double perspective on both the characters and their feelings. Viewers felt a character's melancholy but at the same time necessarily sensed the way in which that feeling was constructed—the conventions giving it existence and its transitory identity. Some of the time, this ironic reflexivity coexisted with the feelings represented in a way that permitted a critical yet profound sense of the character's state of being. Other times, the parodic intervention dissolved any connection to feeling through its presumptuous extravagance. Regardless of the degree of its outrageousness, the parodic presence never permitted characters' feelings to develop in long, unbroken sequences or characters themselves to attain enduring, stable identities.

The combination of humor, shock, and eros served up in these productions appealed not only to the working classes for whom they were a familiar staple but also to the aristocracy whose values they openly satirized.[21] Whereas the working classes relished the opportunity to appropriate and then violate the ennobling myths of the period, the aristocracy delighted in the sexy affront to elevated values. By providing a kind of entertainment to which both classes could enthusiastically respond, the fair theaters complicated and compromised a policy designed to maintain distinct kinds of art for distinct classes of people. Police and other city authorities expressed ambivalence about the fair theaters, at once feeling the pressure to uphold the high standards of the king's authorized artistic tradition as exemplified by the Opéra and Comédie Française, but also subscribing to the prevalent belief that a populace, diverted by entertainment, would be more controllable and less given over to discussions of flagrant social injustice.

Still, the subversive impact of the productions may have extended further than authorities could anticipate by involving viewers from disparate social classes in a commentary on social class itself. The productions must have simultaneously assaulted and involved all viewers with their unpredictable sequencing of events in different mediums, enhanced by the viewers' physical proximity to the stage. For not only did the small size of the theaters, as compared to the main houses at the Opéra or Comédie Française, situate viewers close to the explosive barrage of sensations onstage, but it also required them to rub shoulders with one another. Although boxes were available for aristocratic spectators, all classes interacted at close range. Tidy boundaries between populations dissolved in such an intimate space, where theatrical lighting and makeshift architecture destabilized clear indications of rank—whether in terms of dress, comportment, or companions. The fact that in these theatrical productions actors were representing identities other than their own further problematized the grounds on which social identity was determined. Could one assume the rank of an aristocrat simply by acting like one?

21. One of Isherwood's main theses in *Farce and Fantasy* is that popular entertainment in Paris consistently appealed to and was viewed by all classes of people, and that at such entertainment the rich and poor brushed shoulders constantly.

One anonymous description, apparently by a lady of high birth, elaborated on the disquieting confusion generated by these productions in a vivid account of pre-performance "entertainments" by actors and audience members. Having entered the well-known fair theater Opéra Comique early because of the cold, she was confronted by a number of players gearing up for the performance:

A young Musketeer, one knee on the floor, declaimed tragicomically at the feet of a fairly pretty actress and kissed the hand that she indifferently allowed him to hold; another actress feebly fought without any difficulty against the advances of a dull councillor who desired to return to its place the garter she had removed so as to show him its fine workmanship; a third dallied with an impudent fop whose hand caressed her bosom.

Un jeune Mousquetaire un genou en terre déclamoit tragicomiquement aux pieds d'une assez jolie Actrice, & lui baisoit une main qu'on lui abandonnoit sans façon; une autre Actrice combattoit foiblement avec un fade Conseiller, qui vouloit absolument lui remettre sa jarretière, qu'elle avoit détachée pour lui faire admirer la beauté de l'ouvrage; une troisième badinoit avec un Petit-maître impudent, qui lui passoit la main sur la gorge.

A duke with whom she was acquainted arrived and escorted her to her seat, but the performers continued to regard her with such effrontery "that I changed appearance twenty times from embarrassment, which in turn served as the subject of a vast number of nasty jokes which they delivered loudly enough to be heard" (que je changeai vingt fois de visage, mon embarras leur fournit quantité de mauvaises plaisanteries, qu'ils débitèrent assez haut pour être entendue). Arriving at her seat, a new series of impertinences assaulted her as twenty sets of opera glasses turned toward her and she overheard loud inquiries as to her identity and comments on her appearance. Soon she was rescued from this scrutiny by the arrival in an adjacent box of another young woman who seemed to relish the opportunity to perform for the audience:

[She] made faces, took some snuff, whispered to some kind of servant who had accompanied her, took from her embroidered purse a small gold box which she handled so as to assure its visibility to the spectators below, and returned it to the purse, ostentatiously tying its knot; then, to dispel the fatigue that this pitiful exercise had caused, but also to be able to display a portrait ringed with diamonds that she wore as a bracelet, she leaned her head on her elbow and tried out for a fairly long time an interesting pose. Unfortunately for her, the actors then appeared, stealing from her the better part of the viewers' attention.

> [Elle] fit des mines, prit du tabac, parla bas à une espèce de Suivante qu'elle avoit avec elle, tira d'un sac brode une navette d'or qu'elle fit briller aux yeux des Spectateurs, la remit dans son sac après avoir fait un noeud; & pour se délasser de la fatigue que lui avoit causé ce pénible exercice, & montrer un portrait enrichi de diamans qu'elle portoit en forme de bracelet, elle appuya sa tête sur son coude, & essaya assez long-tems une attitude intéressante. Malheureusement pour elle, les Acteurs parurent, & lui enlevèrent la plus grande partie des Spectateurs.[22]

This description cast audience members and actors in a series of scenes performed in the lobby, and it likewise described audience members performing for one another—all prior to the commencement of the production. It even intimated the continuation of audience performances throughout the performance onstage. The snide irreverence of the actors and the hyperbolic gestures of the young woman who could afford a box seat derived their meaning from a class-conscious critique of aristocratic privilege. If this anonymous account is at all accurate, then the performances encouraged audience members along with actors to demonstrate their knowledge of the codes of class-based comportment both on and off the stage.

In their transgressive experimentation with bodily movement and gesture, the fair theaters constructed a critique of absolutism. By satirizing the very conventions through which aristocratic identity was maintained, performances intimated the existence of a more egalitarian site from which to exercise the state's power. This ironic egalitarianism differed from the humanistic conception of citizenship subsequently elaborated in the action ballets choreographed by Noverre and others. In those ballets the body, as the vehicle for individuated expression, functioned as a territory controlled by the individual to ensure adherence to the state's prescribed behavior. No bodies behaved outrageously; all bodies faithfully portrayed the characters assigned them. The ironic pantomime, in contrast, cultivated a protean body capable of conformance and then excess, docility followed by grotesquerie. Any consistency in its satiric stance resided in its relentless critique of absolutist values and not in the body through which such a critique was manifested.

This ironic stance toward dance and world, however, was not to prevail as the choreographic model for ballet's subsequent development out of opera and into an autonomous art form. Instead the action ballet, with

22. Anon., *Lettre de Madame *** à une de ses amies sur les spectacles, et principalement sur l'Opéra Comique*, 9–11, 15–16; Bibliothèque de l'Opéra.

its humanistic characterization of people and circumstances, came to define late-eighteenth-century theatrical dance. Where fair theater productions elaborated a collective and contingent responsiveness to situations, the action ballet focused on the logical reactions of individual characters. These characters manifested qualities of good samaritanism, domestic loyalty, and the work ethic, as well as empathic sensitivity to others, the *sensibilité* so championed by Diderot and others. And unlike the fair theaters, in which bodies reacted unpredictably, maintaining their allegiance only to social critique, action ballet developed docile bodies, bodies loyal to the subjects whose thoughts and desires they portrayed.

Sallé's parents had both performed in the fair theaters, and her uncle was a famous harlequin.[23] Her own first performances took place on fair theater stages. Her career as *première danseuse* at the Opéra also brought her into contact with London theater producer John Rich, whose various projects included the development of pantomime theater in that city. Although she was not alone in undertaking the kind of choreographic experimentation with ballet and pantomime that marks her choreographic oeuvre, her mastery of two distinct movement repertoires and her prestigious position at the Opéra endowed her pioneering explorations with special distinction.

Historians of dance have seldom credited Sallé with any influence over the shape of choreographic change, preferring instead to focus on her great skill as a dancer.[24] Credit for the choreographic breakthroughs that led to the development of the story ballet has typically gone not to Sallé, but to Jean Georges Noverre, who may well have been a young audience member at her performances.[25] Noverre not only choreographed but also wrote

23. See Pierre Aubry and Emile Dacier, *"Les Caractères de la Danse": Histoire d'un divertissement pendant la première moitié du XVIIIe siecle* (Paris: Honoré Champion, 1905), 17.

24. Many eighteenth-century authors identify Sallé's work as the direct source and inspiration for the reforms in dance advocated by mid-eighteenth-century choreographers. Algarotti, for example, cites her ballets *Pygmalion* and *Les Ballets de la rose* as the ones choreographers should emulate (*Essai sur l'opéra*, 66); and Charles Compan describes her as the innovator of the genre of *ballet d'action* (*Dictionnaire de Danse* [Paris: Chez Cailleau, 1787], 4). Twentieth-century scholars, however, have largely ignored her central influence on the establishment of narrative in dance, with two notable exceptions: Peter Brinson, in *Background to European Ballet* (New York: Arno Press, 1980), 164–66; and Artur Michel, "Ballet d'Action," 68. Michel (65) traces her influences through Hilverding, who saw her in Paris in 1735, and through her partner Lany, who produced a version of her *Pygmalion* in Berlin in 1745, which Noverre saw.

25. Deryck Lynham presumes an association between Noverre and Sallé during the early 1740s though their alliances with the director of the Opéra Comique, Jean Monnet; see *Le Chevalier Noverre* (1950; London: Dance Books, 1972), 13–15.

about the choreographic reforms that would enable dance to narrate.[26] His books and scenarios for his productions made history where her dances did not. Dance histories have also failed to acknowledge the experimental ingenuity of fair theater performers who pioneered in the use of gestural narration. Even though Noverre, like Sallé, began his career in the fair theaters, histories have typically established distinct paths of development for aristocratic and popular entertainment traditions, delineating for theatrical dance an exclusively aristocratic heritage.

This text's body has moved against canonical dance histories by advocating interest in the resistive ingenuity of popular culture. It also chose to dance with Sallé rather than Noverre in an attempt to problematize not only his fame but also the preference for the written over the danced, which his place in dance history represents. By the time of Noverre's notoriety the ballet's sensible body had established a clear image of egalitarian premises, which the Revolution further attempted to realize. Yet this vision of liberation from absolutism entailed the subjugation of the body to both anatomy and narrativity. Only two generations earlier, Sallé had performed her vision of dance's future at a time when the body, still a powerful medium for articulating and not merely enhancing identity, could also begin to narrate its circumstances. Dancing in the midst of epistemic motion, she could coalesce at the site of her body a physicalized sociability, an individuated sensibility, and an ironic critique.

This text's politics worked to complicate traditional accounts of the political mobilization that led to the French Revolution by focusing on changes in the conception of the dancing body across that period. In an effort to dismantle the exoskeletal structure of absolutism that kept all bodies in their proper places, choreographers constructed new techniques of performance and of representation that imbued each dancing body with an endoskeletal system of control. As partner to this new system, a polarized opposition between aesthetics and politics replaced the subtle yet persuasive politicking of which the baroque dancer was capable. Sallé, whose choreography theorized these relationships between body and identity, stands for and at a moment when the aesthetic and the political might still dance together on the same stage.

26. Noverre's *Lettres sur la danse et les ballets* was published in 1760 and expanded and revised as the two-volume *Lettres sur les arts imitateurs en général, et sur la danse en particulier* (Paris: Léopold Collin, 1807).

8

The Theater of Punishment

Melodrama and Judicial Reform in Prerevolutionary France

SARAH MAZA

Many of the essays in this volume explore the political culture of the Old Regime at its apogee under Louis XIV, a system that revolved around the sacred body of the king. In what follows I look at the end of the politico-cultural system of French absolutism, the period in the prerevolutionary decades when that system came under attack and began to fall apart.

Some scholars have described the cultural transition that took place in the late eighteenth century as a shift from an iconic system centered on the body of the king to a logocentric universe that enshrined the word of the law—in Napoleon's long-lived Civil Code, for instance.[1] I follow this line of argument in pointing to the importance of a certain category of legal documents, the trial briefs in which eighteenth-century lawyers narrated their versions of the cases they defended. But I also seek to complicate the picture by noting the theatrical element of these legal narratives, and to the close kinship between their style and the physically expressive techniques of contemporary drama.

The broader historical context for the trial briefs I examine here is the eighteenth-century movement to reform France's system of criminal justice. Following Michel Foucault, I argue that the transition was not a neat one from corporal punishment to an abstract legal system: progres-

1. For instance, see Marie-Hélène Huet, *Rehearsing the Revolution: The Staging of Marat's Death* (Berkeley: University of California Press, 1982); and Joan Landes, *Women and the Public Sphere in the Age of the French Revolution* (Ithaca: Cornell University Press, 1988).

sive reformers in the age of Enlightenment still conceived of punishment as body-centered. But the performance of punishment at this juncture no longer implicitly glorified the monarch; it was directed instead at the education and reform of the spectators. If eighteenth-century punishment was still imagined as a spectacle, the audience now shared the limelight with the performers: the body on stage was theirs, not the king's.

My discussion centers on a near miscarriage of justice that became a cause célèbre in France in 1785–86: the case of Victoire Salmon, a young servant accused of poisoning her masters.[2] The context for this affair was the culmination in the 1780s of a decades-long movement for the reform of France's ancient and complex system of criminal justice, as codified in the great Criminal Ordinance of 1670.[3] Two of the salient characteristics of the ordinance were the privacy of proceedings and the all-powerful role vested in the judge, who dispensed justice in the name of a divinely ordained monarch. Under the Old Regime, criminal investigations—from the questioning of the plaintiff, defendant, and witnesses to the final deliberations—took place in private, behind closed doors, under the eyes only of the judges and their clerks. Secrecy, arbitrariness, and the defendant's lack of access to counsel were among the features of the system, which in the later eighteenth century increasingly came under attack, often through a contrast with contemporary English procedure.

Lawyers did play a role in this system, although in criminal cases it was confined to the written word (they were allowed to plead orally only in civil cases). Barristers composed trial briefs or memoranda (*mémoires judiciaires*), which they presented to the judges on their clients' behalf. *Mémoires* in important cases had long been printed up and disseminated widely, and by the late eighteenth century such documents had acquired a pivotal status in the legal culture of the old regime (in part because they were the only form of pamphlet literature to escape any form of preventive censorship).[4] Increasingly sensational, popular, and sought after, *mémoires judiciaires* were the only link between the criminal courtroom and

2. For a fuller account of the context of this case, see Sarah Maza, *Private Lives and Public Affairs: The Causes Célèbres of Prerevolutionary France* (Berkeley: University of California Press, 1993), chap. 5. I wish to thank the University of California Press for granting permission to use material from this book.

3. The following remarks on the system of criminal justice are drawn from André Laingui and Arlette Lebigre, *Histoire du droit pénal*, 2 vols. (Paris: Cujas, 1979), 2:81–103.

4. Sarah Maza, "Le Tribunal de la nation: Les Mémoires judiciaires et l'opinion publique à la fin de l'ancien régime," *Annales E.S.C.* 42 (1987): 73–90; and idem, *Private Lives and Public Affairs*, 34–38, 120–31. See also Hans-Jürgen Lüsebrink, "L'Affaire Cléreaux: Affrontements idéologiques et tensions institutionnelles autour de la scène judiciaire au XVIIIe siècle," *Studies on Voltaire and the Eighteenth Century*, no. 191 (1980): 892–900.

the world beyond it, and their use came to open up a widening breach in the hermetic system of prerevolutionary justice. It was through such documents that in the mid-1780s the French reading public learned of the case of Victoire Salmon—one of a handful of highly publicized *affaires* that were used to challenge the judicial system of the Old Regime and, through it, the very bases of public authority.

In the dark hours just before dawn, on 1 August 1781, a young woman in her early twenties walked on the road to Caen in Normandy.[5] Victoire Salmon, a laborer's daughter who worked as a domestic servant, was traveling in search of the employment she needed to support herself and to put together a decent dowry. She could not possibly have imagined the extraordinary events that would occur a mere week after her arrival in Caen, or the upheavals in her life that would take place in the next five years.

By what seemed a stroke of good luck, Salmon found work on her very first day in Caen—employment as a maid-of-all-work for a petit-bourgeois family named Huet-Duparc: parents, three children, and two grandparents. On the first Monday after she was hired, Salmon prepared a porridge of milk and flour for the eighty-eight-year-old grandfather, as she had been ordered. She later testified that she saw her mistress throw salt, or something like it, into the old man's *bouilli*. When she returned from errands later that morning, she learned that the grandfather had suffered a violent colic, and that a doctor and priest had been summoned. He died that same evening, around six. On the following morning, Madame Duparc scolded Salmon for wearing the new calico pockets she used on Sundays, and told her to put on the striped ones she wore every day. This was before Victoire helped her mistress and the latter's daughter prepare the family's midday meal: a fresh soup for the masters, a leftover one for Salmon and another servant, and a plate of cherries for dessert. The story at this point gets somewhat muddled. It seems that several family members felt ill after the meal, and that the mistress exclaimed that she smelled burnt arsenic. Rumors were soon circulating which resulted in the arrival of a surgeon and police officer, who discovered a white glittery substance presumed to be arsenic in the pockets the young girl was wearing. She was arrested on the spot.

Thus began Victoire Salmon's long ordeal in the courts and prisons of Caen, Rouen, and Paris. Arrested in early August of 1781, she was not to

5. The following summary of the case is based on the trial briefs cited below, on reports in contemporary newspapers and gazettes, and on Armand le Corbeiller, *Le Long Martyre de Françoise Salmon* (Paris: Perrin, 1927). Salmon's first names were Marie Françoise Victoire. I refer to her as Victoire because that is the name she seems to have used herself.

recover her freedom until May 1786. After a lengthy investigation involving dozens of witnesses, the *bailliage* (lower court) of Caen found her guilty on 18 April 1782 of poisoning the old man and attempting to poison her other masters with the intention of robbing them, and the Parlement of Rouen, where the case went on appeal, upheld the conviction a month later. Salmon was condemned to be tortured for the names of possible accomplices, to beg forgiveness in public barefoot and carrying a torch, and to be burned at the stake (the standard punishment for poisoners).

Although a scaffold was erected for Salmon in Caen, her execution was delayed owing to two developments: first, she was able to gain a respite by declaring that she was pregnant; and second, an enterprising young lawyer from Rouen named Pierre-Noël Lecauchois was convinced to take an interest in her case, which resulted in his obtaining in extremis a stay of execution from the king. The hundreds of bundles of documents pertaining to the case were then trundled up to Paris, where the king's *conseil privé* ordered a retrial and lobbed the case back to the Parlement of Rouen. It was while the case was being retried by the Rouen magistrates in the winter of 1784–85 that Lecauchois published the first of several trial briefs that were to make the case nationally famous; it was printed up in thousands of copies and sent all over France. On 12 March 1785 the Rouen parlement annulled the original verdict, and the case, along with Salmon herself, went back up to Paris, where another barrister, Jean-François Fournel, also produced highly successful briefs in her defense. On 26 May 1786, the Parlement of Paris granted Victoire Salmon a full acquittal. She emerged at the top of the great staircase of the Palais de Justice to find Paris both literally and figuratively at her feet. Salmon had been in prison for five years, but that summer dawn when she had walked on the road to Caen must have seemed light years away.

An event that followed shortly upon Salmon's acquittal deserves some mention here. After the verdict, Victoire Salmon and her defender were lionized by Parisian high society, paraded through the houses of the great, and plied with gifts. In June 1786, the pair were invited to attend a performance at the Comédie Française, the theater of the Parisian aristocratic elite. Salmon and Lecauchois were ushered onto the balcony, where they received an ovation from the crowd, and when a character onstage delivered a line about the triumph of truth, the spectators once again turned to the balcony and burst into applause.[6] The curious cultural syncretism in this scene seems neatly emblematic: a severely clad lawyer and a work-

6. Bibliothèque Nationale [hereafter cited as BN], fonds français, MS. 6685, Journal of Siméon-Prosper Hardy, entry of 8 June 1786.

ing-class woman made into a spectacle for the rich and titled, amid the rococo finery of the Comédie Française. But while it is tempting to see in the theater the world of the past, and in the law that of the future, the story, as we shall see, is more complicated than that.

The trial briefs written by Pierre-Noël Lecauchois and Jean-François Fournel played a crucial role in the reversal of the case against Victoire Salmon, and there is abundant contemporary testimony of readers' enthusiastic response to them.[7] The *Gazette des Tribunaux*, for instance, informed its readers that Fournel's first brief "caused the greatest sensation in the Palais [de Justice] and among the public" and went on to praise the lawyer's "gracious and fluid style," "good taste and wisdom," and "vigorous argumentation."[8] What I want to suggest is that the effectiveness of the *mémoires* in the case was dependent on the successful enlistment of readers in two capacities—as an audience for a certain *type* of performance, and as jury. First, it should be noted that, to borrow some terms from literary criticism, *mémoires judiciaires* are quintessential discourses (rather than histories) in that the narrative is explicitly addressed to an inscribed (rather than implied) reader.[9] In theory, the readers of *mémoires* are the judges who will pronounce on the fate of the accused, and accordingly Lecauchois's first brief for Salmon—a first-person narrative in the voice of the young woman—opens with conventional invocations addressed to "venerable magistrates" and "upright judges."[10]

For the most part, though, the briefs for Salmon are framed to address a broader reading public of laypersons to whose sympathy the narrator recurrently (and shamelessly) appeals. "Unfortunate maid!" she exclaims. "Aged only twenty-one; a defenseless young girl! But forgive me, reader, if I stray from my account: my situation, my sex, my age deserve some consideration."[11] Lecauchois's first-person account makes copious use of a technique that will be familiar to readers of eighteenth-century fiction: rather than assert Salmon's innocence, virtue, and charms, the lawyer has her describe herself as she is perceived by (usually male) others, as do fe-

7. For instances of the public's response to the briefs, see [Louis Petit de Bachaumont et al.,] *Mémoires secrets pour servir à l'histoire de la république des lettres en France*, 36 vols. (London, 1777–89), 31:277 (which mentions the public's "avidity" for such reading material); *Gazette des tribunaux* 16 (1786) ("this work caused in the Palais [de Justice] and in the public the greatest sensation"); and BN, ms. fr. 6685, 11 May 1785.

8. *Gazette des Tribunaux* 16 (1786): 5.

9. Susan Suleiman and Inge Crosman, eds., *The Reader in the Text: Essays on Audience and Interpretation* (Princeton: Princeton University Press, 1980), 14–15.

10. Pierre-Noël Lecauchois, *Mémoire pour Marie-Françoise Victoire Salmon* (n.p., 1784), 1–2.

11. Ibid., 17.

male narrators in the novels of Richardson, Marivaux, and Diderot. One of the judges instrumental in obtaining the harshest sentence against her had met Salmon, or so she claimed, at her first employer's house in the countryside, where he had made an unsuccessful pass at her: "He saw me there; my youth, my figure, and my bearing struck him; he had the kindness to tell me that I should come and serve [him] in Caen."[12]

The memoir-novel in the female voice thus served as an inspiration for texts that were aimed at a broad readership beyond the legal milieu; but the prominence of gesture and visual staging in these accounts also suggests a theatrical model. Because Salmon's experiences had indeed been wrenching (she very narrowly escaped execution on two occasions), the narrative of the case offered the authors of these briefs the opportunity to send readers hurtling from one emotional climax to the next. One of the most gripping scenes in Lecauchois's second brief occurs in the prison at Rouen, where Salmon is waiting for the outcome of the parlement's first deliberation. One of the wardens, perhaps out of compassion, informs her wrongly that the death sentence has been overturned. Giddy with relief, Victoire returns to her cell to make a cabbage soup, the first meal she has been able to swallow in days. But a fellow prisoner knows the truth and brutally informs her that she is going back to Caen to be executed: "At this terrible news, the touching features of this unfortunate girl took on a deathly hue. Her eyes rolled back, she cried: Ah! Great God! Horrors! And then fell to the ground senseless."[13]

Jean-François Fournel's account of the same scene describes it in more detail, and more explicitly clues the reader in to its meaning. He prefaces his account—this one a third-person narrative—with the observation that the guilty and the innocent react very differently to the news of imminent execution; the former lose all courage and implore the judges and the heavens for mercy, while the latter are galvanized into furious outcries against human injustice, and when they implore God, "it is less to ask for mercy than to demand justice."[14] Salmon's reaction to the news, her gestures and the words she uses, spell out her innocence in terms that cannot be mistaken by those who witness the scene: "She appeals with loud cries to Divine Justice; she calls upon all the heavenly judges against her persecutors; she cites them before the Tribunal of the Sovereign Judge; now with her brow to the ground which she drenches with her tears; now on

12. Ibid., 11.

13. Pierre-Noël Lecauchois, *Justification de Marie Françoise Victoire Salmon* (Paris, 1786), 6–7.

14. Jean-François Fournel, *Consultation pour une jeune fille condamnée à être brûlée vive* (Paris, 1786), 74.

her knees with her hands out to the heavens as the source of all justice, she begs for an act of their almighty power to rescue innocence."[15]

This scene can be called theatrical in a general sense, for instance in the fact that within the text it takes place before an audience: Salmon's assembled fellow prisoners, but also three priests who, convinced of her innocence, will be the ones to search out the lawyer Lecauchois and ask him to defend the girl. More specifically, most elements of this scene are what we might term melodramatic: pathos, exclamation, hyperbolic expressions and gestures, sketchy characterization, all belong to the melodramatic mode as analyzed by Peter Brooks.[16] Melodrama in its heyday, Brooks has argued, arose as a response to the waning of the traditional sacral authorities of church and monarchy. The flowering of melodrama in the late eighteenth and early nineteenth centuries was symptomatic of an urge to "resacralize" the world by locating good and evil in the drama of ordinary life and by replaying over and over, in unambiguously legible terms, the triumph of virtue and the defeat of vice.

Salmon's anger, her bowed head and tears, imploring gestures and howling for divine justice, as well as the relentless classifying and labeling typical of *mémoires* in this style ("Odious monster!" "Unfortunate maid!"), all belong to the linguistic and gestural repertoire of melodrama, which is, writes Brooks, "about virtue made visible and acknowledged, the drama of a recognition."[17] During the heyday of melodrama in France, in the first decades of the nineteenth century, plays in this genre frequently included a trial scene that represented "a final public reading and judgment of signs which brings immanent justice into the open, into operative relation with men's lives." Brooks cites a trial scene from Ducange's early melodrama *Thérèse* in which the villain Valther is tricked into accusing himself; he does so in terms that echo Salmon's, but in the mode of villainy: "Ah! . . . Divine justice! . . . yes, yes, I am your murderer, I confess my crime . . . spare me. I will publish your innocence, my crimes. . . . Here are the proofs."[18] In such climactic scenes, gesture and language serve as signs that lead to the uncovering and making public of concealed, albeit simple, moral truths.

Although classic melodrama did not flourish in France until the early nineteenth century, it had its origins in a form of theater that became pop-

15. Ibid.

16. Peter Brooks, *The Melodramatic Imagination: Balzac, Henry James, Melodrama, and the Mode of Excess* (New York: Columbia University Press, 1985), 11–23.

17. Ibid., 27.

18. Ibid., 45.

ular around the middle of the eighteenth century, known as the *genre sérieux* and later dubbed *drame bourgeois* or simply *drame*. In 1757, Denis Diderot articulated the need for a new form of theater, one that would replace the abstractions of classical tragedy and the frivolities of contemporary comedy with something more germane to the experiences of ordinary spectators—the everyday tensions between members of a family, or the interactions of persons of different social conditions.[19] The essence of the *genre sérieux* was, according to Diderot, its didactic conveying of a moral lesson that would impress upon spectators "the love of virtue and the horror of vice."[20]

One characteristic of the *genre sérieux* was its predilection for the portrayal of persons of middling or lower conditions, as the titles of some of the most successful dramas in this style suggest: *Les Gens de lettres, La Brouette du vinaigrier, L'Indigent, Les Trois Fermiers*. Authors of *drames* also relied heavily on the visual representation of emotion by means of individual gesture or of dramatic painterly groupings called *tableaux*. In his seminal treatise on the genre, Diderot recommended the use of what he called "pantomime" as a support for dramatic action, and the replacing of contrived *coups the théâtre* (dramatic plot twists) with visually striking tableaux.[21] It is likely that the authors of the briefs for Salmon had the new theatrical conventions in mind when they included in their accounts episodes such as the scene in the prison yard or an earlier scene in which Salmon is shown weeping at the deathbed of the old man she was later accused of poisoning.

This is all the more plausible in that there is substantial evidence, in the writings of progressive thinkers of the later eighteenth century, of a belief that an ideally open courtroom (or, in its absence, published trial briefs) could fulfill the same exemplary function as this new form of drama—indeed, that the two could feed off one another. Louis-Sébastien Mercier, a prominent author of *drames*, suggested in his treatise *Du théâtre* (1773) that great court cases be reenacted onstage so that the public could witness them and then "confirm, through their cheers, the triumph of the law."[22] In his futuristic fantasy *L'An 2440* (1770), Mercier imagined wak-

19. Denis Diderot, *Paradoxe sur le comédien, précédé des Entretiens sur "Le Fils naturel"* (Paris: Garnier-Flammarion, 1967), 97–98.

20. Ibid., 97. The major study of this genre of theater remains Félix Gaiffe, *Le Drame en France au XVIIIe siècle* (Paris: Armand Colin, 1910).

21. Diderot, *Paradoxe*, 83, 105–9.

22. Louis-Sébastien Mercier, *Du théâtre, ou nouvel essai sur l'art dramatique* (Amsterdam, 1773; repr. Geneva: Slatkine, 1970), 153.

ing up, Rip van Winkle style, in the future when the theater had indeed become "a public school for morality and taste" and going to see a play about the Calas affair.[23] Did Mercier know in 1770, one wonders, that several playwrights had indeed already used the Calas case as a subject for theatrical melodramas, none of which, however, were allowed onstage in France before the Revolution?[24] The conventions of contemporary stage melodrama, then, were pressed into service by Victoire Salmon's lawyers to interest readers in the fate of an obscure woman, to have them identify with her terrors, and above all, through gestures and words whose meaning could not be doubted, to make them bear witness as spectators to the unmistakable signs of her innocence.

Readers, then, were inscribed in the text of Lecauchois's and Fournel's accounts as spectators of a drama whose very telling proved the young woman's innocence. But the aims of these authors—and of many other ambitious barristers of their generation—went beyond the mere winning of a case. The Salmon affair was one of a series of cases that, in the mid-1780s, were used to dramatize the need for a drastic reform of France's system of criminal justice, and this purpose also governed the style and content of the *mémoires*.[25] Old Regime legal briefs were customarily divided into two parts: first a narration of the facts of the case (*les faits*), which could be aimed at the general reader, and then a technical discussion of points of law and precedent (*les moyens*), aimed at legal specialists and especially at the judges who would be pronouncing on the case. As the eighteenth century progressed, and lawyers increasingly courted the support of the general public, fame-seeking barristers involved in sensational cases often neglected the legal technicalities to concentrate on novelistically crowd-pleasing accounts of their client's case.[26]

Although, as we have seen, Lecauchois did not skimp on sensational storytelling in his account of Victoire Salmon's ordeals, he also included in his briefs some discussions of technicalities; these were not, however,

23. W. D. Howarth, "Tragedy into Melodrama: The Fortunes of the Calas Affair on the Stage," *Studies on Voltaire and the Eighteenth Century*, no. 174 (1978): 125–26. The Calas affair of 1762 was Voltaire's first great judicial crusade. The writer managed, through publications and petitions, to rehabilitate the memory of a Protestant man, Jean Calas, who had been wrongly accused and executed for the murder of his own son. See Maza, *Private Lives and Public Affairs*, 27–33.

24. Ibid.; Gaiffe, *Le Drame en France*, 378.

25. Maza, *Private Lives and Public Affairs*, chap. 5.

26. Ibid., passim; also David Bell, "Lawyers into Demagogues: Chancellor Maupeou and the Transformation of Legal Practice in France, 1771–1789," *Past and Present*, no. 130 (February 1991): 107–41.

aimed at specialists, but at laypersons. Along with his first *mémoire*, the lawyer published an *Introduction to the Defense of Miss Salmon*, which begins thus: "Since this brief will be coming before the eyes of a number of persons of different estates, the greater number of whom are not instructed in the points of departure from which criminal justice proceeds in order to acquire proof. . . . "[27] He goes on to detail for his readers the bases on which criminal convictions are secured: confession, written proof, the testimony of witnesses, clues or circumstantial evidence (*indices*), and inanimate objects (*témoins muets*).

There was, of course, an immediate reason for this exposition; indeed, Lecauchois segues from it into explanations both of the absurdity of some of the rules for establishing guilt and of ways in which procedure had been bungled or misapplied in the Salmon case. He objected, for instance, to the use of *indices* as fractions of truth that could be added up: how, he asked, can one speak of a quarter or an eighth of truth?[28] Lecauchois then mounted his case for the defense on a wide array of grounds: forensic evidence from the autopsy of the old man, procedural flaws in the investigation, contradictions in the testimonies of the witnesses, the suspicious behavior of the Duparc family, lack of evidence against the accused and of solid motive for the crime, and so on.[29] Thus, Lecauchois used the case to show up some of what he considered to be faulty premises in contemporary jurisprudence, at the same time arguing that even within the parameters of the law as it existed the case against Victoire Salmon was severely flawed.

Lecauchois's defense of Victoire Salmon contained both explicit and implicit attacks on Old Regime criminal law, attacks that echoed a whole body of recent writings on the subject. The reform movement of the late eighteenth century—which would come to dramatic fruition in the Revolution's overhauling of France's judicial system—was touched off in the 1760s by Voltaire's involvement in the Calas case and by the publication and translation of Cesare Beccaria's treatise on crime and punishment.[30] By the late 1770s and early 1780s, the trickle of publications on the sub-

27. Pierre-Noël Lecauchois, *Introduction aux défenses de la fille Salmon* (n.p., n.d.), i.

28. Ibid., i–v.

29. Lecauchois, *Justification*, 45–54.

30. Peter Gay, *The Enlightenment: An Interpretation*, vol. 2: *The Science of Freedom* (New York: W. W. Norton, 1977), 423–37; David Jacobson, "The Politics of Criminal Law Reform in Late-Eighteenth-Century France" (Ph.D. diss., Brown University, 1976), 59–71. The Milanese nobleman Cesare Baccaria's *Del delitti e delle pene* (1764), which argued for reforms to make European judicial systems more rational and humane, became a blueprint for reformers in several countries in the later eighteenth century.

ject had grown into a torrent. In response to contests on the subject organized by provincial academies, prize-winning essays calling for reform were penned by ambitious young lawyers whose names were soon to become famous: Jacques-Pierre Brissot, Jean-Paul Marat, Maximilien de Robespierre.[31]

In criticizing not only the way this particular case was handled, but also some of the system's basic features, Lecauchois was drawing on ideas commonly articulated by such reformers. He objected, for instance, to the fact that charges were drawn up in the absence of the accused (who thus often didn't know what he or she was accused of) and to the fact that the defendant's lawyer did not have access to the records of the case. In a ghoulish passage, he invoked the victims of other famous miscarriages of justice, a familiar litany in the reform literature of the age: "Ghosts of Lebrun, of the Danglades and Fourrés . . . bring forth your grief-stricken, ruined families; uncover your bloody corpses, some cruelly mangled by torture and mutilated on the gallows, others crushed with blows, crawling, expiring on the galleys."[32] A powerful critique of contemporary institutions was also implicit in the way the lawyer framed his brief. By instructing his lay readers in the rules for weighing evidence and determining guilt—even as he criticized some of those rules—Lecauchois rhetorically cast his audience in the role of a jury. Such institutions, however, did not exist in France, as they were antithetical to the basic premise of Old Regime jurisprudence, the dispensing of justice from on high in the name of a divine-right monarch.

What, finally, is the link between the two rhetorical strategies adopted by Victoire Salmon's defenders—that which made readers into the spectators of a melodramatic performance, and that which cast them in the role of a jury? I want to end by arguing that the link is that suggested by Scott Bryson in his stimulating volume *The Chastised Stage*. Commenting on the many analogies in late-eighteenth-century discourse between penal and theatrical reform, Bryson suggests that the essence of these parallel systems (the playwright as lawmaker, the stage as tribunal) is the desire to educate and, through education, to control. Bryson posits that penal and aesthetic reform—as advocated for instance by Beccaria and Mercier—both point to a profound shift in the nature of authority as it is made manifest onstage and in proposals for new ways of judging and punishing: "These reforms conceive of representation whether legal, theatrical, or pictorial, no longer as a static, idealized, reflection or image of

31. Jacobson, "Politics of Criminal Law Reform," chap. 7.
32. Lecauchois, *Justification*, 33.

power, separate and aloof from the public, but as a dynamic strategy of manipulation and control."[33]

Bryson's approach to the question is of course much indebted to Foucault. In *Discipline and Punish*, Foucault argues that the logic of Old Regime penology, of public torture, *amende honorable*, and ceremonial public executions, was that of vengeance and expiation.[34] The body of the condemned criminal was the locus on which the heinous nature of the crime was first affirmed and then obliterated. A criminal was considered to have offended not his or her fellow subjects, but the divinely ordained society and polity incarnated in the monarch. And just as power was vested in and displayed through the body of the king, punishments that spelled out the hideous nature of the crime were performed on the body of the criminal—a branded letter for theft, a severed tongue for blasphemy, a body reduced to ashes for crimes such as parricide that defiled society.[35] Both the criminal and the public assembled for the execution of a sentence were to participate actively in a ritual expiation thanks to which a crime was "manifested and then annulled"—the condemned by (ideally) showing remorse and begging for forgiveness, the crowd by serving as witness to a drama of physical agony and spiritual redemption that washed away the crime.

The late-eighteenth-century reformers, most of them men of law like Fournel and Lecauchois, who began to chip away at Old Regime penology, argued against torture and cruel punishment and for the publicity of proceedings, the right to counsel, jury trials, and the like—and it takes all of Foucault's gleeful perversity to argue that none of this represented "progress." But it *is* the case that some of the ideas put forth by these early reformers seem just as barbaric as the system they were designed to replace. One of the standard-bearers of the movement, Michel de Servan, argued in all his writings that in order for punishments to be socially effective they should be both swift and certain: "Here is the moment to punish crime, do not let it escape, make haste in convicting and judging, erect scaffolds, set stakes aflame, drag culprits into the public squares, call the People with loud cries. . . . You will see joy exploding, and that virile insensitivity that comes from the love of peace and the horror of crime."[36]

33. Scott Bryson, *The Chastised Stage: Bourgeois Drama and the Exercise of Power* (Stanford: Anima Libri, 1991), 5.

34. Michel Foucault, *Discipline and Punish: The Birth of the Prison*, trans. Alan Sheridan (New York: Vintage Books, 1977). The following synopsis is based on pages 3–69.

35. Ibid., 43–47.

36. Michel de Servan, *Discours sur l'administration de la justice criminelle* (Geneva, 1767), 36; see also Charles Prud'home, *Michel de Servan (1737–1807): Un Magistrat réformateur* (Paris: Larose & Tenin, 1905).

Reformers also, following the example of Beccaria, drew up elaborate taxonomies precisely relating the crime with its punishment. François Vermeil, for instance, wrote that the penalty should be that "most contrary to the vicious predisposition that produced the crime . . . the most suited to repress it and the most efficacious."[37] Thus, adulterers should be banished from the community, crimes of "idleness" like theft should be punished by forced labor, and so on. This preoccupation with congruence between crime and punishment could also involve a sadism every bit as lurid as that practiced under the old system: arsonists should be thrown alive into the flames, poisoners have a cup of poison tossed at them before being thrown alive into a vat of boiling water, parricides left to rot away in a cage suspended above the ground.[38] Foucault argues that this is not, however, merely a slight modification of traditional penology; the purpose of classifications like Servan's or Vermeil's was not symbolic expiation but didacticism, the penalty being calculated "not in terms of the crime but of its possible repetition."[39]

In the new codes, chastisement took on the more abstract qualities of a language, a decipherable set of signs that were not replicas of the crimes but compressed narratives of the action committed and its effects on society. The purpose of punishment was no longer a "symmetry of vengeance," a biblical "eye for an eye," but a lesson that could be read for the edification of onlookers. François Vermeil imagined, in a properly reformed society, the public's reaction to the acquittal of an innocent man or the conviction of a guilty one: "Prepared for either one of these events by an illuminating report and a wise discussion, the Public would find in this exposition a moral lesson all the more persuasive in that example and precept would be conjoined and punishment would follow closely on crime."[40] The spectacle of punishment, then, would no longer serve to reflect the glory of a monarch and restore the integrity of the body politic; its object would not be primarily retribution, but the enshrining within the consciences of spectators of the word of law.

In Scott Bryson's view, the new aesthetics of the "bourgeois drama" sought to provoke a similar internalization of moral norms.[41] In classical

37. François Vermeil, *Essai sur les réformes à faire dans notre législation criminelle* (Paris, 1781), 30.

38. Ibid., 66–157.

39. Foucault, *Discipline and Punish*, 93.

40. Vermeil, *Essai sur les réformes,* 236–237.

41. The next two paragraphs draw on Bryson, *The Chastised Stage*.

drama, the source of authority, the ultimate referent, be it the king, the Christian god or the gods of antiquity, or the timeless truths of character, lay outside the sphere of representation. The function of the audience within this "classical" system of representation was to serve as a witness to dramas that reflected a higher reality. In the new aesthetic code pioneered by playwrights like Diderot and Mercier, moral truth was located not beyond the visible stage but within a fiction that reflected the dynamic realities of history, of daily experience, and of social or familial relationships.

Paradoxically, the new aesthetic, whether in the plays of Mercier or in the paintings of Greuze, presented closed, self-absorbed worlds, which appeared to negate their spectators but in fact by this very act of negation drew them in all the more. In Bryson's view, then, the new theater resembled the penal codes drawn up by reformers in that both narrated stories in whose telling the public was implicated: the actions of a criminal or the dynamics of a family partook of a collective history that was shared by the public and that led to the acceptance and internalization of legal norms and moral standards. Bryson's argument helps us to make sense of the apparently hybrid nature of eighteenth-century *mémoires judiciaires* such as those written for Victoire Salmon, which function simultaneously as melodramatic performance and as object lesson in the values and procedures of a reformed judicial system.

The transformation in public culture that took place at the end of the Old Regime is therefore somewhat more complex than that suggested by some scholars who describe it as a shift away from the primarily iconic (the body of the king) to the primarily textual (the word of the law).[42] Peter Brooks argues that in the Revolution the spectacular body politics of the Old Regime was displaced not by words alone, but by a new "aesthetics of embodiment." Revolutionary rhetoric was abstract, to be sure, but its Manichaean utterances were given bodily existence, Brooks argues, in contemporary stage melodrama. Melodrama, thus, was "the genre, the speech, of revolutionary moralism; the way it states, enacts, and imposes its moral messages in clear, unambiguous words and signs."[43]

The changing place of the body in eighteenth-century public culture is perhaps best understood diachronically. The static, iconic public sphere of the Old Regime was undermined, as Jürgen Habermas has argued, by

42. See note 1.

43. Peter Brooks, "The Revolutionary Body," in *Fictions of the French Revolution*, ed. Bernadette Fort (Evanston, Ill.: Northwestern University Press, 1991), 42.

commerce and the print medium, and especially by the commercialization *of* the print medium, as represented, for instance, by the *mémoire judiciaire*. The abstractions of print culture created a diffuse "public" of readers, who through the use of their critical reasoning faculties would evolve into a politically oppositional public sphere.[44] In order for that public to be as inclusive as possible, however, writers had to enlist the power of gesture, the visual representation of the body, which they found in the pantomime and tableau of the *genre sérieux*.

In the judicial sphere, the *mémoires* represented a blueprint for what became, in the postrevolutionary judicial system, the oral testimony before a jury. On the subject of the transition from the Old Regime's written, secret procedure to the postrevolutionary open courtroom, Katherine Taylor writes that oral testimony "revolves around facts and acts, described in narrative and gesture. It . . . blends evidence into performance, encouraging the listener to judge the credibility of the speaker as well as the statement."[45] In the judicial sphere then, the transition process comprised two stages: the printed *mémoire judiciaire* undermined traditional "representation" (inasmuch as the all-powerful judge "represented" the king), but the print medium in turn relied, for greater impact, on the stage melodrama's new "aesthetics of embodiment." The public culture of postrevolutionary France was the product of a mutually reinforcing exchange between the print medium and the stage.

Sébastien Mercier dreamed in 1773 of a theater that would be "a sovereign court to which the enemy of the nation would be summoned, and before which he would be delivered to infamy, the audience's cheers sounding to his ears like the thunder of posterity."[46] He could never have imagined that his wish would come true twenty years later, with a king of France in the role of the nation's foe. As Michael Walzer suggests, the public trial and execution of Louis XVI disposed simultaneously of *both* of the king's bodies. By making Louis the king answerable to the nation as embodied in a public assembly, the deputies of the National Convention disposed of the transcendent, ahistorical monarch, the linchpin of the Old Regime's society and polity. But they also killed Louis Capet, a man whose historical actions and destiny had placed his mortal body in

44. Jürgen Habermas, *The Structural Transformation of the Public Sphere: An Inquiry into a Category of Bourgeois Society*, trans. Thomas Burger and Frederick Lawrence (Cambridge, Mass.: MIT Press, 1989), esp. chap. 2.

45. Katherine Taylor, "The Representation of Criminal Justice in Second Empire Paris" (typescript), 15.

46. Mercier, *Du théâtre*, 62.

jeopardy.[47] The readers and spectators of the trial of Louis Capet were implicated through the narrative of the Revolution in his bodily fate, just as less than a decade earlier readers had been drawn through other narratives into the historical, bodily destiny of an obscure woman, Victoire Salmon.

47. Michael Walzer, *Regicide and Revolution: Speeches at the Trial of Louis XVI* (Cambridge: Cambridge University Press, 1974), 1–34.

9

Sex, Savagery, and Slavery in the Shaping of the French Body Politic

ELIZABETH COLWILL

In 1791, two years after the French Revolution had shattered the remnants of the absolutist state, a slave revolution exploded in Saint-Domingue, the jewel of the French empire in the Caribbean.[1] In February 1794 the French Convention ceded to necessity and abolished

I am grateful to participants in the New York Area French History Seminar and the UCLA Center for Seventeenth- and Eighteenth-Century Studies/Clark Library conference "Constructing the Body in the Seventeenth and Eighteenth Centuries" for stimulating discussions of the issues raised here. Special thanks to Sara Melzer, Kathryn Norberg, Bryant T. Ragan, Stephanie McCurry, Laura Mason, and Margaret Waller for their invaluable written comments on an earlier draft of this essay.

1. My discussion of the revolution in Saint-Domingue draws on a rich historiographical tradition. I am especially endebted in what follows to Carolyn Fick, *The Making of Haiti: The Saint Domingue Revolution from Below* (Knoxville: University of Tennessee Press, 1990); C.L.R. James, *The Black Jacobins: Toussaint L'Ouverture and the San Domingo Revolution* (New York: Vintage Books, 1989); Yves Bénot, *La Révolution française et la fin des colonies* (Paris: Editions la Découverte, 1987); Julius Sherrard Scott, "The Common Wind: Currents of Afro-American Communication in the Era of the Haitian Revolution" (Ph.D. diss., Duke University, 1986); Robin Blackburn, *The Overthrow of Colonial Slavery, 1776–1848* (London: Verso, 1988); and the extensive scholarship of David Patrick Geggus, including *Slavery, War, and Revolution: The British Occupation of Saint Domingue, 1793–1798* (Oxford: Clarendon, 1982) and "Racial Equality, Slavery, and Colonial Secession During the Constituent Assembly," *American Historical Review* 95, no. 5 (December 1989): 1290–1308. Several outstanding books that illuminate the issues raised in this essay appeared after the article was written. See especially Joan Dayan, *Haiti, History, and the Gods* (Berkeley: University of California Press, 1995); Sue Peabody, *"There Are No Slaves in France": The Political Culture of Race and Slavery in the Ancien Régime* (New York: Oxford University Press, 1996); David Barry Gaspar and David Patrick Geggus, eds., *A Turbulent Time: The French Revolution and*

slavery in the French colonies.[2] The dual revolutions displaced the political order of early modern France and destroyed, if temporarily, the colonial slave regime; in the process they altered categories such as "slave," "citizen," and "woman" within which identity was conceived and contributed to the transformation, in Foucault's words, of "the way in which the body itself [was] invested by power relations."[3] In the response of French officials and colonial planters to the slave insurrection, the threat of African "atrocities" merged almost imperceptibly with the specter of black passions, even as self-identified bearers of (European) civilization jockeyed to devise the appropriate modes of corporeal repression and containment. Just as proslavery discourses unfolded according to a series of conventions concerning the "corps sauvage" and its control by the forces of civilization, French revolutionaries reconfigured political power and social order in the metropolis by anchoring allies and enemies at opposite poles of civilization and savagery. They did so by rooting their political arguments in what appeared to be the incontestable ground of the body. To mark particular enemies with a lust for bodies and blood was to stigmatize them with passions incompatible with political or moral responsibility. Sex, savagery, and slavery appeared in the political rhetoric of the revolutionary epoch as metaphors for the shifting boundaries of power, but also as a means to reconfigure social relations.[4]

French and colonial commentators, journalists, deputies, missionaries,

the Greater Caribbean (Bloomington: Indiana University Press, 1997); and David Barry Gaspar and Darlene Clark Hine, eds., *More than Chattel: Black Women and Slavery in the Americas* (Bloomington: Indiana University Press, 1996).

2. Eugene D. Genovese, *From Rebellion to Revolution: Afro-American Slave Revolts in the Making of the Modern World* (Baton Rouge: Louisiana State University Press, 1979), interprets the Saint-Domingue insurrection within the context of the European revolution as the first revolutionary slave movement in history. On the other hand, in *Testing the Chains: Resistance to Slavery in the British West Indies* (Ithaca: Cornell University Press, 1982), esp. 161, Michael Craton expresses skepticism that slave rebellions synchronized closely with the bourgeois democratic revolutions, including the French.

3. Michel Foucault, *Discipline and Punish: The Birth of the Prison* (New York: Vintage Books, 1977), esp. 24, 182–83. Foucault defines the body politic as "a set of material elements and techniques that serve as weapons, relays, communication routes and supports for the power and knowledge relations that invest human bodies and subjugate them by turning them into objects of knowledge" (28). I use the term *body politic* to connote both the ways in which all parts of the body social are implicated in the construction of power and the processes of exclusion that define certain groups as unfit for the exercise of formal political rights.

4. I draw here on Joan Scott's definition of gender as both a means of representing power and a constitutive element of social relations; see her *Gender and the Politics of History* (New York: Columbia University Press, 1988).

and pamphleteers defined civilization—and by extension the new citizenry—against an astonishing parade of transgressive bodies. In political pamphlets, "seductive" financiers, "immodest" clerics, "infamous courtesans," "vile prostitutes," unnatural nuns, sinful celibates, and lusty "nègres" illustrated the state of savagery produced by centuries of real and metaphorical "slavery."[5] Revolutionaries sought to link degenerate aristocrats with African lusts the better to discredit the old social hierarchy.[6] Competing political factions on both sides of the Atlantic struggled to appropriate power, in the name of civilization, by stigmatizing their enemies with the epithet *sauvage*. The French Creole Milly, *avocat en parlement*, drew for his audience the shocking tableau of the African *femme sauvage*, who so lacked maternal feeling that she abandoned her infants to "the voracity of tigers," while the antislavery missionary Abbé Sibire presented the colonists, not the slaves, as "barbarous" and "lustful," bestial and bloodthirsty.[7] For the royalist Abbé Solignac, unruly and violent Parisian women who abandoned the "compassion natural" to their sex presented a spectacle of "barbarism" to rival those of Algiers, Tunis, and Constantinople.[8] The *femme sauvage* assumed many masks in the age of revolution. Even Marie Antoinette, the embodiment of civilization in the Old Regime, emerged in the pornography of the Revolution as a "tiger with a taste for human blood," convicted of adultery, incest, bestiality, and tribadism.[9] The imaginary encounters in the pamphlet literature defined civilization relationally:

5. Bordel, *Opinion sur la régénération des moeurs* (Paris: Imprimerie de Dufart, Year II), 6.

6. Pierre Manuel, *La Police de Paris dévoilée*, 2 vols. (Paris, Year II), 1:348.

7. Père Jean-Baptiste Labat, a missionary in the West Indies, quoted in M. Milly, *Discours sur la question relative à la liberté des nègres, discours prononcé le 20 février 1790* (Paris, 1790); Abbé Sibire, *L'Aristocratie négrière, ou réflexions philosophiques et historiques sur l'esclavage et l'affranchissement des noirs* (Paris, 1789), 18–19.

8. Abbé Solignac, *Relation intéressante, exacte, politique et morale, des événements désastreux du Fauxbourg Saint Antoinne [sic], Quai de la Ferraille, et autres quartiers de Paris, les 24 et 25 Mai 1790*, 1–2; Cornell University French Revolution Collection, Department of Rare Books, DC 141, F87, v. 263, 424868B. On the activism of women of the people, see Dominique Godineau, *The Women of Paris and Their French Revolution* (Berkeley: University of California Press, 1998); originally published as *Citoyennes tricoteuses: Les Femmes du peuple à Paris pendant la Révolution française* (Aix-en-Provence: Alinéa, 1988).

9. Silvain, *Liste civile, suivie des noms et qualités de ceux qui la composent, et la punition dûe à leurs crimes* (n.p., 1789). Philosophes and journalists of the Enlightenment found evidence of the high development of French civilization in the status of aristocratic women and in the sexual enslavement of woman in "her primitive state" who lost "the charms of her sex in enduring the fatigues of the other" (La Croix, *Le Spectateur français avant la Révolution* [Paris, Year IV], 218–23). On the political pornography of the Revolution, see Lynn Hunt, *The Family Romance of the French Revolution* (Berkeley: University of California Press, 1992); Sarah Maza, "The Diamond Necklace Affair Revisited (1785–1786): The Case of the Missing Queen," in *Eroticism and the Body Politic*, ed. Lynn Hunt (Baltimore: Johns Hopkins University Press, 1991), 63–89; Jacques Revel, "Marie-Antoinette in Her Fictions: The Staging of Hatred," in *Fictions of the French Revolution*, ed. Bernadette Fort (Evanston, Ill.: North-

fraternity against the planters' "monstrous pleasures"; the sacred duties of wife and motherhood against the faithless bodies of market women; the rule of law and nature against slaves' thirst for vengeance; the republican body politic against Marie Antoinette's "corps impure."[10] Images of sodomitical clerics, African bloodlust, and *femmes sauvages* drew on older representational conventions in the course of reconceptualizing power and reinventing difference.

The project of grafting savagery and civilization onto the contours of gendered bodies was not, of course, specific to the revolutionary epoch. Felicity Nussbaum, for instance, has recently explored the "interpenetration between the domestic and the exotic, the civil and the savage, the political and the sexual," in the formation of the eighteenth-century British empire.[11] Throughout the age of European expansion, political and sexual orders, reciprocally defined within a binary opposition between civilization and savagery, were as intimately interwoven as the metropolitan and colonial regimes themselves. By the eighteenth century, as Julia Douthwaite has shown, conceptual devices for talking about savagery and civilization in France ran "the gamut from pseudo-scientific inquiries into humanity's original nature and institutional schemes for improving society through control of 'undesirables' to sensational fictions of exotic peoples and eyewitness views of anthropomorphic apes."[12] Natural man, envisioned variously as the bestial Hottentot, the noble American native, or the wild and solitary European, figured centrally within Enlightenment classificatory schemes, providing sites of speculation about the nature of just social and political order. "Exotics" such as the "savage" chieftain imported from Africa by Bougainville and displayed at the French court in 1769, then described in great physical detail in the *Mémoires secrets*, provided a measure of the heights achieved by French civilization. This chieftain, so went the story, confirmed his savagery when he showed "no emotion at the sight of the magnificence of the château of Versailles" but a

western University Press, 1991), 111–29; and Chantal Thomas, *La Reine scélérate: Marie-Antoinette dans les pamphlets* (Paris: Seuil, 1989).

10. On Marie Antoinette, see *La Confession de Marie-Antoinette, ci-devant reine de France, au peuple Franc, Catherine de Médicis dans le cabinet de Marie-Antoinette à St. Cloud, premier dialogue, de l'Imprimerie royale* (n.p., n.d.).

11. Felicity A. Nussbaum, *Torrid Zones: Maternity, Sexuality, and Empire in Eighteenth-Century English Narratives* (Baltimore: Johns Hopkins University Press, 1995).

12. Julia Douthwaite, "Rewriting the Savage: The Extraordinary Fictions of the 'Wild Girl of Champagne,'" *Eighteenth-Century Studies* 28 (1994–95): 62–91, esp. 63–64. On competing visions of the savage in the Renaissance, see Margaret T. Hodgen, *Early Anthropology in the Sixteenth and Seventeenth Centuries* (Philadelphia: University of Pennsylvania Press, 1964), esp. 354–85.

great and undiscriminating "passion for women."[13] French understandings of sociability, sensibility, and science derived in large part from investigation into the primitive and exotic. As Londa Schiebinger has argued, eighteenth-century anatomists analyzed non-European men and all women as deviations from the (European) masculine norm, with scientific interest focusing especially on the "black male (the dominant sex of the inferior race) and white women (the inferior sex of the dominant race)." African sexuality fell under the objectifying gaze of the French, it seems, in proportion to the state's elaboration of new methods of sexual regulation in the metropolis.[14]

By the 1790s, discourses of sex, savagery, and civilization, however formulaic, held new and radical political implications, for the slave revolution in Saint-Domingue unfolded in conjunction with a revolution in France that posed in the sharpest terms the question of which "savages"—male or female, sans-culotte or *petit blanc*, black or white—would be incorporated in the new body politic, and in what ways.[15] This essay examines the changing nature of proslavery discourses in the revolutionary period, then compares two antislavery treatises that deployed the familiar trope of civilization and savagery to new political ends. In the process, it suggests both the impact of the slave revolution in Saint-Domingue on the meanings of freedom in France and the political constraints inherent in metropolitan constructions of abolition. The conflation of debates over slavery, sex, and citizenship also provides a striking historical example of the ways in which "race" is a gendered category. Sexual hierarchy and the slave regime posed interrelated moral and practical dilemmas for French revolutionaries. The dual revolutions that forced the issue of emancipation and inspired unprecedented numbers of women on both sides of the Atlantic to political action brought the promise of universal rights into direct conflict with French republicans' struggles to obtain political legitimacy at home, retain control of their empire abroad, and establish new forms of "free" and domestic labor. Inventive justifications for racial and sexual hierarchy were necessary to revolutionaries whose political survival

13. *Mémoires secrets pour servir à l'histoire de la République des Lettres en France* (London, 1780), 4:266–67 (10 July 1769). For another example of exoticism, see the description of the "white Negress" displayed in France and Italy in *Mémoires secrets*, 10:174 (9 July 1777).

14. Londa Schiebinger, *Nature's Body: Gender in the Making of Modern Science* (Boston: Beacon Press, 1993), 144; Robert Purks Maccubbin, ed., *'Tis Nature's Fault: Unauthorized Sexuality During the Enlightenment* (Cambridge: Cambridge University Press, 1987).

15. For the revolutionary period, see Jean-Claude Halpern, "Représentations populaires des peuples exotiques en France, à la fin du XVIIIe siecle" (Thèse doctoral, Histoire, Paris I, 1992).

required mitigating abstract political idealism with more restrictive notions of citizenship and an apprenticeship in civilization. The pro- and antislavery treatises examined here thus illuminate what Thomas Holt has termed the "problem of freedom" in postemancipation societies, and expose it as a gendered problem.[16]

To study discourses of sex, savagery, and slavery at the juncture of revolution on both sides of the Atlantic is to glimpse in microcosm the impact of political rupture on early modern conceptions of hierarchy, social order, and difference.[17] Proslavery theorists of the early modern period had conceived of the slave system, like the sexual order, as one part of an organic social and political hierarchy sanctioned by king and Church.[18] The assertion that all men were not born with the same faculties or the same rights would have seemed self-evident to most eighteenth-century French subjects of European descent, despite the challenges posed by the likes of Locke, Montesquieu, and Rousseau.[19] Privileges did indeed derive from race, but until the late eighteenth century the term referred not to "scientific" sets of fixed physical characteristics, but rather to a broader notion of "race" as bloodline or lineage.[20] The extent to which Europeans' generally negative view of "savages" derived from "racial difference" itself remains a controversial subject among scholars, in part because the historical malleability of the term *race* occludes the subject under debate. We know, however, that the category *sauvage* was flexible enough to accommodate the Irish as well as the African, among others, in the early modern period. The fact that travelers and political emissaries not only recognized linguistic, political, and religious distinctions between African peoples but also honored individual African leaders would seem to undermine the ahistorical assumption that racial antipathy proceeded "naturally" from differences of color.

16. Thomas Holt, *The Problem of Freedom: Race, Labor, and Politics in Jamaica and Britain, 1832–1938* (Baltimore: Johns Hopkins University Press, 1992).

17. On slavery as a sexual, though not fully gendered, system, see Ronald G. Walters, *The Antislavery Appeal: American Abolitionism After 1830* (New York: W. W. Norton, 1978).

18. For an example of relationships of authority conceived within familial metaphors of king and colonies, see M. Dutrône la Couture, *Vues générales sur l'importance du commerce des colonies, sur le caractère du peuple qui les cultive, & sur les moyens de faire la constitution qui leur convient* (n.p., 1788).

19. [Anon.], *Catéchisme des colonies, pour servir à l'instruction des habitans de la France* (Paris, 1791), 38. See Edward Derbyshire Seeber, *Anti-Slavery Opinion in France During the Second Half of the Eighteenth Century* (New York: Greenwood Press, 1937).

20. Jean-Louis Flandrin, *Families in Former Times: Kinship, Household, and Sexuality*, trans. Richard Southern (London: Cambridge University Press, 1979), 11–12.

Nor did slavery itself generate modern racism.[21] Before the age of revolution, slave traders and planters could define the "nègre" as peculiarly suited for enslavement without resorting to biological explanations for the subject status of the enslaved. Scientific racism and sexism reached their apogee in the wake of—not prior to—emancipation.[22] In the eighteenth century, French philosophes were more likely to attribute cultural variation to historical evolution or climactic variation than to biological difference per se. In an era in which many naturalists still perceived age, sex, and nation as more salient categories than "race" for differentiating among humankind, Europeans' sense of superiority over the "primitive" obtained not from cranial measurements but rather from an ethos of politeness and sociability linked to commerce and civilization itself.[23] Nonetheless, race provided an essential principle of social organization in early modern Europe. If, as Tessie Liu has argued, "the operating definition of race was based not on external physical characteristics but on blood ties—or, more precisely, some common substance passed on" through heterosexual relations and birth, then race was a way of imagining community that embraced both class and gender.[24]

The dual revolutions in France and Saint-Domingue transformed this early modern terrain by shifting the theoretical and corporeal grounding of social hierarchy. The anonymously authored *Catéchisme des colonies, pour servir à l'instruction des habitans de la France* resembled its early modern precursors in insisting on the natural inequality among men. Yet this proslavery tract, published in the revolutionary year 1791, differed in im-

21. Barbara Jeanne Fields, "Slavery, Race, and Ideology in the United States of America," *New Left Review*, no. 181 (1990): 95–118. For the classic statement of an opposing view, see Winthrop Jordan, *White over Black* (New York: W. W. Norton, 1977). See, in the French context, Pierre Boulle, "In Defense of Slavery: Eighteenth-Century Opposition to Abolition and the Origins of Racist Ideology in France," in *History from Below*, ed. Frederick Krantz (Oxford: Oxford University Press, 1988), 219–46.

22. Fields, "Slavery, Race, and Ideology," 116. On the changing terminology of race in antislavery literature, see Serge Daget, "Les Mots esclave, nègre, noir, et les jugements de valeur sur la traite négrière dans la littérature abolitionniste française de 1770 à 1845," *Revue française d'histoire d'outre-mer* 60 (1973): 511–48.

23. On naturalists, see Schiebinger, *Nature's Body*, 117; on sociability, see Daniel Gordon, *Citizens Without Sovereignty: Equality and Sociability in French Thought, 1670–1789* (Princeton: Princeton University Press, 1994), esp. 134–35, 149–50. William B. Cohen, *The French Encounter with Africans: White Response to Blacks, 1530–1880* (Bloomington: Indiana University Press, 1980), 60–99, stresses the philosophes' generally negative view of blacks, but recognizes the differences between their theories of inequality and nineteenth-century scientific visions of race as immutable.

24. Tessie Liu, "Teaching the Differences Among Women from a Historical Perspective: Rethinking Race and Gender as Social Categories," *Women's Studies International Forum* 14 (1991): 265–76, esp. 270–71.

portant ways from the proslavery thought of the Old Regime, for it invoked the revolutionary slogan of liberty as buttress for the autonomist aspirations of French and Creole colonists.[25] By the first months of 1791, colonists in Saint-Domingue had joined political clubs, denounced "ministerial despotism" and the restrictions imposed on colonial trade by the French metropolis, elected a renegade colonial assembly, and achieved colonial representation in the French National Assembly. There, in the company of absentee planters in the Massiac Club and their allies on the French Colonial Committee, colonial representatives proceeded to act as a powerful lobby against those *gens de couleur* who demanded the extension of the Declaration of the Rights of Man and Citizen to the large population of free, property-holding, and in many cases slave-holding men of mixed race in the colonies.[26] Meanwhile, *petits blancs* in the colonies had extended the assault on class privilege and claimed the rights of man, which they gained only to wield ever more violently as a club against *gens de couleur* with similar aspirations to citizenship.[27] In February 1791, after an unsuccessful insurrection by *gens de couleur* in Saint-Domingue, Vincent Ogé and Jean-Baptiste Chavannes were broken on the wheel and beheaded, their heads exposed on stakes as an example to those of mixed race insolent enough to aspire to a piece of the liberty the white colonists had claimed for themselves.[28]

These bloody events in the colonies unfolded in uneven and awkward tandem with the revolution in France, which by the beginning of 1791 had demolished royal "despotism," abolished feudalism, and established a constitutional regime. By the time of the publication of the *Catéchisme des colonies*, Abbé Sièyes had redefined the Third Estate as the "nation,"

25. David Brion Davis, *The Problem of Slavery in the Age of Revolution, 1770–1823* (Ithaca: Cornell University Press, 1975).

26. Fick, *Making of Haiti*, 78, shows that the Massiac Club, initially formed in Paris by colonists opposed to colonial representation in the French Assembly, soon made common cause with the colonial deputies in their attempts to block the aspirations of the *gens de couleur*.

27. See, for example, the violent denuncation of the terms *grands blancs* and *petits blancs* by Baillio l'aîné, *L'Anti-Brissot, par un petit blanc de Saint-Domingue* (Paris: Girardin, [1791]), 10–11.

28. John Garrigus, "Blue and Brown: Contraband Indigo and the Rise of a Free Colored Planter Class in French Saint-Domingue," *Americas* 2 (October 1993): 233–63, argues that the movement for reform by the free colored population on the southern coast contributed to the destabilization of the slave regime. As David Brion Davis demonstrates in *The Problem of Slavery*, 143–46, not until May 1791 would the Girondin ministry grant rights to all men born of free parents. Only in the spring of 1792, when confronted with the need to ally with *gens de couleur* in the interests of pacifying the insurgent slaves, would the Legislative Assembly enfranchise all free men of color.

Parisian women had brought the royal family to Paris to remain under the surveillance of the people, and French patriots were well on their way to war with "foreign despots." Shorn of the familiar clerical foundation of hierarchy and privilege, and in the context of increasing hostility toward colonial interests, the unadorned argument that "all men are not equal" required a new evidentiary buttress both in France and in the colonies.

The age of revolution that transformed the meaning of antislavery forced proslavery ideologues to rethink the foundations of social hierarchy and, in the words of David Brion Davis, moved debates over slavery "irresistibly to the ground of race."[29] As Barbara Jeanne Fields has argued, in the United States "racial ideology supplied the means of explaining slavery to people whose terrain was a republic founded on radical doctrines of liberty and natural rights."[30] Even prior to the republican era, revolution in France and its colonies dislodged old rationales for slavery and altered the terrain of proslavery thought. The *Catéchisme des colonies*, for instance, reconciled autonomist ambitions and the interests of civilization and the slave regime with a retreat to the secure terrain of nature; however, unlike its proslavery precursors, it retreated not to the natural hierarchy inherent in lineage, but to the political implications of color. Blacks, explained the author, differed from whites not merely in skin color but in build, behavior, organs, senses, appetites, ideas, and mental faculties; indeed, he insisted, the intellectual divergence was so profound that blacks themselves readily conceded that their race was "incapable of perfection" and that white man was "man par excellence, the model of human perfection."[31] Since "one must follow nature, and not command it," it

29. Davis, *Problem of Slavery*, 303; Blackburn, *Overthrow of Colonial Slavery;* Holt, *Problem of Freedom*. Edward Seeber, *Anti-Slavery Opinion*, provides ample evidence of eighteenth-century Europeans' fascination with the meanings and origins of "color." According to Robert Dirks, *The Black Saturnalia: Conflict and Its Ritual Expression on British West Indian Slave Plantations* (Gainesville: University of Florida Press, 1987), 31–32, slaves were sometimes described earlier in the eighteenth century as a separate "species," but the same term was also used to differentiate between French and English and aristocrat and peasant. Although, as Dirks says, the French and English might define themselves against the African as "members of a single race," race appeared more a question of degree than of kind. Despite the elaborate classification systems based on color in the West Indies, the essential determinant of both species and race was less one's color than one's position within the broader religious and political hierarchy.

30. "Slavery got along for a hundred years after its establishment without race as its ideological rationale. The reason is simple. Race explained why some people could rightly be denied what others took for granted: namely, liberty. . . . But there was nothing to explain until most people could, in fact, take liberty for granted" (Fields, "Slavery, Race, and Ideology," 114).

31. *Catéchisme*, 37–39, 45. On the intimate relationship betweeen colonial science, medicine, and slavery in prerevolutionary Saint-Domingue, see James E. McClellan III,

would be impossible to establish equality constitutionally. Instead, the legislator should devise regulations to govern the drives, or passions, specific to each race.

Thus relieved by nature of the revolutionary dictates of equality, the author was at liberty to reconstruct political order as racial hierarchy, which made a theory of the "intrinsic value" of each race the basis of an equality of classes. If the "sacred" Declaration of Rights of Man made no distinction between categories of men, that was because "no physical or moral differences [existed] between the diverse classes of inhabitants of France." The colonies, however, presented a different case, for the black, condemned to an eternal childhood by the weakness of his faculties, had so little "intrinsic value" that he was unfit to partake in the society of "free and enlightened men." The man of mixed race acquired value in proportion to the percentage of white (paternal) blood that ran through his veins. But only the white man, invested with the highest intrinsic value, had, "essentially," the right to citizenship.[32]

The comprehensive racial program of the *Catéchisme des colonies* rooted hierarchy in gendered bodies, black and white. In so doing, it erased gender difference within the category "race," constructed paternity as the determinant of race, rendered French women invisible within the universal "man," and proposed "race" as substitute for class as the "natural" physical and moral foundation of social order.[33] One can glimpse in the identification, examination, and classification of "racial" characteristics the development of a repertoire of signs of blackness that in their very essence defined inferiority. The author of the *Catéchisme des colonies* thus reconfigured the older binary oppositions between civilization and savagery, intellect and passion, black and white, model man and his inverse, around

---

Colonialism and Science: Saint Domingue in the Old Regime (Baltimore: Johns Hopkins University Press, 1992).

32. *Catéchisme*, 44–45, 47–78.

33. I am not suggesting that race simply replaced class as a "naturalized" category of social order. After various eighteenth-century assaults on privilege, however, defenders of class distinction tended to represent social distinction in racial and gendered terms. In that discursive sense, class became race in the age of revolution. On shifting understandings of the "nature" of sexual, racial, and/or class difference, see Dorinda Outram, *The Body in the French Revolution: Sex, Class, and Political Culture* (New Haven: Yale University Press, 1989); Michel Foucault, *Histoire de la sexualité*, 2 vols. (Paris: Editions Gallimard, 1976); Thomas Laqueur, *Making Sex: Body and Gender from the Greeks to Freud* (Cambridge, Mass.: Harvard University Press, 1990); Julia Epstein and Kristina Straub, *Bodyguards: The Cultural Politics of Gender Ambiguity* (New York: Routledge, 1991); Londa Schiebinger, *The Mind Has No Sex? Women in the Origins of Modern Science* (Cambridge, Mass.: Harvard University Press, 1989); and Henry Louis Gates Jr., ed., *"Race," Writing, and Difference* (Chicago: University of Chicago Press, 1986).

a racial order that elided gender difference among those with the least "intrinsic value."[34] In so doing he was typical of French proslavery theorists of his epoch, who with increasing regularity derived a "natural" propensity toward slavery from Africans' "natural" state of moral degeneracy represented by passion, paganism, and sloth. Colonists in the years of revolution tended to embellish Bougainville's voyeuristic charge that in African lands, "men and women deliver themselves without modesty to the sins of the flesh," copulating in broad daylight "on the first mat they find."[35] The slave system, which represented to proslavery theorists an "amelioration" of the African condition, thus emerged as intrinsic to the civilizing mission itself.[36]

Even French opponents of the slave trade tended to agree with Monsieur de Milly that slaves summoned too soon to the banner of liberty were likely to confuse liberty with license. The better to represent the threat, Milly presented "evidence" that Africans, unchecked by civilization, inscribed their passions on the body in blood. He walked his readers through the "flesh markets" of the Gold Coast replete with disemboweled dogs and mutilated natives; introduced them to a savage kingdom where bodies received no decent burial and were consumed by panthers and birds of prey; displayed for their view a dozen freshly cut heads mounted as trophies for the pleasure of a king who dipped his feet in his victims' blood and held his wives in seclusion to await his desires.[37] To the "barbaric" practices of ritual sacrifice, mutilation, and polygamy, Milly added the obligatory reference to cannibalism. Quoting another European traveler, he confided: "The Anicos eat their slaves; human flesh is as common in their markets as beef is in ours." Indeed, cannibalism could be a family affair: "The father devours the flesh of his son, the son that of the father; the brothers and sisters eat one another," and the mother callously feeds upon her newborn infant.[38] The tale of primitive passions that Milly invented for his readers culminated, then, with the taboos that distinguished man from beast. The *femme sauvage* who consumed her own infants in a brutal state of nature figured the "nègre" as devoid of family

34. On race and Manichaean analogies, see Abdul R. JanMohamed, "Sexuality on/of the Racial Border: Foucault, Wright, and the Articulation of 'Racialized Sexuality,'" in *Discourses of Sexuality: From Aristotle to AIDS*, ed. Domna C. Stanton (Ann Arbor: University of Michigan Press, 1992), 106.

35. *Mémoires secrets*, 4:266–67.

36. Milly, *Discours sur la question relative à la liberté des nègres, prononcé en l'assemblée générale du district des Filles-Saint-Thomas* (Paris: Didot jeune, 1790), 3, 9–10.

37. M. Gourg, royal administrator on the Gold Coast, quoted in ibid., 21–27.

38. Drapper, quoted in ibid., 20.

feeling, therefore beyond the boundaries of civilized society. Against this backdrop of African bloodlust Milly invoked the specter of an American bloodbath. The mere rumor of freedom, he reminded his audience, had already caused agitation in Guadeloupe and Saint-Domingue, and an insurrection in Martinique. The slaves, he warned, were "not disposed to become the fellow citizens of their masters"; it was far more likely that slaves would become their executioners.[39] This self-proclaimed sympathizer with the slaves concluded, then, by defining fraternity along racial lines.

If the prospect of a massacre was a useful club to wield against the Amis des Noirs and their allies, Creole planters and their French supporters outdid themselves to depict the impact of black passions unleashed after the slave revolution that erupted in Saint-Domingue the night of 22 August 1791. The slaves on the Gallifet plantation who rose according to a carefully orchestrated plan against one of the wealthiest and most murderous slave regimes in the western hemisphere were soon joined by thousands across the Northern Plain and eventually the West and South. In C.L.R. James's classic statement, their acts of vengeance were real, but hardly in proportion to the daily death they had suffered under slavery or, for that matter, to the terror unleashed by the "forces of order" in response to the revolt itself.[40] Yet French commentators joined Creole colonists in denouncing the murderous passions of the insurgent slaves rather than their masters. In fact, the response of many French revolutionaries to the "calamity" in Saint-Domingue suggests that pro- and antislavery forces both found the prospect of an "empire of blacks" threatening, if for different reasons.[41] In the account of one French citizen, a witness to the slave uprising in Saint-Domingue, black "monsters" coupled with foreign foes and vermin clerics presented an unholy fraternity responsible for the devastation. The blacks, he claimed, massacred children "on the breasts of their mothers," impaled babies on pikes, and butchered young girls after they had "satiated the brutality of the brigands and endured indignities that the pen refuses to trace."[42] The letters from Saint-Domingue that trickled into the metropolis as the months passed confirmed earlier suspicions of black savagery. Colonial deputies disseminated tales of *gens de couleur* who pinned whites' ears to their caps in place of cockades and slaves who

39. Ibid., 10–11.
40. James, *Black Jacobins*, 88–89.
41. Sibire, *L'Aristocratie négrière*, 69.
42. Baillio l'aîné, *L'Anti-Brissot*, 8–9.

tore a fetus from a pregnant woman and forcibly fed it to her husband.[43] In such narratives, black men's naked exercise of power despoiled civilization's sacred objects—mothers, virgins, and children—and made beasts of civilized men. The familiar trope of the imposition of savagery on civilization, deployed by colonists in defense of the slave regime, served in the context of slave revolution to refigure the terrain of both racial and gender difference.

The Manichaean boundaries of colonial discourse, however, reveal only one part of the story. If "savages" were a mere discursive effect, slaves were not. Behind the planters' vocabulary of savagery and civilization lay a revolutionary drama in which former slaves, male and female, forced themselves as historical actors on the consciousness of colonists and government officials and claimed liberty for themselves.[44] Between the opening days of the insurrection in August 1791 and the French Convention's emancipation decree on 16 Pluviôse Year II (4 February 1794), the relationship between France and its colonies had changed dramatically. By Year II, having established a republic, executed their king and queen, and declared war on domestic and foreign foes, the French had sent troops and commissioners to subdue the planters (by this time largely royalists), to enforce the rights of the *gens de couleur*, and to crush the insurgent slaves. Despite the recall of the Girondin commissioners as opinion turned against Brissot and his followers in the Convention in late 1792, Commissioner Léger-Félicité Sonthonax refused his summons and set about fulfilling his mission. The steady advance of royalist planters in the company of Spanish and British troops, however, drove Sonthonax back on the mercies of the *gens de couleur* and the former slaves and forced him into a series of concessions that culminated in his emancipation proclamation of the North on 29 August 1793. Commissioner Poverel soon followed suit in the South and West. In the wake of this momentous decree, Sonthonax sent three emissaries to France with the unenviable mission of justifying an emancipation proclamation that had not emanated from the French Convention itself. The task of defending the commissioners' actions fell to the white deputy from the Northern Province of

43. De Laval, "Extrait d'une Letter des Cayes du 30 janvier 1792," *Nouvelles de St. Domingue;* Archives Nationales [hereafter cited as AN], W13 (Juridictions Extraordinaires—Parquet du Tribunal Révolutionnaire), no. 45.

44. For illuminating analyses of the ways in which an exclusive focus on colonial categories of knowledge can flatten the experiences of the subaltern, see the contributions of Gyan Prakash, Florencia E. Mallon, and Frederick Cooper to the forum in *American Historical Review*, 99, no. 5 (December 1994): 1475–1545.

Saint-Domingue, Louis Pierre Dufay, Parisian born but a longtime *greffier* and landholder in Saint-Domingue. His speech before the Convention on 16 Pluviôse Year II (4 February 1794) invoked the familiar opposition between savagery and civilization, but this time in opposition to, rather than in service of, the slave regime.

Dufay's defense of the emancipation decree was a masterpiece of political artistry. First, he depicted the slave revolution of 1791 as a conspiracy orchestrated by outsiders, representing the former slaves as incapable of initiative, self-organization, or political leadership. Spanish and British gold and the planters who had "propositioned Pitt" and regarded themselves as a "privileged race" were, he claimed, responsible for the atrocity of insurrection. Next, he constructed the *gens de couleur*, the "evil, undisciplined men, cruel and ferocious beings" of planter narratives, as the "true sans-culottes of the colonies."[45] In his narrative, these manly troops, along with loyal black workers, had provided a law-abiding bulwark for the deputies against the bloodthirsty Galbaud, "minister of the vengeance of his caste." Once Dufay had inverted the planters' equation of black with passion and re-created blacks as faithful servants who shared with the deputies a common enemy, he had arrived at a justification for emancipating those black soldiers who had served the French *patrie*.

His response was far cooler toward those former slaves who after two years in rebellion reappeared en masse armed with weapons and revolutionary vocabulary to strike a bargain with the French delegates. In Dufay's recollection, they explicitly demanded the rights of man in the course of claiming their freedom. "'We are French Nègres,' they said. 'We will fight for France, but in recompense we demand our liberty.'" It was, for Dufay, a humiliating moment: "We were confused," he confessed; "they felt their strength; they could even have turned their weapons against us." Law thus followed the logic of necessity. Unable to force these self-emancipated men into the posture of supplicants, the French delegates granted liberty to all men, regardless of color, who fought for the French republic against foreign or domestic foes. In the days that followed the initial manumissions, Le Cap burned while, in Dufay's inflammatory description, "all" the former slaves of the Northern Province were "delivered to themselves, without brake, without guide, knowing no other law than their will."[46] Having summoned for his audience of *conventionnels* the fa-

45. [Louis Pierre] Dufay, *Compte rendu sur la situation actuelle de Saint Domingue* (Paris: Imprimérie Nationale, 1794), 3–4, 14–21.

46. Ibid., 6–9.

miliar specter of black savagery, he sought to vindicate the deputies' actions and reconstitute their authority by placing the blame for the destruction squarely on Galbaud's perfidy.

Dufay's justification for the sweeping emancipation proclamation of 29 August, however, took the form of a narrative in which former slaves earned the status of citizens when they insisted on the rights of their sex. By the end of August, freedmen, invested with new powers, had assumed the prerogatives of masters of households by demanding freedom for their families. In Dufay's account, freedmen appeared as republican husbands and fathers who claimed their children as personal "property" and represented their wives as patriotic helpmeets and model mothers. "'It isn't our wives' fault that they are unable to take up arms for France. Should they be punished for the weakness of their sex?'"[47] At least two speakers—Dufay and the former slaves—are present in this text, and two audiences sit in judgment: the colonial deputies who weighed the rebels' argument for emancipation in Saint-Domingue, and the members of the French Convention, who were to determine the fate of the colonial emancipation proclamation of August. We would be mistaken to conclude from Dufay's memory of events that the insurgent slaves shared with French Jacobins a "naturalized" conception of bourgeois womanhood.[48] Slave women had never enjoyed the privileges of the "weaker sex" in Saint-Domingue, nor had they acted as "ladies" in the years of revolution.[49] In fact, on this occasion, slave women had organized in their own interests. When the municipality of Le Cap sent a delegation to the French commissioners demanding freedom for the families of black soldiers, "an immense crowd of women," armed with the liberty cap and dragging their children with them, "followed the petitioners, crying 'Long live the French Republic! Long Live Liberty!'"[50]

47. Ibid., 9.

48. Ibid., 4–6. As John K. Thornton has shown in "'I Am the Subject of the King of Congo': African Political Ideology and the Haitian Revolution," *Journal of World History* 4 (1993): 181–214, two-thirds of the slaves in Saint-Domingue on the eve of revolution had been born and raised in Africa, and thus brought to the revolution their own republican and monarchist ideologies of resistance.

49. See Barbara Bush, *Slave Women in Caribbean Society, 1650–1838* (Kingston, Jamaica: Heinemann, 1990); and Arlette Gautier, *Les Soeurs de solitude: La Condition féminine dans l'esclavage aux Antilles du XVIIe au XIXe siècle* (Paris: Editions Caribéennes, 1985).

50. Députés de la Partie du Nord de Saint-Domingue, *Relation détaillée des évènemens malheureux qui se sont passés au Cap depuis l'arrivée du ci-devant général Galbaud, jusqu'au moment où il a fait brûler cette ville et a pris la fuite* (Paris: Imprimérie Nationale, 1794), 73–74. For the broader context of women's revolutionary resistance, see Bernard Moitt, "Slave Women and Resistance in the French Caribbean," in *More than Chattel,* eds. Gaspar and Hine, 239–58.

Significantly, Dufay chose to exclude from his narrative the initiative women took in their own emancipation. Instead he refashioned slave women as republican mothers and slave men as masters of households endowed with paternal rights—rights entirely at odds with the planters' "right" to property in persons. In domesticating black passions within a European familial model, Dufay deftly assimilated "savages" into civilization.[51] His speech before the Convention thus reveals the complex ways in which the savagery/civilization trope, whether deployed in service of the slave regime or the new republic, drew its force from the juxtaposition of "primitive" passions to a "civilized" familial order. On the one hand, sexual order paved the route to emancipation. On the other, the dynamic of revolution itself provided its own rationale: "The blacks of the Northern Province were already free in fact; they were the masters." What was the civil commissioner to do but take the "prudent" path and free the remaining slaves?[52]

It would have been unseemly to leave the republic's delegates thus "mastered." Dufay hastened to assure the *conventionnels* that the decree of 29 August had "subjected" the former slaves to a severe discipline, "bound them to the soil," and put them to work for a daily wage. Properly disciplined, freedmen and -women would indemnify France by producing workers for the *patrie*. A new regime, Dufay declared, had come into being, based on the rights of commerce and property and the rule of law.[53] If recently blacks had "merited some reproaches for indiscipline, excuse them, citizens." Freedmen needed enlightened "guides" on the road to emancipation, just as "a necessary passage" existed between "youth to manhood [*virilité*]."[54]

The analogy was apt. As Dufay traced the road to emancipation on the (white male) body, he constructed a bridge between proslavery paternalism and an antislavery Jacobinism that would gently draw the former slaves from savagery toward civilization through an apprenticeship in republican virtue. To preserve whites from the potential dangers of a black apprenticeship in "manhood," Dufay drew a portrait of black "nature" as

51. Cf. M. Jacqui Alexander, "Not Just (Any)Body Can be a Citizen: The Politics of Law, Sexuality, and Postcoloniality in Trinidad and Tobago and the Bahamas," *Feminist Review* 48 (autumn 1994): 5–23, on the relationship between nation-building and the heterosexual family in a colonial context.

52. Dufay, *Compte rendu*, 8–10.

53. On the labor provisions of the emancipation proclamation of Sonthonax, see Robert L. Stein, *Léger Félicité Sonthonax: The Lost Sentinel of the Republic* (London: Associated University Presses, 1985), 89–90. Fick, *Making of Haiti*, 168, specifies that the labor codes were not put into practice for several months.

54. Dufay, *Compte rendu*, 21–22.

the mirror image of European womanhood. By assimilating the "natural" black—male or female—to the virtues of woman—"patient," "generous," "sweet," "charitable," "respectful"—he stripped them of the passions that could threaten French rule. Schooled in republican virtues by French patriots, the emancipated slave could figure as the quintessential "new man," mascot of the beneficent transformation wrought by the Revolution.

In Dufay's attempt to reconcile the new boundaries of the republican body politic with liberal notions of property, slaves, like peasants, were to "redeem" their obligations to a regenerated French nation. But it would prove impossible both to erase "caste" distinctions based on color within a single national identity and to confine former slaves within a modern coercive labor regime.[55] Dufay's was a contradictory vision that the *conventionnels* confirmed as "tutelary divinities" when they decreed universal emancipation in the colonies on 16 Pluviôse Year II (4 February 1794).[56] The brief emancipation proclamation, which abolished slavery and granted all men in the colonies the rights guaranteed by the constitution, explicitly redrew the boundaries of citizenship without specifying the nature of the labor system that would replace slavery. Yet education, labor, and family would serve as watchwords in the project of reconstructing the black savage as French subject. Just as a feminine liberty could represent the fledging republic while the rights of citizenship remained the rights of man, the emancipated slave could receive Dufay's "fraternal embrace" without fully realizing the promise of equality.[57] Despite the extraordinary radicalism of the emancipation decrees of Sonthonax and the Convention, empire and tutelage rooted in fears of black passions marked the boundaries of their vision of the "new man." Dufay's text reveals the coercive force of that vision. Most important, it reveals the changing shape of the body politic as the product of negotiation with black revolutionaries, male and female, who had claimed freedom for themselves as full historical subjects.

If Dufay's account had hesitantly incorporated new men into the French body politic following the dictates of political expediency, Pierre Gaspard Chaumette, in his official capacity as representative of the Paris Commune, explicitly designed his speech for the festival at the Temple of

55. Ibid., 24.

56. Bénot, *Révolution française*, 180–83, notes that the emancipation decrees played a critical role in cementing the alliance between white republicans and black insurgents in Saint-Domingue. They brought the leading black generals, including Toussaint L'Ouverture, into the republican forces and turned the tide of the war in Saint-Domingue in France's favor.

57. Dufay, *Compte rendu*, 23–26.

Reason on 30 Pluviôse Year II (18 February 1794) to celebrate the principle of emancipation declared by the Convention. Whereas Dufay's conversion to the cause of emancipation had been a recent one, by the time of abolition Chaumette, *procureur* of the Paris Commune from December 1792 and then *agent national*, had gone on record as an advocate for blacks and *gens de couleur*. On 15 June 1793 he had led a delegation of blacks and whites before the Convention to present a petition in favor of abolition. Less than two weeks later he initiated the Commune's "adoption" of an orphaned black child, whom he christened "Ogé, martyr of American liberty."[58] It was again Chaumette who assumed responsibility at the Festival of Reason on 30 Pluviôse for redrawing the boundaries of the French body politic so as to incorporate former slaves as citizens.[59]

His speech, delivered in the name of the Paris Commune and in the presence of a delegation from the Convention, conflated antislavery, civilization, and fraternity and defined them in opposition to a state of savagery where passions reigned.[60] In his text, the "barbarian" was not the slave but the master "who first charged his brother with irons" and destroyed "man in man by opposing nature to nature." For Chaumette, slavery, "the greatest of evils," was in its essence an assault on manhood. Slavery served as a metaphor for the subjugation of all men, the degradation of the species prior to the Revolution when France was a nation of "brigands," "slaves," and "ferocious animals." The revolution that had abolished feudal slavery in France would, in destroying colonial slavery, regenerate manhood at home and abroad.[61]

Women were absent from Chaumette's text when discussion focused exclusively on fraternity, but they emerged occasionally within the familiar antislavery formulas of dusky maidens sacrificed to the unchaste embrace

58. On the delegation that Chaumette led to the Convention, see *Archives parlementaires*, vol. 66, 4 June 1793; and Bénot, *Révolution française*, 171. For Chaumette's role in ensuring the success of the colonial deputies at the Convention, see Bénot, *Révolution française*, 83–85. On the adoption, see *Affiches de la Commune de Paris*, no. 1, 14 June 1793.

59. *Nouvelles politiques, nationales et étrangères* 85 (25 Pluviôse Year II/13 February 1794), 339; and 92 (2 Ventôse Year II/20 February 1794). Chaumette would pay the price for his militant leadership of the Parisian sans-culottes. While Dufay survived the Terror, sat briefly on the Council of Five Hundred, and held minor juridical posts until 1815, Chaumette, advocate of de-Christianization, was guillotined as an "apostle of atheism" just two months after his speech in the Temple of Reason (AN, W345 [Juridictions Extraordinaires-Tribunal Révolutionnaire], no. 676, pt. 1, pièce 26, Procès Chaumette).

60. Pierre Gaspard Chaumette, *Discours prononcé par le citoyen Chaumette, au nom de la Commune de Paris, le décadi 30 pluviôse an II (18 février 1794), à la fête célébrée à Paris, le décadi 30 pluviôse an II (18 février 1794), en réjouisance de l'abolition de l'esclavage* (Paris: Imprimerie Nationale, [1794]).

61. Ibid., 3–4, 10, 13–14.

of their masters and maternal instinct violated by slavers' greed.[62] Their appearance, if fleeting, was vital to the ideological work of associating the slave system, rather than slaves themselves, with a state of savagery. Just as Dufay had invoked slave women's familial roles to justify their emancipation, Chaumette summoned images of mothers who suffocated their beloved children from "tenderness and pity" so as to condemn slavery as an institution that denatured motherhood. Chaumette supplanted the proslavery cliché of the African mother as a natural cannibal with the representation of the slave system itself as a violation of both maternal sympathies and the female body. Sex was essential to the Chaumette's realignment of proslavery paradigms, for in his text the rape of woman violated the rights of man. "Follow the greedy merchant of men," he urged. "Watch him pile his victims one upon the other in a close, foul, stifling space; [see him] bruise beneath a sinuous rope the breast still swollen with milk; see the young wife torn from her husband, her children . . . ; hear the moans of these wretched creatures."[63] The masculine counterpart to the sadistic romance with the bound body of African woman typical of the male antislavery literature was a masochistic fascination with black passions expressed as male violence. In Chaumette's speech, the slavers' rape of beautiful Africa had transformed "a people sweet by essence" into a herd of "wild beasts" engaged in a "war of vengeance" that left the earth "strewn with cadavers." He evoked for his listeners the specter of the slave uprising, in which three hundred thousand slaves metamorphosed into three hundred thousand armed men who ravaged the countryside. "What do I see? . . . black men! . . . the homicidal arrow in your hands!" The traffickers in man had created a monster of slavery indistinguishable from its manifestation as black rage.[64]

Just as Dufay had evoked black passion only to reconstruct paternal authority, Chaumette lowered the curtain on black rage and opened it on a panorama of French nationalism. Now that the *conventionnels*, "ministers of the morality of the nations," had listened to the voice of nature and passed the "immortal" emancipation decree, the slaves, Chaumette

62. The antislavery missionary Abbé Sibire considered the destruction of the African family one the most powerful images in his antislavery arsenal. See, for instance, his description of a young wife and mother who was attacked while tending her fields and pushed violently "toward the abyss" (*L'Aristocratie négrière*, 57–58). Sibire left to the imagination of his audience the "*épouvantables* disgraces" suffered by the young wife at the hands of her "inflexible ravishers," and in the process sexualized her maternal sufferings.

63. Chaumette, *Discours*, 13–14, 16.

64. Ibid., 17–19.

promised, would respond with loyalty and gratitude. Now, he urged, was the time for the remaining black insurgents to abandon their English and Spanish allies, join the republican forces, and adopt as their battle cry "France" and the "National Convention." Linking an emancipatory French nationalism to traditions of resistance among men of color, he advised freedmen to erect a monument "as simple as [their] hearts" to honor the "male virtues" and martyrdom of Ogé, inscribed "Decree of the National Convention That Abolished Slavery."[65] Chaumette thus redrew the boundaries of the French body politic from the common manhood of citizens and former slaves. His address, like the Code Noir discussed by Joseph Roach in this volume, constituted "an act of incorporation, an expansion of the body politic," which, unlike its precedents, reconstructed difference along a divide marked by gender rather than by color. But Chaumette's discursive metamorphosis of slaves into French subjects left even freedmen something short of citizens. Fraternity, he warned, could not immediately obliterate all distinctions among men. Too sudden an ascent into liberty in the new republican order might "excite among the [former slaves] movements that could be fatal, for them" and, significantly, "for us." Just as passengers allow the pilot to guide the ship, freedmen should "celebrate the eternal designs of nature" and count on the "experience" and the "paternal solicitude" of the National Convention. "Vive Egalité! Vive Liberté!"[66]

It would appear that fraternity had foundered on the shoals of paternalism. Chaumette's speech invested the *conventionnels* with guardianship of the paternal powers stripped from the master class, not to mention the king. His attempt, like Dufay's, to reconcile "the sacred laws of nature" with the "principles of civilization" and the "rights of man" subjected slaves' passions to a definition of civilization predicated on a strict labor regime under French national authority. The discourses of emancipation thus add another dimension to Lynn Hunt's analysis of the family romance of the Revolution: the patriarchal order of the Old Regime suppressed by the Revolution seems to have emerged in a different incarna-

65. Ibid., 20–21.

66. Ibid., 21–22. Chaumette's speech bears comparison with the female antislavery discourses of the time. See, for example, Olympe de Gouges, who, self-identified as a royalist and a patriot, angrily denies that she is the pawn of the Amis des Noirs, in *Réponse au champion américain, ou Colon très aisé à connaître* (n.p., [1790]). Cf. Moira Ferguson, *Subject to Others: British Women Writers and Colonial Slavery, 1760–1834* (New York: Routledge, 1992); and Jean Fagan Yellin, *Women and Sisters: The Antislavery Feminists in American Culture* (New Haven: Yale University Press, 1989).

tion as paternalism in the colonies.[67] In Chaumette's understanding, civilization was inseparable from the reconstitution of masculine authority in the Convention. Slavery was annihilated at the moment the "oracle of truth" sounded in the "breast" of that "assembly of wise men."[68] Although freedmen forced themselves on the stage as (albeit unwanted) actors in Dufay's historical drama, in Chaumette's text they served as objects, never subjects, of the civilizing process.

Meanwhile, in Chaumette's speech, as in Dufay's, freedwomen's silence spoke loudly indeed. Chaumette proposed no statues of heroines to stand beside the martyr Ogé. Amid the language of fraternity and paternalism, women seemed to vanish not only from the category "brother," but also from the category "slave," emerging from the shadows only occasionally—and then often in tears. Nonetheless, as we have seen, his remapping of the French body politic in the Temple of Reason conjoined debates over slavery and sex. Chaumette cast slave women in cameo roles as ravished wives and despairing (but model) mothers to expose the slave system as the essence of savagery and the antithesis of nature—a project to his mind inseparable from the construction of domesticity as measure of the triumph of French civilization.

Over the course of the previous year, Chaumette himself had played an instrumental role in encouraging French women to act in accordance with their domestic nature. In his capacity as *procureur* of the Paris Commune, he had served on the committee that interrogated Marie Antoinette's daughter in the search for evidence that the "Austrian wolf" had committed incest with her son. Although the incest charge was never proven, the Revolutionary Tribunal convicted the former queen on grounds that mirrored the charges in the pamphlet literature.[69] Marie Antoinette, as constructed in the *acte d'accusation*, was at root a *femme sauvage*, as ready as her cannibalistic African counterpart to immolate the republic's "first-born child, liberty."[70] The queen's execution was followed in short order by the closing of women's political clubs and the trial and execution of the Girondin *salonnière* Madame Roland and playwright Olympe de Gouges, also accused of abandoning the "duties of their sex." On 27 Brumaire Year II (17 November 1793), a group of women wearing the red cap of liberty appeared before the Commune to protest the closure of women's political clubs. Lynn Hunt's essay in this volume helps

67. Hunt, *Family Romance*.

68. Chaumette, *Discours*, 4.

69. Hunt, *Family Romance*, 89–123.

70. Elizabeth Colwill, "'Just Another Citoyenne'? Marie-Antoinette on Trial, 1790–93," *History Workshop* 28 (autumn 1989): 63–87.

explain the jeering that broke out in the galleries at the sight of these women, for their controversial dress and political demands called into question the very boundaries of the new French body politic. On this occasion, it was Chaumette who mastered the day by condemning women's liberty caps as an "insult to nature" that justified women's exclusion from the proceedings. When a member of the crowd protested, Chaumette interrupted with the voice of moral authority. "Since when," he demanded, is "it permitted to give up one's sex?" Morals, enforced by the laws of man, had their foundation in the laws of nature. "Is it to men that nature confided domestic cares? Has she given us breasts to breast-feed our children? No, she has said to man: 'Be a man: hunting, farming, political concerns, toils of every kind, that is your *appanage*.' She has said to woman: 'Be a woman. The tender cares owing to infancy, the details of the household, the sweet anxieties of maternity, these are your labors.'" The record reports that the women replaced their red caps with "a headdress suitable to their sex."[71] The Commune unanimously banned women's deputations from presenting their requests before the Council.

Chaumette's words represented far more than mere regression to the patriarchalism of the Old Regime. When he constructed "the divinity of the domestic sanctuary" against the excessive appetites and ambitions of unnatural women, he redefined the boundaries of civilization itself. The law would have its way. Shorn of the *femme sauvage* in her multiple and threatening incarnations, the full rights of citizenship would remain exclusively male.[72] The new contours of the French body politic were thus chiseled, in part, on the feminine form: the transgressive bodies of the *femme sauvage* and the quiescent body of the mother, slave and free. The republican project of domesticity, expressed overtly in the Marie Antoinette pornography and covertly in the antislavery literature, did not repress sexuality in one set of feminine bodies to project onto another; it invested certain bodies with sexual aggression and others with a supine, titillating passivity. The antislavery literature's aching maternal breasts and ravished wives—victims of the savage passions of the planters—stood at the opposite end of the spectrum from Marie Antoinette's orgiastic frenzy, but both were cast within a sexual script that by 1793 sought to define fraternity through the exclusion of women.

To represent this story solely as women's defeat by a masculine frater-

71. *Actes de la Commune de Paris, 1793–1794*, 27–28 Brumaire Year II, nos. 145–46, preface by Albert Soboul (Paris: EDHIS, 1975).

72. *Réimpression de l'Ancien Moniteur* (Paris, 1847), 18:450–51, in *Women in Revolutionary Paris, 1789–1795*, ed. Darline Gay Levy, Harriet Branson Applewhite, and Mary Durham Johnson (Urbana: University of Illinois Press, 1979), 219–20.

nity, however, would be to simplify the transformation of the body politic wrought by the dual revolutions. Revolutionary pornography, the forcible domestication of the *femmes du peuple*, and the subjection of freedmen to the authority of the French Convention were all part of a broader republican project to domesticate passions, to discipline the uncivilized body, and to recast difference. Chaumette had begun his speech for the festival of emancipation with a parable that traced the fall of man from the paradise of patriarchalism and "primitive morals" to the moment at which man first deviated from nature's dictates. The "degradation and debasement of the human species" that followed was an age of "absolute empire" in which passions reigned and slavery made wild beasts of men.[73] In the cathartic moment of emancipation, the *conventionnels* mastered the passions unleashed in the age of despotism: explicitly, those of the slaves and their masters; but implicitly, those of the courtiers, priests, and queens exposed in multiple revealing postures in the pornographic pamphlets. Chaumette's speech provides a window on this process through which the early modern order founded on an organic hierarchy of masters and slaves, king and subjects, husbands and wives, was displaced by a structure of power rooted in the "incontestable" ground of a normalized body, male and female, white and nonwhite.[74] The transformation of the French body politic was predicated on the elimination of the older "primitive" hierarchy of orders. The repression of "public woman," then, was just one element of the reconfiguration of difference, which assumed the defeat of the old master classes in their various guises as sodomitical monks, merchants of flesh, and aristocratic *femmes sauvages*.[75]

Nor did legislation against women's political organizations involve the repression of "the female subject" in any simple or linear sense. The Jacobins who excluded women from full rights of citizenship would enlist the category "woman" in the revolutionary war of civilization against savagery. The feminine breast or heart in tandem with the masculine mind would colonize the new *corps social*. The vision assumed a new understanding of nature itself. In early modern Europe, medicine, religion, and

73. Chaumette, *Discours*, 1–3.

74. My evidence is consistent with David Brion Davis's case for the United States that "both parties in the Revolutionary debate helped to make race the central excuse for slavery" and that "antislavery ideology had less to do with race per se than with the discipline of a potentially disruptive lowest class" (*Problem of Slavery*, 303–4), but it shifts the emphasis to discursive constructions that elide class in race.

75. Cf. Joan Landes, *Women and the Public Sphere in the Age of the French Revolution* (Ithaca: Cornell University Press, 1988).

law posited woman as inferior to man and superimposed the dichotomies civilization/nature and man/woman on the same vertical axis. By 1793 the axes had shifted in a manner that appeared to rehabilitate both Woman and Nature. Woman, in fulfilling her domestic role, would become an agent of civilization and a link between man and nature.[76] It was a role that offered certain female subjects new possibilities. But which women could properly act the part that nature had assigned? The common physical space occupied by universal Woman and Nature, reconfigured within the realm called Civilization, defined a normative ideal that assumed the bifurcation of both Nature and Woman, not to mention Man. Nature, long understood as civilization's inverse, splintered in the modern era, one part conflated with the imperatives of civilization, the other cast back into a state of savagery.

This was the fractured "natural" landscape in which Chaumette sought to locate the newly emancipated slaves. But for which side of nature—the savage or the civilized—were they suited? The rationale for emancipation rested on an argument of fraternity that assumed the freedmen's humanity. Chaumette, however, considered freedmen, brothers or no, unprepared for the responsibilities of citizenship. His political challenge, then, that day at the Temple of Reason, was to place them deep enough within the realm of savagery to avert any claim to immediate equality, yet on the road toward enlightenment, so as to vindicate the emancipation proclamation and the promise of revolution. Chaumette followed a pragmatic script that begged the question of the "nature" of difference between slaves and citizens. Insofar as he framed his argument for emancipation in terms of the radical implications of fraternity, freedmen appeared as quintessential "new men," symbols of a regenerated French civilization. Insofar as he resorted to paternalism, he assimilated blacks into the civilizing process, but not fully into civilization itself. The freedwoman was of use in his text only in that her abused body provided proof of the outrage of slavery. Reconstructed on the model of European domesticity, the freedwoman would provide a bridge between nature-as-savagery and nature-as-civilization.

But a relationship between men conceived as both fraternal embrace and paternal surveillance was unstable from its inception. As Napoleon's quest for empire severed the revolutionary partnership of fraternity, liberty, and equality, the passageway that Chaumette had envisioned from savagery to civilization narrowed. Napoleon's genocidal campaign to re-

76. See Schiebinger, "Why Mammals Are Called Mammals," in *Nature's Body*, 40–74.

store slavery in the colonies with an armada and a force of twenty thousand men marked the decisive end of France's brief flirtation with the implications of fraternity. Reports of the black "atrocities" committed in the bloody war of liberation that ensued provided many Frenchmen with evidence of a "natural" savagery that they found more compelling than the claim to common humanity. If the Jacobins had contributed to the process of naturalizing gender difference, Napoleon institutionalized gender and racial inequality as he cynically restored slavery in Guadeloupe and Martinique under the banner of revolution.[77] Make no mistake, Napoleon's racial empire constituted an outright betrayal of the radical program of Jacobins like Chaumette who castigated the slave system as "a vast cancer." Nonetheless, one can find in the emancipatory vocabulary of Chaumette and Dufay a precedent for linking authoritarianism, in its diverse manifestations, in France and its colonies. Precisely because they inverted rather than abandoned the trope of civilization and savagery, because they sacrificed fraternity to tutelage in the interest of metropolitan profits, because they linked "natural" sex subordination to a "naturalized" colonial program, Napoleon's initiative could have appeared to many nineteenth-century French nationals consistent with both natural law and revolutionary nationalism.[78]

Just as the slave insurrection of 1791 shaped in fundamental ways Dufay's vision of the French body politic, the world-shaking war of liberation by the freedmen and -women in Saint-Domingue who proclaimed themselves the liberators of blacks and established the first independent black nation in the western hemisphere marked the limits of Napoleon's racial empire.[79] But these victories did not prevent nineteenth-century Eu-

77. See David Nicholls, *From Dessalines to Duvalier: Race, Colour, and National Independence in Haiti* (New York: Macmillan Caribbean, 1979). According to Cohen, *French Encounter with Africans*, 119, Napoleon not only banned Antillean blacks and people of mixed race from entering France, he also ordered General Leclerc to deport from Saint-Domingue white women who had sexual contact with blacks.

78. On the ways in which European women both resisted and were implicated within domestic and racial ideologies, see Nussbaum, *Torrid Zones;* Margo Hendricks and Patricia Parker, eds., *Women, "Race," and Writing in the Early Modern Period* (London: Routledge, 1994); Moira Ferguson, *Subject to Others;* and Doris Y. Kadish and Françoise Massardier-Kenney, *Translating Slavery: Gender and Race in French Women's Writing, 1783–1823* (Kent, Ohio: Kent State University Press, 1994).

79. In the process, they subverted the meaning of racial privilege. As Nicholls, *From Dessalines to Duvalier*, 13, 35–36, has argued, Haitians used race as the basis for their claims for independence, and defined all Haitians as black in their first constitution. See also Hilary McD. Beckles, "'An Unnatural and Dangerous Independence': The Haitian Revolution and the Political Sociology of Caribbean Slavery," *Journal of Caribbean History* 25 (1991): 160–77.

ropeans from imagining a physical geography of the body in a manner that inscribed European superiority. As revolutionary openings to equality narrowed, the more rigid became the triangulation of a physical geography that posited the brain (European male) and heart (European female) as forces of civilization whose role was to hold the (black) nether regions in check. Within this European map of a global body politic, black woman had no designated space; or rather, given her irreducibility to a single point within that map, she was fractured, like nature itself.[80] During the years of slave insurrection, antislavery writers domesticated her, while the planters magnified her sexuality to monstrous proportions.[81] Nineteenth-century Frenchmen, following political winds, would either assimilate her with both nature and civilization as noble (but domestic) savage or cast her back to nature as a sexualized *femme sauvage*. The ideal of passionlessness and new "scientific" evidence of racial difference etched a deep and "natural" divide between European and non-European women.[82] Even the "wild girl of Champagne," to whom some attributed Antillean origins, could reform, repent her state of savagery, and come clean after several washings.[83] The European woman might fall from virtue, betraying her destiny and her nature, but only the foreign *femme sauvage* was ineluctably associated with the primitive, her sexual essence a marker that placed her outside the bounds of womanhood itself.

80. On man as universal racial subject and the equation of "universal woman" with middle-class European women, see Schiebinger, *Nature's Body*, 148, 181.

81. During the Revolution in Saint-Domingue, the *femme sauvage* of African origin has a particular symbolic resonance for the planters, but she is absent from the rhetoric of Chaumette, for whom the *femme sauvage* of aristocratic origins proved a more compelling target.

82. Nussbaum, *Torrid Zones*, 47–48; Sander Gilman, *Difference and Pathology: Stereotypes of Sexuality, Race, and Madness* (Ithaca: Cornell University Press, 1985); Ludmilla Jordonova, *Sexual Visions: Images of Gender in Science and Medicine Between the Eighteenth and Twentieth Centuries* (Madison: University of Wisconsin Press, 1989).

83. Douthwaite, "Rewriting the Savage," 165.

10

Freedom of Dress in Revolutionary France

LYNN HUNT

"Freedom of dress" is not usually counted as one of the inalienable human rights central to modern democratic politics. It might be related to Jefferson's "pursuit of happiness" in the Declaration of Independence, but freedom of dress hardly seems central to life, liberty, or the protection of property. Even so, dress, with both its freedoms and constraints, turned out to be one of the most hotly contested arenas of revolutionary cultural politics. It provided the most visible marker of both adherence and resistance to new social and political conceptions, including notions of gender definition. Its powers of signification went far beyond the vagaries of *la mode*, beyond even the identification of political groupings; it touched on the very definition of the new body politic and especially on the definitions of the many different bodies, both male and female, that made up that new body politic.

As in many other questions of cultural politics, French revolutionaries veered between two extremes in their attitude toward dress: on the one hand, they wanted to erase all the supposed legal encumbrances of the Old Regime and make what one wore yet another arena for free choice (and market forces); on the other hand, they harbored a more repressive wish to insist on consensus by enforcing completely new regulations about personal adornment. The cockade is a prime example of the latter impulse. The red, white, and blue cockade appeared on men's hats as early as 16 July 1789, spontaneously signaling adherence to the new nation. Over the years, however, the appearance of the cockade, its size, and the material used in making it all became the subject of controversy. Large woolen ones soon seemed more democratic than small silk ones. On 5 July 1792 the Legislative Assembly ordered all men to wear it by law, a requirement repeated by the National Convention on 3 April 1793.[1]

These laws apparently did not apply to women. When the Society of Republican and Revolutionary Women was founded in May 1793, one of their first acts demanded that members wear the cockade (fig. 10.1). The club also sent an address to the forty-eight sections of Paris inviting all women to follow their example. In the summer of 1793, a "cockade war" broke out pitting club militants against market women who made a practice of ripping off the cockade to show their disdain for the female Jacobines and their mimicry of men. At the beginning of September, a group of women from another club initiated a petition drive to force the municipal and national governments to take action. In response, the city government forbade women to appear in public without a cockade. The National Convention, meanwhile, temporized, and street battles erupted once again. On 21 September the Convention finally ordered all women to wear the cockade, promising a six-year prison term as punishment for tearing off someone's cockade.

Matters did not end there. In October, the struggle shifted to the red liberty cap, frequently worn by female club members during their meetings. On the twenty-eighth of that month a pitched battle erupted during one of the meetings of the Republican and Revolutionary Women. Some of the women who had come to watch shouted, "Down with the red cap, down with the Jacobines, down with the Jacobines and the cockade."[2] Faced with a full-scale melee, the club members fled.

The next two days their opponents took the floor of the Convention. A deputation of women appeared to present a petition complaining of the efforts of "supposedly revolutionary women" to force them to wear the red liberty cap. The president assured them that the Committee on General Security was in the midst of preparing a report on the subject. Fabre d'Eglantine then took the floor in an angry mood:

There has already been trouble over the cockade. You decreed that all women must wear it. Now they want the red cap: they won't rest there, they'll soon ask for a belt with pistols, in such a way that this will coincide perfectly with

1. Lynn Hunt, *Politics, Culture, and Class in the French Revolution* (Berkeley: University of California Press, 1984), 57–59.

2. For the most complete account, see Dominique Godineau, *The Women of Paris and Their French Revolution* (Berkeley: University of California Press, 1998); originally published as *Citoyennes tricoteuses: Les Femmes du peuple à Paris pendant la Révolution française* (Aix-en-Provence: Alinéa, 1988), 163–77.

Figure 10.1 *Citoyenne au pied*, anonymous engraving, ca. 1791. By permission of the Bibliothèque Nationale.

the maneuver of raising crowds about bread, and you will see lines of women going for bread like men march to the trenches. It is very adroit on the part of our enemies to attack the strongest passion of women, that is, their attire [*ajustement*].

Fabre went on to attack women's clubs, claiming, to much applause, that they were composed of "adventuresses, wandering female knights, emancipated girls, and amazons." He called for a decree forbidding all efforts to force changes in dress. The Convention then ruled that "no person of either sex may constrain any citizen or citizeness to dress in a particular manner, each individual being free to wear whatever clothing or attire of its sex that pleases him, under pain of being declared suspect." At the same time, and in somewhat contradictory fashion, the Convention explicitly maintained its previous decrees requiring the cockade.[3]

The next day, 30 October, Amar delivered the eagerly awaited report of the Committee on General Security. He began with a description of recent troubles: "Several women, so-called Jacobines, of a Society that pretends to be revolutionary, promenaded this morning at the markets . . . in pantaloons and red liberty caps; they tried to force other women to adopt the same costume. . . . A crowd of some 6,000 women formed. All the women agree in saying that violence and threats will not force them to wear a costume that they honor but which they believe to be reserved to men."[4] He went on to develop at some length the rationale for the exclusion of women from the public, political sphere and for the suppression of women's clubs as dangerous to public order and to the natural division of sexual functions. The Convention thereupon officially suppressed all women's political clubs.

Thus the conflicts over women's fashions ended in the simultaneous declaration of freedom of dress and the suppression of women's political organizations. A curious progression in concerns had developed in the course of these disputes. The deputies to the Convention wanted to enforce wearing the cockade as a badge of revolutionary belonging, but they drew the line when it came to women forcing other women to wear more controversial tokens of revolutionary enthusiasm such as the red liberty cap. Such women supposedly played on "the strongest passion of women,"

3. *Gazette nationale ou le Moniteur universel*, no. 39 (9 Brumaire Year II/30 October 1793), recounting the session of 8 Brumaire Year II. All translations from the French, unless otherwise noted, are mine.

4. *Moniteur universel*, no. 40 (10 Brumaire Year II/31 October 1793), recounting the session of the preceding day.

their concern for dress, and turned it into a form of masculinization, wearing "a costume reserved to men." Dress had become too public an issue for women, and it signaled their intrusion into a public sphere seen as masculine (thus requiring masculine dress). The answer, it seems, was to reaffirm freedom of dress for women as long as their choice of dress remained confined to the private sphere and to feminine sartorial options. It would soon become apparent that men did not enjoy the same freedom of dress.

The declaration of freedom of dress obviously grew out of motives much more complicated than a simple break with Old Regime sumptuary laws. As Daniel Roche has argued, sumptuary laws had long been disregarded and were in any case caught up as much in royal monetarist policy as in efforts to defend the distinctiveness of the nobility.[5] The revolutionaries, however, had been habituated by their reading of the philosophes, especially Voltaire, to see in sumptuary regulation an attack on liberty.[6] Lying behind this conception of liberty was some notion of the operation of the market, but this was never fully elaborated either in the discussion of sumptuary regulation or in the many revolutionary discussions of dress.[7]

In 1789 the crown seemed to revive sumptuary legislation when it insisted that the deputies of the three orders wear distinctive costumes for the opening session of the Estates General: the clergy wore clerical costumes reflective of rank; the nobility wore hats with white feathers and clothing adorned by lace and gold; and the deputies of the Third Estate wore the sober black and three-corner hats of the magistrature (fig. 10.2). These prescriptions revived the spirit if not the letter of sumptuary laws and instantly politicized the question of dress. On 10 May 1789 Mirabeau published a letter from Jean-Baptiste Salaville denouncing the distinction in costume decreed by His Majesty's master of ceremonies as "absurd,"

5. Daniel Roche, *La Culture des apparences: Une Histoire du vêtement (XVIIe–XVIIIe siècle)* (Paris: Fayard, 1989), 54.

6. Old Regime sumptuary laws have apparently attracted only the attention of legal historians interested in the long-term development of the practice. See, for example, Etienne Giraudias, *Etude historique sur les lois somptuaires* (Poitiers, 1910). I have not been able to locate any source that discusses eighteenth-century sumptuary laws in detail.

7. In the eighteenth century the *marchandes de modes* suddenly increased in number; they were first attached to the *merciers* and then, after 1776, to the *plumassiers-fleuristes*. See Madeleine Delpierre, "Rose Bertin, les marchandes de modes et la Révolution," in Madeleine Delpierre et al., *Modes et révolutions, 1780–1804* [Catalogue of an exposition at Musée de la mode et du costume, Palais Galliera, 8 February–7 May 1989] (Paris: Delpierre Editions Paris-Musées, 1989), 21–25.

Figure 10.2 Deputies of the three Estates, anonymous engraving, 1789. By permission of the Bibliothèque Nationale.

"ridiculous," and "the height of despotism and debasement." The prescription of different dress for the different orders, he charged, only reinforced "that unfortunate distinction between orders that can be regarded as the original sin of our nation." Yet even Salaville did not conclude from this that all notions of official costume should be discarded; instead he argued that the National Assembly should be responsible for adopting any such costume, operating on the principle that all deputies represented the "universality of the kingdom" and hence should be dressed exactly the same.[8] This same tension between dressing for difference and dressing for equality would appear again and again. For the moment, however, Salaville's suggestion fell on deaf ears; the deputies soon opted for the elimination of signs of difference between the three orders, leaving to each deputy the choice of individual costume.[9]

Freedom of dress had a very ambiguous history during the revolutionary decade because the deputies followed competing agendas: they wanted to wrench French society away from past habits of social dis-

8. *Lettre du comte de Mirabeau à ses commettans*, as published in the *Moniteur*'s account of the early days of the Estates General, *Réimpression de l'Ancien Moniteur* (Paris, 1847), 1:27 (6–14 May 1789).

9. Jean-Marc Devocelle, "D'un costume politique à une politique du costume: Approches théoriques et idéologiques du costume pendant la Révolution française," in Delpierre et al., *Modes*, 83–103.

tinction and at the same time underline the legitimacy of the new regime, in part by introducing distinctive markings for officials and also, of course, by maintaining gender differentiations. New kinds of functional distinctions had to replace the old objectionable social ones. On 20 May 1790, for instance, the National Assembly voted to dress all mayors in a tricolor sash.[10] In April 1792, in contrast, the Legislative Assembly decreed that members of the suppressed religious orders could no longer wear their customary costume. In proposing this decree, Bishop Torné explicitly rejected the argument that this constituted an attack on freedom of dress (*la liberté des vêtements*):

> Would it be permitted to one sex to wear indistinctly the clothing of one or the other sex? Do not the police prohibit masks and cockades that might be a sign of a party opposed to the Revolution? Do not the police prohibit clothing that undermines morals? And if the simple clothing of a citizen is susceptible to a multitude of wise regulations, would religious costume, which can entail so many abuses, then not be submitted to any police rule?[11]

Freedom of dress could not mean complete absence of regulation, at least not for men.

Thus, it is not surprising that the Convention did not explicitly declare freedom of dress until confronted with the very particular problem of women's political insignia. Long after they rendered their declaration, moreover, dress continued to be a subject of potential regulation, especially insofar as official costume was concerned. In March 1794 a local Parisian deputation appeared on the floor of the Convention to demand the suppression of judge's costumes "because they seem to us to recall monarchical, feudal, and chivalric ideas; because the robe, by its form and its color, retraces the memories of nobles and priests, which contrasts too violently with our republican sentiments."[12] Decrees requiring the cockade were repeated all during the Directory government, but at the same time, the government also restated its insistence on freedom of dress in order to prevent street fights over the color of clothing, black collars in particular being associated with royalism.[13] Dress had to be regulated in its

10. Ibid., 85.

11. *Réimpression de l'Ancien Moniteur*, 12:62 (7 April 1792).

12. Ibid., 20:64 (8 Germinal Year II/28 March 1794).

13. See, for example, ibid., 28:490 (26 Brumaire Year V/18 November 1796; requirement to wear the cockade); 28:770, 771 (30 Thermidor Year V/17 August 1797; reaffirmation of freedom of dress and troubles over black collars); 28:797 (21 Fructidor Year V/7 September 1797; troubles over a black costume).

official modes, free in its absolutely private ones, and was therefore a subject of constant contention in the areas in between (in particular the private/public wearing of the cockade).

Despite the best efforts of revolutionary legislators, dress necessarily crossed over the line separating private and public, especially since the distinction between public and private itself came under intense pressure with the politicization of many aspects of daily, private life. As the case of the Society of Republican and Revolutionary Women shows, the question of dress intersected at least two different axes of concern: the gender axis of the appropriate differentiation between men and women, and the political axis of the necessary differentiation between friends and enemies, insiders and outcasts, in the new revolutionary order.

Gender and political differentiation operate in every society, but during the French Revolution they became especially charged because their very definition came into question. The system of gender differentiation by dress underwent a profound transformation, what J. C. Flügel called "The Great Masculine Renunciation." As he put it, "Men gave up their right to all the brighter, gayer, more elaborate and more varied forms of ornamentation, leaving these entirely to the use of women. . . . Man abandoned his claim to be considered beautiful."[14] Men began to dress alike, whereas women's dress took on more of the burden of class signification. I will return to Flügel's argument in greater detail below; for now I want simply to suggest that disputes about appropriate female dress involved more than a simple reassertion of gender distinctions. They took place against a backdrop of subtle but momentous realignments of the gender/dress system.

Similarly, the very foundations of the political system shifted. A body was no longer defined by its place in a cosmic order cemented by hierarchy, deference, and readily readable dress; each individual body now carried within itself all the social and political meanings of the new political order, and these meanings proved very difficult to discern. With sovereignty diffused from the king's body out into the multiple bodies of the nation, the old codes of readability broke down and new ones had to be elaborated. The uncertainty of this situation was reflected in the seesaw of regulatory practice concerning dress.

The body assumed such significance in the French Revolution because the long-term shift from a sacred to a secular framework of legitimacy made the workings of the social both more visible and more problem-

14. J. C. Flügel, *The Psychology of Clothes* (New York: Hogarth Press, 1969), 111.

atic. In an important theoretical work on the role of the French Revolution in the process of secularizing legitimacy, Brian Singer offers what he calls "a history of social visibility." Using concepts first developed by Cornelius Castoriadis, Singer argues that the Revolution fundamentally altered the relation of visible powers to the larger society. Under the Old Regime, schematically speaking, society seemed to be given from without, transcendentally, that is by the will of God, with the king—the only visible power—embodying the presence of the divine. Society had no immanent, self-given status; society was only appearance or façade. The separation of state and society did not become possible, Singer insists, until society was successfully designated as the source of its own power. The Revolution completed the auto-institution of society, and it was this transference that made the revolutionary process revolutionary (and, some would argue, violent, because auto-institution is inherently unstable). The Revolution was made possible by the claim that society provided its own legitimation, and it was driven forward by disputes over the exact meaning of this claim.[15]

The development of a secular, societal framework for legitimacy does not mean that all notions of the sacred disappeared. Sacrality was still present but now displaced from the king's single body into the collectivity of bodies in the nation. As a result, the social came more closely into focus, and the bodies of individuals were even more intensely invested with significance. In other words, the Revolution brought into consciousness a new awareness of the social as a category. Bodies had to be closely examined for their meanings, but the system of decodification was constantly in flux. The strangest incidents of the Revolution can only be explained in this way, from the concern over the greenish putrefaction of Marat's body during his funeral to the executioner's slap of the severed head of Charlotte Corday, causing it to blush. All bodies had to be examined closely because all bodies now made up the body politic; every body literally embodied a piece of sovereignty, or at least some connection to it. As a consequence, the whole subject of appearance was valorized in new and particularly significant ways.

This long-term shift explains, as well, why the body is so central to the disciplinary practices analyzed by Michel Foucault. Almost all of Foucault's investigations concerned the body in the crucial transition period toward modernity: the seventeenth, eighteenth, and early nineteenth cen-

15. Brian C. J. Singer, *Society, Theory, and the French Revolution: Studies in the Revolutionary Imaginary* (New York: Macmillan, 1986), esp. 5.

turies.[16] This is the period of the secularization of legitimacy, the challenge to divine-right theories and the rise of socially immanent ones as a replacement. Although he never says so, Foucault's image of the dispersion of power rests on the eruption of democracy in the eighteenth century, and much of the characteristic postmodern problem of differentiating between democracy and totalitarianism can be traced back to Foucault's own inability or unwillingness to distinguish between the two. For him, all forms of bodily discipline are essentially the same: democracy and totalitarianism are equally carceral. Although both democracy and totalitarianism are made possible by the shift of sovereignty from the king to the nation, their common sources of enablement do not make them the same phenomenon.

We do not yet have a history of the body that enables us to distinguish clearly between totalitarian and democratic forms of discipline.[17] The question of dress provides an especially significant window onto this set of problems because dress was the field in which both gender and political differentiation were played out, and at times played upon, as the case of the Society of Republican and Revolutionary Women shows. Foucault did not discuss dress, just as he did not discuss gender (except in the most abstract terms), yet it seems likely that dress—and gender, one of whose most visible components is dress—are crucial to modern conceptions of the individual, and by extension to the modern conception of democracy. Anne Hollander makes the link in *Sex and Suits* when she argues that the modern aesthetic principles of fashion reflect the modern democratic "ideal of self-perpetuating order, flexible and almost infinitely variable."[18]

Democracy, especially in practice, creates enormous tensions about the various forms of social and gender differentiation.[19] In the most radical moments of the French Revolution, the idea of social differentiation itself came under attack. There is no need to belabor the obvious signs of the disintegration of a body politic based on deference and the clearly read-

16. It might be argued that Foucault's chronological focus steadily shifted from the seventeenth century toward the nineteenth century from the time of his writing *Madness and Civilization* (first published 1961) to *The History of Sexuality: An Introduction* (1976). Only in his last two posthumous volumes did he shift away from this central period.

17. Dorinda Outram certainly does not provide it, since her work is fundamentally confused on just this issue; see *The Body and the French Revolution: Sex, Class, and Political Culture* (New Haven: Yale University Press, 1989).

18. Anne Hollander, *Sex and Suits* (New York: Alfred Knopf, 1994), 9. She does not, however, recognize that this same ideal may be more closely tied to the operation of the capitalist market than to democracy.

19. I discuss the tensions surrounding gender differentiation in Lynn Hunt, *The Family Romance of the French Revolution* (Berkeley: University of California Press, 1992).

able signs of social status: the killings of the king and queen, the elimination of titles of nobility, the drive to repress the *vous* formal form of address and the title *Monsieur* and replace them with a universal *tu* and *Citoyen*, the imitation of the dress of the sans-culottes by various political figures, and so on. Even the recommended style of writing letters changed. According to *Le Secrétaire des républicains*, a letter-writing manual of 1793, those who had been reduced by misfortune to serving "their equals" should no longer be called lackeys or domestics but rather "homme ou femme de confiance." Letters should be simply signed "salut" or "salut et fraternité."[20] This attack on an ancien régime based on deference and evident social distinctions inevitably created anxiety about the legitimacy of any form of social difference (class especially, but also to some extent race and gender).

This is not to say that most revolutionaries dreamed of a society utterly without distinctions. They wanted to install a new system of signs, marking individuals by their utility and republican virtue (and, of course, maintaining gender differentiations as well). Thus festivals instituted new kinds of functional divisions. More sinister forms of marking were suggested but not taken up. One deputy proposed in October 1791 that all nonjuring priests should wear a badge on the left breast reading, "Priest, suspected of sedition." Others suggested that prostitutes be forced to wear special colors. Saint-Just proposed that injured soldiers wear gold stars on their clothing over the spots of their wounds.[21] These all reflected an obvious concern with transparency, inspired by Rousseau: clothes should reveal the inner person, not provide a means of dissimulation.

At the center of anxiety about social differentiation stood the body, the preeminent site for revolutionary signification and symbolization.[22] Although the body was central to the revolutionary reformulations of political and social meaning, its clothing always raised more questions than it could solve. Clothing inevitably underlined political and social differences, whereas republicans wanted to emphasize sameness and consensus (except in the arena of gender, where the republicans insisted on differ-

20. As quoted in Janet Gurkin Altmam, "Teaching the 'People' to Write: The Formation of a Popular Civic Identity in the French Letter Manual," in *Studies in Eighteenth-Century Culture*, vol. 22, ed. Patricia B. Craddock and Carla H. Hay (East Lansing: Michigan State University Press 1992), 159–60.

21. Nicole Pellegrin, *Les Vêtements de la liberté: Abécédaire des pratiques vestimentaires en France de 1780 à 1800* (Aix-en- Provence: Alinea, 1989), 123–24.

22. On the meanings of the French word *corps* and its allegorical and symbolic development during the Revolution, see the remarkably rich work of Antoine de Baecque, *Le Corps de l'histoire: Métaphores et politique, 1770–1800* (Paris: Calmann-Lévy, 1993).

ence). As a consequence, contemporary clothing came to seem virtually incompatible with republican ideals. Rarely did either Liberty or Hercules, two of the most current republican icons, appear in contemporary garb in revolutionary allegories. Roman dress and nudeness both had the effect of erasing the reference to contemporary social distinctions and enforcing the sense of consensus that stood above social differentiation. Pornography, the underside of revolutionary idealization, operated in a similar fashion. The nude pornographic scene made the basic materialist point that all bodies are alike. Clothing in pornography—showing monks or nuns in their customary dress, for example—served to inject a social distinction into the action, but by implication, such figures were in the process of losing their clothing too, of becoming like everyone else.[23]

To control the signifying possibilities of clothed bodies in the revolutionary festivals, organizers tended to rely on either uniforms or special dress. As Mona Ozouf explains, the revolutionaries tried to reduce social man to biological man in the festivals. In the Festival of the Supreme Being of June 1794, everyone had an indispensable part to play, "whether as father or husband, mother or daughter, rich or poor, young or old." Yet when one club in Compiègne suggested that a simple village girl march alongside an elegant citizeness, the festival organizers rejected the proposal because it would call too much attention to social divisions. Even rich and poor were to be alike in some fashion in the festivals. The program for the Festival of the Supreme Being called for young ladies to use powder with restraint and to bunch up their skirts in the Roman style. In other festivals women most often appeared in white dresses crowned with oak wreaths.[24]

Given the heightened importance of the social and its signification by the body, it might be presumed that men's and women's public appearances would be equally freighted. Or alternatively, men's dress might matter more than women's because men mattered politically whereas women presumably did not (women could not vote or hold office, and after October 1793 they could not even form their own political clubs). The story is more paradoxical, however, than either of these formulations would suggest. Put most schematically, men's dress mattered more politically, but the result was to make it more uniformlike over the long run; in other

23. For more on the relevance of pornography to these questions, see Lynn Hunt, ed., *The Invention of Pornography: Obscenity and the Origins of Modernity, 1500–1800* (New York: Zone Books, 1993).

24. Mona Ozouf, *Festivals and the French Revolution*, trans. Alan Sheridan (Cambridge, Mass.: Harvard University Press, 1988), 114–15.

words, because of its greater potential political signification, it came to be evacuated of some of the most obvious signs of difference.

The long-term shift in the coding of men's dress has recently attracted attention from film and literary critics and art historians much more than from historians. At issue is "The Great Masculine Renunciation," the homogenizing of male dress at the beginning of the nineteenth century to eliminate the obvious sartorial display that characterized aristocratic society.[25] The sumptuary legislation that had once guaranteed the accurate display of social rank for both men and women under the Old Regime gave way to a more implicit code of masculine sameness and female difference. As Kaja Silverman has argued, this historical shift provides the grounds for the modern equation of spectacular display with female subjectivity (that women are objects to be looked at by men), and the very fact that it is historical undermines all the psychoanalytic explanations (insofar as they are ahistorical) of the controlling male "gaze," so central to film theory. In the past, men were as much subject to being looked at as women. The difference between beholding and being beheld is therefore not part of an intrinsic gender identity, whether imagined as biological or cultural.

Silverman only sketches out her argument, but it is very suggestive. The history of fashion shows ornate dress to have been a class rather than gender prerogative during the fifteenth, sixteenth, and seventeenth centuries, a prerogative protected by law. (The eighteenth century represents a transitional period in this regard, one in which commercial fashion steadily replaced sumptuary legislation in the determination of dress.)[26] Under the ancien fashion régime, extravagance in clothing signified aristocratic power and privilege; it was, as Silverman insists, "a mechanism for tyrannizing over rather than surrendering to the gaze of the (class) other."[27] The elegance and finery of male dress at least equaled that of female dress during the classical period—and indeed, since the end of the Roman empire; hence visibility was a male as much as or even more than

25. Flügel relates this shift to the French Revolution and the idea of fraternity, but his main center of interest lies elsewhere than in a historical account. Hollander explicitly dismisses Flügel's thesis only to reincorporate it into her own analysis: speaking of the eighteenth century, she claims, "men gradually came to look similar; and to desire to look similar" (*Sex and Suits*, 97; cf. 22).

26. Jennifer Jones of Rutgers University is preparing a book on this transitional period. I have benefited from the observations she offers in her introduction.

27. Kaja Silverman, "Fragments of a Fashionable Discourse," in *Studies in Entertainment: Critical Approaches to Mass Culture*, ed. Tania Modleski (Bloomington: Indiana University Press, 1986), 139–52, quote 139.

a female attribute. Most commentators seem to agree that a major change took place in the eighteenth and early nineteenth centuries, but no one has offered a compelling explanation of just why and how it occurred then. Why did men give up their hair, for example, their long locks, their wigs—or as one observer puts it, their century and a half of immunity to the crowning injustice of nature?[28]

In other words, class distinctions within male dress blurred toward the end of the eighteenth century, while gender distinctions between men's and women's dress became all the clearer. (Thus French republicans could insist on all men wearing the cockade even while insisting on freedom of dress for women.) Women's dress carried all the messages of social distinction, while men's dress began to shun them. Eventually all men wore trousers of somber colors, rather than expressing their class differences by the length and color of their pants (silk, brightly colored breeches for the rich; gray or brown woolen trousers for the working poor). Trousers, according to Philippe Perrot, constituted one of the rare examples of a fashion moving up rather than down the social scale.[29] Men also now wore their own and only their own hair rather than wigs or powdered hair for the upper classes. They stopped using makeup, except on the stage. In short, they cut off all resemblances to female finery.

The Revolution did not transform the dress codes overnight, and men's dress continued to carry some of the freight of social distinction. Yet the Revolution did put enormous stress on male dress and on the signification of the male body. Mona Ozouf has remarked, for example, that women and children in processions and festivals often appeared indiscriminately, without social categorization, while men were always carefully ordered and categorized.[30] The presence of women and children was taken to symbolize the community as a whole rather than any particular social station or function (other than motherhood or childhood, the biological categories). Men had more individual representativity, as it were.

As a consequence, it was perhaps inevitable that the republican government would consider the introduction of uniforms not only for all officials but for all male citizens. As early as 1792 David made sketches for a new national male costume. According to John Moore, his sketches at

28. Quentin Bell as cited in ibid., 140.

29. Philippe Perrot, *Fashioning the Bourgeoisie: A History of Clothing in the Nineteenth Century*, trans. Richard Bienvenu (Princeton: Princeton University Press, 1994), 31.

30. Ozouf, *Festivals*, 41.

that moment resembled "the old Spanish dress, consisting of a jacket with tight trowsers, a coat without sleeves above the jacket, a short cloak which may either hang loose from the left shoulder or be drawn over both; a belt to which two pistols and a sword may be attached, a round hat and a feather."[31] In 1794, on official request, David designed a national male costume that combined Renaissance and antique motifs with a tight-fitting tunic, a cloak, and classical tights (fig. 10.3).[32] The pantaloon and tights obviated the choice between breeches and trousers.

The Popular and Republican Society of the Arts defended the idea of a national costume on the grounds that it fulfilled the goal of "announcing or recalling everywhere and at every instant the fatherland, of distinguishing French citizens from those of nations still branded by the irons of servitude; it would offer easy means for designating both the age and the diverse public functions of the citizens, without altering the sacred bases of equality."[33] In other words, a national costume would reinforce the break with the Old Regime and mold republican citizens for the new one. Here freedom of dress for men has clearly been much attenuated, if not effaced altogether.

Although the government never manufactured these civil uniforms, Denon produced an engraving of David's sketch, and discussion of appropriate dress continued even after the fall of Robespierre.[34] *La Décade philosophique*, soon to be one of the leading Directorial journals, carried lengthy discussions of dress throughout the summer of 1794. One of the contributors to the journal recommended a new style of men's dress that in many ways resembled a uniform: tunics with sleeves that did not go below the elbow (so that men's muscles would be evident—"that is the beauty of men"); unpowdered hair falling just below the neck; no hats except when traveling because they were not healthy; simple slippers or sandals that left the toes free and could be taken off at the doorway; and a formless coat, "a kind of portable tent." Similar but much briefer recommendations were offered for women's dress: they should also wear tunics and similar shoes and wear their own hair held back in a simple knot, washed and lightly perfumed with ribbons as decoration.

31. Aileen Ribeiro, *Fashion in the French Revolution* (London: B. T. Batsford, 1988), 101.

32. For more on David's uniform, see Jennifer Harris, "The Red Cap of Liberty: A Study of Dress Worn by French Revolutionary Partisans, 1789–1794," *Eighteenth-Century Studies* 14 (1981): 283–312.

33. As quoted in *La Décade philosophique, littéraire et politique* 1 (10 Floréal Year II): 62.

34. On previous projects for civil uniforms, including some for children's dress, see Devocelle, "D'un costume politique," 89–90.

Figure 10.3 Denon, after David, sketch for a new national costume, 1793. By permission of the Bibliothèque Nationale.

La Décade went on at some length about the inconveniences of women's wigs.[35]

The Directorial republic eventually established official costumes for all branches of government, and the Consulate and Empire continued the practice.[36] When Grégoire presented the official report of the Committee of Public Instruction on the subject of official costumes on 14 September 1795, he specifically referred to the emotions caused by dress regulations at the opening of the Estates General, a long six years before:

> The suppression of orders, which had presupposed a difference between civil and political modes of existence, brought in its train the suppression of costumes; but the Constituent Assembly was wrong not to substitute a costume common to its members. From that moment the dignity of its sessions steadily diminished. The harm worsened until the epoch when the tyrants who oppressed the National Convention did all but put cleanliness and decency on the list of counterrevolutionary crimes and prided themselves on wearing their contempt for propriety on their sleeves.[37]

The legitimacy of the government seemed to depend on being able to represent itself coherently in an immediately apprehendable fashion. But navigating between the excessive social distinctions of the ancien régime and the erasure of all social distinctions under the Terror proved nearly impossible.

The official costumes now seem quaint and sometimes even bizarre, yet they did announce an important break with Old Regime habits. In the royal court uniforms appeared only on exceptional occasions, such as the crowning of the king, and most often they had a religious significance; secular dress codes for the various professions conveyed social status and rank. Revolutionary and Napoleonic uniforms, in contrast, signaled the representativity of power: an official carried the marks of popular sovereignty rather than of his specific position within a social order defined by relative proximity to the body of the king. Even the uniforms introduced in Napoleon's imperial court to reestablish links to the monarchy signaled different purposes: they served as a kind of livery with a touch of militarism.[38]

35. *La Décade philosophique, littéraire et politique,* 2 (30 Thermidor Year II): 136–43 (Lettre de Polyscope au Rédacteur de la Décade sur les costumes); esp. 2 (20 Fructidor Year II): 279–86 (Troisième lettre de Polyscope); and 3 (30 Vendémiaire Year II): 147 (on wigs). I am grateful to Elizabeth Colwill for bringing this discussion to my attention.

36. Hunt, *Politics, Culture, and Class*, 75–81. See also Devocelle, "D'un costume politique," 92–97.

37. *Réimpression de l'Ancien Moniteur*, 25:763 (3eme jour complémentaire Year III/19 September 1795).

38. For brief remarks on this subject, see Madeleine Delpierre, "Le Retour aux costumes de cour sous le Consulate et l'Empire," in Delpierre et al., *Modes*, 33–39, esp. 38.

Figure 10.4 *Incroyables*, anonymous engravings, 1795. By permission of the Bibliothèque Nationale.

The efforts to enforce uniformity of male dress predictably produced reactions, even among ardent revolutionaries. While some men donned the red liberty cap and mimicked the dress of the sans-culottes in 1793–94, others stuck by their middle-class forms of dandyism. Robespierre, for example, always wore a powdered wig, knee breeches, buckled shoes, and silk shirts. After the end of the Terror, sartorial opposition became the order of the day, the most spectacular examples of which were the *incroyables* and *muscadins* (a word used in the mid–eighteenth century for scented fops) who appeared in 1795 in the aftermath of the fall of Robespierre. They usually wore knee breeches in the old style, powdered hair or shaggy side locks falling like spaniel's ears, and fancy footwear (fig. 10.4). Their costumes seemed designed to emphasize individuality of choice rather than any consistent form of royalist dress. In Paris they roamed the streets looking for a fight, singing anti-Jacobin songs (including the taunting "Remettez vos culottes"), effacing revolutionary inscriptions, and ripping the cockade off suspected Jacobins. "Remettez vos culottes" played on the different possibilities of the term "sans-culottes," which could mean (in addition to simply "without culottes") not a wearer of knee breeches and hence someone who wore trousers instead. One verse ran: "Don't trust the intriguer / Who praises the indecent costume of our false patriots. / Don't push liberty to the point of letting down your pants, / Put your pants back on! [*Remettez vos culottes*]." The other side in these costume street battles would grab a *muscadin* and tear off his black or green collar (considered counterrevolutionary colors) and shear his hair "à la Titus," that is, in the new short style associated with neoclassical austerity and republican virility.[39]

Still, the trend toward the Great Masculine Renunciation was clearly present, even if vehemently resisted by the *incroyables* and later by Napoleon himself. Napoleon tried to reinstitute much of ancien régime fashion after 1804, wearing the kind of coat worn at the court of Louis XVI and gradually replacing his republican pantaloons with aristocratic knee breeches (in part to hide his increasing portliness). Certain trends, however, were not reversible. More and more men wore English-inspired tailored costumes in dark colors with few adornments. Although returning aristocrats tended to favor powdered hair and tight-fitting knee breeches in the old style, most middle-class men wore trousers or pantaloons and kept their hair in a natural style, whether tousled or à la Titus. Even Napoleon kept the Titus cut of his youth (fig. 10.5). Whereas women wore clothes to show their sex, especially in the transparent whites of the Directorial period, men began to dress to look alike.[40]

The trend toward masculine sameness already attracted commentary during the decade of revolution. In February 1792, for instance, the *Journal de la mode* announced that "for some time now, men's apparel has hardly been worthy of attention . . . coats, for the most part, are brown or black; frock coats of the worst taste; vests are almost all red."[41] In contrast, women's fashion changed at a vertiginous pace, which the *Journal de la mode* attributed to the disappearance of the nobility: "Since the abolition of titles, many women can only distinguish themselves by a continual variety in their attire." Such comments were appearing as early as August 1790.[42]

The fashion journals that sprang up after the end of the Terror sounded similar notes. In 1800, *Le Mois* offered a little history of French fashion in its pages, claiming that "in the first centuries of the monarchy, the clothing of men varied more in its major forms than that of women."[43] This was no longer true. The post-Thermidor fashion journals showed continual variation in women's fashion and commented little if at all on men's

39. The best brief account is in Ribeiro, *Fashion*, 115–17.

40. It should be noted, however, that in 1796 women also started wearing a version of the Titus cut. The mode lasted until 1809 with several variations. See Françoise Vittu, "1780–1804, ou vingt ans de 'révolution des têtes françaises,'" in Delpierre et al., *Modes*, 41–57, esp. 51. Most commentary on this fashion for women seems to have come after 1800.

41. *Journal de la mode*, 5 February 1792, 2.

42. *Journal de la mode*, 5 August 1790, 2.

43. *Le Mois*, [Prairial] Year VIII, 288 (at this time the journal no longer specified the month; Prairial was determined here by counting backward).

Figure 10.5 Bonaparte as first consul, 1800.
By permission of the Bibliothèque Nationale.

fashion. The *Journal des modes et nouveautés*, for example, claimed in the spring of 1799 that the Titus cut so dominated among men that even those who had to wear wigs to cover their baldness wore wigs with a Titus cut. In 1797 the same journal insisted that women's fashion changed all the time: "The fashion now is to follow none. In a circle of thirty women, you will not see two hairstyles, two dresses, two get-ups that resemble each other."[44] In his *Encore un tableau de Paris* published in 1800 (Year VIII), Charles Henrion claimed that "in the past, [a fashion] lasted three or four months, and sometimes a whole semester; now, it changes every fifteen days, and there is never one pronounced enough to enjoy preference over the others. This comes from the fact that there is no longer a court, and as a result, no longer a rallying point for a fashion. In the olden days, *Versailles* set the tone."[45]

44. *Journal des modes et nouveautés*, 15 Ventôse Year VII, 516; 20 Frimaire Year VI, 10.
45. Charles Henrion, *Encore un tableau de Paris* (Paris, Year VIII), 125.

Men's fashion seemed to fall into oppositional categories rather than multiple variations, no doubt because of the politicization of the revolutionary decade. According to a 1799 issue of *Le Mois*, for instance, "men are divided into two classes for hairstyles only, the *Titus* and the *Powdered*" —and powdered hair was definitely losing out. In 1800, the same journal described "a great quarrel" that had arisen between the *pantalonistes* (trouser wearers) and the *culotistes* (*sic*, wearers of knee breeches). In its view, the *pantalonistes* were bound to win because the new consuls and ministers gave their audiences in trousers.[46] The trend in men's clothing was there to be seen, even if the final outcome remained in doubt in the 1790s and early 1800s.

The post-Terror fashion journals carried forward the same ambivalence about women's fashion that had characterized their eighteenth-century precursors.[47] The Rousseauian disdain for women's use of their adornment to get their way still appeared in the very journals that sold precisely because they provided women with indicators of the latest fashions. *Le Mois*, for instance, reproduced the Rousseau line in 1800: "Women, this enchanting sex, born for the happiness of one part of our sex and for the torment of the rest, women, I say, discontent with the little that the laws have done for them in the distribution of direct power, have sought in all epochs to acquire by cunning what they cannot reasonably hope to obtain by open force." Clothing was obviously central to this cunning. Yet the same journal concluded that "we must be fair; women dress infinitely better today than in the past, with more taste and lightness."[48]

Women's dress seemed to elude all facile categorizations such as the purported divisions between men who wore powdered hair and those who wore Titus cuts or those who wore trousers and those who wore knee breeches. Yet one stylistic innovation in women's wear does catch the eye and call out for further investigation: the white muslin dress worn in an antique manner. White gowns in neoclassical style had appeared in fashionable and artistic circles during the neoclassical revival of the 1780s. Vigée–Le Brun held a famous "Greek supper" in 1788 in which she and her female guests wore white draped like a tunic. In September 1789 the painter David's wife and other wives and daughters of leading artists dressed in white with tricolor cockades in their hair when they went to

46. *Le Mois*, Germinal Year VII, 18; Prairial Year VIII, 283–85.
47. On the eighteenth-century journals, see Roche, *Culture des apparences*, 447–76.
48. *Le Mois*, Prairial Year VIII, 286–87, 302.

publicly donate their jewelry to the National Assembly (fig. 10.6). David then chose the same style of dress for his festivals (fig. 10.7). Manon Roland and Lucille Desmoulins wore simple white dresses to their own executions, perhaps to make the point that they were the true republicans, not their executioners.

A similar style dominated Directorial fashions. Louis-Sébastien Mercier complained in 1798 that there is "not a *petite maîtresse*, not a *grisette*, who does not decorate herself on Sunday with an Athenian muslin gown, and who does not draw up the pendant folds on the right arm, in order to drop into the form of some antique or at least equal Venus *aux belles fesses*."[49] The *Tableau général du goût, des modes et costumes de Paris* that appeared in 1799 published twenty fashion plates; of the fifteen that depicted women's dresses, nine showed women in white dresses and six showed women in dresses of all other colors. The journal concluded that "white is so advantageous to women that the use of it is constant, even though it is the most costly."[50] The style was immortalized in David's 1800 portrait of Madame Juliette Récamier. Napoleon, however, explicitly discouraged the style, which depended on expensive English muslins, in favor of French made silks.[51]

But what are we to make of this fashion? Can it be termed a kind of uniform for women, since it figured so prominently in republican festivals and portraiture (or at least in David's imagination)? Viewed in this way, and contrasted with the wild variation of the costume of the *incroyables* and the *muscadins*, we might be tempted to conclude that the Revolution drove women toward uniformity and sameness and men toward variation and playfulness, thus inverting Flügel's proposed gender/dress system for a time. Like trousers for men, with their origins in the lower classes, the simple-looking muslin dress, often worn with natural-looking, even untidy hair, had filtered up as a fashion from milliners' assistants and farm girls, having been first adopted by Marie Antoinette and her circle.[52]

49. My account of the white dress comes from Mercier, quoted in Ribeiro, *Fashion*, 128–29.

50. *Tableau général du goût, des modes et costumes de Paris* (Paris, Year VII/1799), 130. This is the only year of the journal I could locate at the Bibliothèque Nationale; the issue in question was supposed to be the first of a series, but many fashion journals disappeared after a year or so.

51. Akiko Fukai, "Rococo and Neoclassical Clothing," in *Revolution in Fashion: European Clothing, 1715–1815*, ed. Jean Starobinski et al. (New York: Abbeville Press, 1989), 109–17, esp. 116.

52. Anne Hollander, *Seeing Through Clothes* (New York: Avon, 1975), 385.

Figure 10.6 *The Patriotic Gift of Illustrious French Women*, n.d. By permission of the Musée de la Révolution Française, Vizille.

Figure 10.7 *The Festival of the Supreme Being*, 1794. By permission of the Musée de la Révolution Française, Vizille.

Many different interpretations might fit the evidence of the white muslin dress draped in antique fashion. Did the white suggest the effacement of difference implicitly required by the republican project of a "new man" (or, in this case, woman)? Did the drapery reinforce the revival of neoclassical austerity and simplicity associated with republicanism? Was it as well an anti-aristocratic, antisilk, probourgeois statement, since the dress depended on fabric provided by the nation of shopkeepers, the English? Or was the naturalness of the line—often coupled with a high waistline that emphasized the maternal in women—a kind of preromantic gesture, a carrying through of Rousseauian ideals for women?

Faced with a plethora of possible meanings, the historian should probably hesitate. Dress can mean many things, perhaps because changes in fashion have no deep rationale beyond the desire to attract the attention of others. That desire takes undeniably historical and social forms, but there is no clear logic to their evolution or to the choices made at any particular moment. As Anne Hollander has argued, "The art of dress has its own autonomous history, a self-perpetuating flow of images derived from other images."[53] Desires for naturalness and simplicity, for purity and rejection of tradition, for sensibleness and practicality can and all do take a myriad of different forms, largely in reaction to the images that came before. Adam Gopnik insists, "The truth is that reason really doesn't have much to do with the reasons of fashion."[54] The white muslin dress, after all, was expensive, and for all their depictions of its multiple variations, fashion journals never offered much in the way of an explanation for its popularity.

Although it is difficult, if not impossible, to make much of specific changes in male or female fashion, it nonetheless remains true that questions of dress more broadly conceived went to the heart of the Revolution in both its democratic and totalitarian aspects. At some moments, republicans clearly hoped to break with the previous aristocratic domination of society by taking over the fashion system and literally redesigning it, that is, by providing a new code of signs for a new kind of society. But who should control these signs? The market with its drive toward constant novelty, constant expenditure, constant wasteful excess? Fashionable women with their reputed taste for luxury and control through bodily presentation?

53. Ibid., 311.

54. "What It All Means: Fashion? Well, Here's the Main Thing: It's Fun," *New Yorker*, 7 November 1994, 16.

The women of the Society of Revolutionary and Republican Women with their penchant for cross-dressing and purported masculinization? Male fashion writers and publishers with their ambivalences toward the very world from which they profited? Or the government that invented those slightly ridiculous official uniforms, half antique, half Renaissance, which never aroused any contemporary enthusiasm (thus proving that fashion could not be legislated)? There was no single answer to these questions, which in itself shows that dress could not be controlled by any one group or agency. This was so because dress was the social itself, the arena in which all social and gender distinction came into being and came under fire. As such it embodied the effervescence, as Durkheim called it, of all social interaction. We can search for its rules, but those rules constantly escape from our grasp, just as social life itself changes form just when we think we know what it is.

Contributors

Elizabeth Colwill is Associate Professor of History at San Diego State University. She has published a series of essays on the political culture of revolutionary France and is currently working on a book-length manuscript tentatively entitled *Sex, Savagery, and Slavery in the French and Haitian Revolutions*.

Susan Leigh Foster, choreographer, dancer, writer, is Professor of Dance at the University of California at Riverside. She is the author of *Reading Dancing: Bodies and Subjects in Contemporary American Dance* and *Choreography and Narrative: Ballet's Staging of Story and Desire*, and editor of two anthologies, *Choreographing History* and *Corporealities*.

Mark Franko is Associate Professor of Dance at the University of California, Santa Cruz. He is the author of three books on dance history and theory, including *Dance as Text: Ideologies of the Baroque Body* and *Dancing Modernism/Performing Politics*, as well as numerous articles in journals and anthologies. He is the director of Novantiqua, a dance company he founded in 1985 and which recently appeared in New York, Berlin, and Los Angeles.

Lynn Hunt is Annenberg Professor of History at the University of Pennsylvania. She is the author of *The Family Romance of the French Revolution* and *Telling the Truth about History* (with Joyce Appleby and Margaret Jacob), and editor of *Histories: French Constructions of the Past* (with Jacques Revel). She is now working on the origins of human rights.

Thomas E. Kaiser is Professor of History at the University of Arkansas at Little Rock. His main area of interest is eighteenth-century French political culture. He has published numerous studies dealing with the politics of royal representation and is currently preparing a book on royalist ideology and public opinion in the reign of Louis XV.

Sarah Maza, a specialist in French cultural history, teaches at Northwestern University. Her most recent book is *Private Lives and Public Affairs: The Causes Célèbres of Prerevolutionary France*. She is currently at work on a study of the bourgeoisie in the French social imaginary between 1750 and 1850.

Susan McClary, Professor of Musicology at the University of California, Los Angeles, writes on relationships between music and the body at various moments in history, from the sixteenth century to the present. She is the author of *Feminine Endings: Music, Gender and Sexuality* and is now working on a book called *Power and Desire in Seventeenth-Century Music*. She received a MacArthur Fellowship in 1995.

Sara E. Melzer is Associate Professor of French and Communication Studies at the University of California, Los Angeles. She is the author of *Discourses of the Fall: A Study of Pascal's Pensées* and coeditor of *Rebel Daughters: Women and the French Revolution*. She is currently working on a book about the relation of classical French discourse in the seventeenth century to the politics of assimilation, with special emphasis on French colonial policy in the New World.

Jeffrey Merrick, Associate Professor of History at the University of Wisconsin–Milwaukee, is the author of *The Desacralization of the French Monarchy in the Eighteenth Century* and many articles about early modern French political culture. Coeditor of *Homosexuality in Modern France*, he is currently working on a documentary volume on same-sex relations in early modern France.

Kathryn Norberg teaches history at the University of California, Los Angeles. She is the author of *Rich and Poor in Grenoble, 1600–1814* and coeditor of *Fiscal Crises and Representative Government*. She has also written articles on pornography, venereal disease, and the history of women in the eighteenth century. She is currently finishing a book on the history of prostitution in France from 1560 to 1822.

Joseph Roach is Professor of English and Theatre Studies at Yale University. He is the author of *Cities of the Dead: Circum-Atlantic Performance* and *The Player's Passion: Studies in the Science of Acting;* the editor, with Janelle Reinelt, of *Critical Theory and Performance;* and the director of many plays and operas.

Abby Zanger is Associate Professor of French at Harvard University, where she is also a member of the Committee on Degrees in Women's Studies. She is the author of numerous essays on subjects concerning classical theater, print culture, and the representation of sovereignty. Her essay in this collection is excerpted from her book *Scenes from the Marriage of Louis XIV: Nuptial Fictions and the Making of Absolutist Power*. She is currently completing a study of theatrical culture in the first decade of the reign of Louis XIV.

Index

Compositor:	Integrated Composition Systems
Music setter:	Mansfield Music Graphics
Text:	10/13 Galliard
Display:	Galliard
Printer and binder:	Data Reproductions